# TABE
## Level D

Test of Adult Basic Education
The First Step to Lifelong Success

Phyllis Dutwin, M.A.

Richard Ku, M.A.

McGraw-Hill

New York   Chicago   San Francisco   Lisbon   London   Madrid
Mexico City   Milan   New Delhi   San Juan   Seoul   Singapore
Sydney   Toronto

10   11   12   13   14       QDB/QDB   1   .5   4   3   2

ISBN 0-07-144689-3

This book is printed on acid-free paper.

Library of Congress Cataloging-in-Publication Data

Dutwin, Phyllis.
   McGraw-Hill's TABE level D/Phyllis Dutwin, Richard Ku.
        p.  cm.
   ISBN 0-07-144689-3  (alk. paper)
   1. Basic education—United States—Examinations—Study guides.  2. Adult education—United States—Examinations—Study guides.  I. Title: TABE level D.  II. Ku, Richard T. (Richard Tse-Min)  III. Title.
   LB3060.32.N67D88  2006
   374'.126—dc22

# CONTENTS

# HOW TO USE THIS BOOK

The TABE tests cover basic skills that you use in your everyday life. You might be surprised to find that you know more than you think you do. You might also be surprised to discover skill gaps you do not know about.

This book will help you target and master the skills you need to succeed:

- With the TABE
- In future situations as a lifelong learner

## Before You Begin

Before you begin to use this book, take some time to explore it. The book offers much more than question-and-answer material. Read the Table of Contents. Notice the following:

- Skills Assessments at the beginning of each section
- Stories, or scenarios about actual students
- Skill building in every subject
- Word study
- Study Tips, Test Tips, and FYIs (For Your Information)

All of these elements give you a process for learning. In fact, each section builds skills. You should read and do all the exercises in order.

You might think that you have a greater skill in a certain subject. Take the Skills Assessment for that subject anyway. If your results are 90 to 95 percent correct, you probably don't have to study that section. However, be sure to take all the posttests in the book.

One section, Spelling, needs a special comment. *You should not study this section through* from first page to last. Correct spelling is best learned slowly and through repetition. Take the pretest. If you find that spelling is not your strong subject, start the section. No matter what else you are working on, study a small part of the spelling section at the same time. Use the tips provided and study consistently. You can improve your spelling.

 **FYI**

*Learning how to succeed in test-taking situations makes good career sense.*

*Adults take tests all the time. Tests are everywhere you look, and you take them for many reasons:*

- *drivers' licenses*
- *technical certification*

- educational placement
- job placement
- advancement exams

## Use This Book as Your Personal Trainer

You should approach this book as you would any fitness program or regimen. Include these three important steps.

Step 1: Develop a fitness plan:
Complete Section 1: "Work Smarter, Not Harder."

Step 2: Warm up:
Take each of the subject area Skills Assessments.
Target the skills you need to strengthen.

Step 3: Work out:
Pace yourself through the exercises.
Achieve your best results.

 **TEST TIP**

Do not study for the Skills Assessments that begin each section. The results of each assessment will help you

- Compare what you already know with what you need to know.
- Make a learning plan for choosing and using the lessons that follow.

Look for these tips throughout the book:

 STUDY TIP    TEST TIP    FYI

## Succeed at Learning

"I *see* and I forget, I *hear* and I remember, I *do* and I understand."

—*An old Chinese proverb*

Research tells us how people learn and remember. This ancient proverb tells the truth. When we learn something new, and do something with that knowledge, understanding comes more quickly.

Now you know what research says. What do you have to say about learning? How would you complete this sentence?

"The best learning experience I ever had was _____."

You do not have to write it—just think about what you would say if someone asked you that question.

There are at least five ways to learn: reading, hearing, seeing, saying, and doing. Combining those ways makes the learning experience even more powerful. Think about this; after two weeks we remember:

- 10 percent of what we read
- 20 percent of what we hear
- 30 percent of what we see
- 50 percent of what we hear *and* see
- 70 percent of what we say
- 90 percent of what we say *and* do
- 95 percent of what we help someone else learn and do

The more active we are in the learning process, the more likely we will remember what we've learned.

You also need to think about how *YOU* learn best. Is listening your best learning style? Or do you prefer to read a lesson? Or would you rather walk around and read out loud? In Section 1, you will have a chance to see how *YOU* learn best.

## Increase Your Percentage of Success

- **Put it to work.** *Do* something with your knowledge. *Put it to work* and get results.

- **Results are valuable feedback.** You might be unhappy with your first results. But making mistakes is a part of the learning process.

- **Mistakes** are learning opportunities. Welcome mistakes as a chance to figure out what is not working and why. Then make it your business to try again.

- **Just do it, step by step.** The path to acquiring new knowledge or skills is a series of steps. Sometimes these are baby steps. That is especially true if you have had no previous experience in an area. Other times these steps might be giant steps. You might take a new bit of information and connect it with knowledge you already have.

- **Use it to make it yours.** To learn something new, you go through these steps. The new idea or skill is stored in short-term memory. Perhaps it will stay there for a minute or an hour, maybe a day. You need to take it out of temporary storage and use it within that time. Otherwise, when you need to use it, it will not be there. You will have to start the learning process over again.

- **Three might be the magic number.** Each time you put a new bit of knowledge to work, you help guarantee that it will move from temporary storage to permanent storage in your memory. Rule of thumb: Use your new skill successfully three times, on three different occasions. After that, you'll probably find yourself saying, "I've got it."

- **Use it again, or risk losing it.** A stored skill, like a stored metal tool, might rust or become stiff with time. Then, when you use it, you'll find it doesn't do the job as well. Then again, you might forget where you left the key! Plan to open that storage door regularly. Put your skill to work.

## How do you prefer to learn something new?

- See it; read about it; write it down?          (See TIPS A)
- Hear it; talk about it?                         (See TIPS B)
- Watch it done, and then do it yourself?         (See TIPS C)

You might have a strong preference for a certain style of learning. Then it makes sense to acquire new information using that style of learning *first*.

TIPS A

1. Think in pictures, colors, and shapes. Make movies in your mind about new ideas.

2. Think on paper. Organize your thoughts by making diagrams, charts, and flash cards.

3. Watch videos, TV, or films about subjects you are learning. Search for study books that have lots of graphics and photographs.

4. Ask yourself questions in writing. Reply to yourself in writing. Draw your ideas.

5. Work in a quiet place. Keep a clear study space that is pleasing to your eyes.

TIPS B

1. Think out loud. Explain things out loud to yourself as you study.

2. Read out loud. Read *under your breath*. As you move your lips, you will *hear* the sound of the words in your head.

3. Make your own tapes of information you want to remember. Get the sound of Standard English in your ear. Do this by taping your voice reading from a textbook or novel.

4. Study with other people. Talk things over. Hold question-and-answer sessions.

5. Listen to information about a topic on video, TV, film, or recorded books.

TIPS C

1. Connect to things you are studying with *movement* and *touch*. Act out ideas. "Talk" with your hands.

2. Watch someone *do* what you need to learn. Then *do* it yourself.

3. Use the computer as a learning tool. Use programs that are multimedia and interactive. Create your own study notes using a word processor.

4. Write about, draw, or build models of what you are learning.

5. Exercise before you sit down to study. Take 5-minute *movement breaks* between 30-minute study sessions. Play background music as you study.

## Don't Limit Your Options

Learning different subjects might mean using different approaches. Consider all the tips above. Ask others about their tips for learning. Watch for study and learning tips in the subject lessons that follow.

## On Your Own, or With Others?

If you work with a partner, or with a small group, you can benefit in these ways. You have the opportunity to

• Pool your experience and knowledge.

• Exchange strategies and study tips.

• Ask and answer questions without fear of embarrassment.

• Give and get suggestions when the going gets tough.

## Ask Questions

Questions are like fishhooks.

Information you hook with your own questions tends to "stick around." You'll store this information in your memory better than information you have received without "fishing" for it.

Learn how to ask good questions. Keep your hook baited and in the water long enough to catch some information.

Take time to do some fishing. Chances are, you will be hooked on learning for a lifetime.

## One Final Thought

The more you understand about the way you learn best, the more you will be able to get what you need to succeed.

***Good luck at discovering how to unlock your potential!***

# SECTION 1 — Work Smarter, Not Harder

## LESSON 1  Identify Your Target

### Where Are You Headed?

*My Goals*

I am studying to upgrade my basic academic skills to: (Check *all that apply*)

❑ Score well on the TABE, Level D

❑ Enroll in an Associate Degree Program

❑ Enter a Vocational Certificate Program

❑ Obtain admission to a Job Training Program

❑ Obtain admission to a Career Advancement Program

❑ Qualify for a promotion at my workplace

❑ Be eligible for Federal Financial Aid under Ability to Benefit guidelines

❑ Qualify for certification in _____

❑ Complete graduation requirements for _____

❑ Successfully exit the Welfare to Work Program _____

❑ Become more independent in handling my affairs

❑ Attain personal satisfaction

❑ Help family members with their schooling

❑ _____

❑ _____

❑ _____

AFTER I upgrade my skills and/or score well on the TABE, I plan to

_____

_____

A vision I have for my future is _____

_____

## When Do You Want to Get There?

My Timeline:

Today's date: _____

I want to upgrade my skills by this date _____

because that is when _____

That date is _____ (months, weeks, days) from today.

If I do not improve my skills as much as I want to by that date, my options will be to _____

## Do You Need to Achieve a Certain Score?

Programs vary in their TABE score requirements.

Are you already in a program with score requirements? _____

Do you want to enroll in, or qualify for, a program that has test score requirements? _____

Do you need to take a test to qualify for scholarship aid? _____

Your answer may be "yes" to any or all of these questions. If so, make sure you know what those requirements are. Take the time to find out this information right now. It will help you focus on your goals for studying the subjects in this book. The information will help you be realistic as you plan your timeline.

Turn to Appendix A for specific information on TABE scoring.

## Do Your Research

Fill in the blank that fits your situation.

1. The program *I am already working in*, requires me to _____

_____

2. The program I want to get into requires me to _____

_____

For my own satisfaction, I would like to _____

## What Do You Already Know about Your Skills?

Take a moment to think in general about the academic subject areas covered in this book, and tested on the TABE: Reading, Math, and Language

Would you say your level of skill is about the same in each area, or is it quite different? _____

How about your level of comfort when you learn about these subjects? Are you just as comfortable learning in one subject area as another? Is there a significant, or major difference in the way you feel about any of them?

_____

_____

## Rank Your Levels of Skill and Comfort

**Skill Level:**                        **Comfort Level:**

Strongest subject area first          Most comfortable subject

1. _____                   1. _____

2. _____                   2. _____

3. _____                   3. _____

Why do you think your skills are stronger in some of these areas?

_____

_____

_____

_____

Why do you think you are more comfortable with some subjects than with others?

_____

_____

_____

_____

## What Do You Need to Succeed as a Test-Taker?

**Reflection: Past Experiences with Tests**

The last time I took a standardized test was _____

My results were:  ____OK  ____Good  ____Excellent  ____A disaster

I think my performance on that test was due to:

_____

In general, I consider myself a  ____Good  ____Fair  ____Poor  test-taker.

My biggest problem with taking tests is _____.

I think I need to _____.

**Test-taking Strategies**

I am familiar with, and am able to put into practice, the following test-taking strategies. I know how to:

| | | | |
|---|---|---|---|
| ❏ Visualize success for self-confidence and best results | Yes | No | Need Practice |
| ❏ Prepare physically for the test day | Yes | No | Need Practice |
| ❏ Identify key words in questions and directions | Yes | No | Need Practice |
| ❏ Recognize pitfalls of multiple choice tests | Yes | No | Need Practice |
| ❏ Use the process of elimination to check multiple-choice questions. | Yes | No | Need Practice |
| ❏ Relax by using breathing techniques | Yes | No | Need Practice |
| ❏ Take 1-minute vacations to relieve stress during the test. | Yes | No | Need Practice |
| ❏ Pace myself during the test to finish within the time limit | Yes | No | Need Practice |
| ❏ Know when to leave a question that is giving me trouble | Yes | No | Need Practice |
| ❏ Use time that is left at the end to check my work | Yes | No | Need Practice |

 **FYI**

Don't worry yet about getting ready for any of the assessments or tests in this book, or the TABE. There are test-taking tips throughout the lessons and a special section devoted entirely to testing strategies. Each of the strategies mentioned in the list above will be discussed, and you will have a chance to try them out.

Take time to complete the next unit: Analyze Yourself as a Learner. You will meet another student in the next few pages. Learn how she uses this analysis to help herself prepare for studying to be test-ready.

## LESSON 2 Analyze Yourself as a Learner

### Self-Assessment and Planning

In this section, you will take steps to better understand yourself as a learner. You also need to examine and manage the time you have to prepare for the TABE. In addition, you will take three important steps. You will identify, understand, and develop strategies to overcome barriers that many adults face as learners. The result will be a plan of action that will help you target success.

To help you through this process, read Anna's story and then walk through the worksheets with her. Once you see how the process is done, you can complete your own.

Anna came to the United States when she was 8 years old. She had learned to read and write in the Spanish language. When she started school in Los Angeles, she knew very few English words. Anna proved to be a good student of the English language. That was not her problem as she grew up. Instead, her problem was that she lacked confidence. By the time she graduated from high school, she had worked at several jobs. The last one was in a small convenience store. Although Anna enjoyed meeting new and old customers every day, she knew she wanted even more responsibility after she graduated.

Working in a bank appealed to Anna. She began looking in the newspaper for help wanted ads. Then she decided to go into her own bank and talk about a job. The manager gave Anna an application and a job description for the teller position. You can see part of the job description below.

Before you read this description, look at the definitions of some words you need to know.

| | |
|---|---|
| Processes | deals with or handles |
| Dexterity | ability to use your hands |
| Transactions | customer business |
| Settlements | adding up all payments and receipts |
| Audit | review, examination |
| Regulatory | rule making |

Category: Branch Position
Title: Customer Service Rep/Teller
Availability: Full time
Job Hours: 40
Location: Wickford
State: RI
Duties:

- Efficiently processes both the paying and receiving of customer transactions in a timely manner. Demonstrates knowledge and dexterity in using computer equipment and systems.

- Takes responsibility for delivering World Class Customer Service that meets and exceeds customer expectations.

- Accurately completes settlements on a daily basis with a minimum of errors and within time guidelines.

- Processes ATM transactions and assists in settlement.

- Seeks out opportunities to learn about bank products and services in order to answer customer questions.
- Understands check-cashing guidelines.
- Understands and obeys all audit, regulatory, and security procedures.
- Recognizes sales opportunities and sells bank products.
- Performs other duties and tasks as requested.
- May be required to help at a neighboring branch.

Qualifications:
High school diploma or equivalent. Person needs 3 months' cash-handling experience and basic computer knowledge. Strong interpersonal and organizational skills required.

Contact: Lucy Quinlan
Fax resume to Lquinlan@sovereignbank.com

Anna read the job description carefully. She thought hard about how her skills would fit the job. Two things bothered her: She had no computer skills and she had taken only the most basic math courses. She knew she was good with customers. Would that be enough? Could she get into banking?

Follow Anna as she learns about herself and what she needs to do to prepare for the future.

## What Kind of Learner Are You?

Because people learn in different ways, it is important for you to understand how *you* learn best. The following information will help you develop a learning plan. The plan targets success on the TABE and on your other learning goals.

Anna thought about her learning experiences. The only computer class she had ever taken was a disaster. She remembered having trouble from the first day. She was confused and felt alone with her problems. The way the teacher expected her to learn just did not work for her. He gave long lectures and she was lost after 5 or 10 minutes. Also, Anna never felt confident enough to go beyond basic math and Algebra 1.

The following is an example of how Anna might complete this worksheet.

**Learner Preference Worksheet**

1. *What time(s) of day or night do you feel better able to study/read/write.*
   Early Morning __✓__ Afternoon _____ Early evening _____ Late night _____

2. *Do you prefer to study or learn by yourself or with other? (Check one)*
   like learning about new things with a study group. _____
   I like learning about new things by myself. _____
   I like learning something new with one other person to help me. _____
   It depends on the subject matter. __✓__ (I need help with computers and math.)

3. *Do you learn best by (Check all that apply.)*
   Reading about something? __✓__
   Seeing a picture or graph? __✓__
   Hearing someone explain something? _____
   Doing what I'm learning about? Writing it down? _____
   Talking about it with or without someone else? __✓__

4. *What length of time do you prefer to spend studying?* _____
   I prefer to work for periods of 2 hours or more. __✓__
   I prefer to work for shorter periods of time (less than an hour)_____
   I can work for as long as time permits. __✓__

5. *How's your concentration? (Check all that apply)*
   I need complete quiet when I study or read. __✓__
   I can study or read with some background noise. _____
   I can study or read in any environment, quiet or noisy. _____

Examine the items Anna checked to get a picture of how best she learns. See how she used the information to fill in the blanks in the Learner Preference Statement that follows.

**Learner Preference Statement**

I prefer to study in the early morning with *the help of others (when I'm doing math or learning computer skills)*. I learn best when I read about it and *see something in a picture or graph* and by *talking about it with other people*. I prefer to spend at least 2 hours studying, and I prefer to study *in complete silence* when I'm not working with others.

You have just seen an example of a completed worksheet. Now complete this one on your own to get an idea of how *you* prefer to learn.

**Learner Preference Worksheet**

1. What time(s) of day or night do you feel better able to study/read/write.
   Early Morning_____ Afternoon_____ Early evening_____ Late night_____

2. *Do you prefer to study or learn by yourself or with others? (Check one)*
   I like learning about new things with a study group. _____
   I like learning about new things by myself. _____
   I like learning something new with one other person to help me. _____
   It depends on the subject matter. _____

3. *Do you learn best by (Check all that apply.)*
   Reading about something? _____
   Seeing a picture or graph? _____
   Hearing someone explain something? _____
   Doing what I'm learning about? Writing it down? _____
   Talking about it with or without someone else? _____

4. *What length of time do you prefer to spend studying?* _____
   I prefer to work for periods of 2 hours or more. _____
   I prefer to work for shorter periods of time (less than an hour) _____
   I can work for as long as time permits. _____

5. How's your concentration? (Check all that apply)
   I need complete quiet when I study or read. _____
   I can study or read with some background noise. _____
   I can study or read in any environment, quiet or noisy. _____

Look at the items you have checked above to get a picture of how you learn best. Use this information to fill in your Learner Preference Statement.

---

**Learner Preference Statement**

I prefer to study in the 1. _____ with (2)_____. I learn best by
(3)_____. I prefer to spend (4) _____
studying. I prefer to study (5) _____.

---

You will use this information to develop your Personal Learning Plan later in this chapter.

You have thought about how you learn and study best. Now you should be aware of, and plan for, obstacles or problems that might get in the way of your success.

As adults we are all faced with a variety of life issues and challenges. If we allow them to, they will stop the accomplishment of our goals. These barriers can be overcome. We need to be aware of the supports that we can draw upon to help us.

You can categorize barriers in three ways: institutional, circumstantial, and individual. Read this discussion of barriers. An exercise will follow to help you plan for and overcome some of these barriers to your success.

## Barriers

**Institutional** barriers are those over which we have no control. They are put in place by a school, program, or class. Institutional barriers can include any of the following:

- Inconvenient class times
- Difficult registration procedures
- Financial aid deadlines
- Other things that keep us from taking a class or continuing with one.

Don't give up! These barriers may be overcome in some cases.

**Circumstantial** barriers are difficult, but more often are within our control. These barriers might include:

- Lack of time
- Lack of money
- Lack of child care
- Lack of transportation

All of the above can make it difficult for us to reach our learning goals.

**Personal** barriers are mainly in our control, yet they are typically the most difficult to overcome. They include long-held beliefs about our abilities as a learner or student.

Personal barriers include:

- Feelings of being too old to take classes or to learn.
- Feelings that we are not smart enough to do well in class.
- Feelings that we are not smart enough to do well in a certain subject. For example, many people have a fear of math and feel they cannot do well in that subject.
- Negative feelings about school or learning because of poor early experiences with school.

These barriers might keep some people from even attempting to go back to school or to take a course. Barriers might also cause someone to drop out of a class or program. The good news is that there are ways to deal with, and overcome, many of these barriers.

## Supports

Many sources of support exist for you. Identify these within your own family, within your circle of friends, and within your neighborhood and community.

### Family

Try to identify people within your close or extended family whom you can ask for help if you need to. Ask yourself these questions:

1. Do I have a parent, sibling, aunt, uncle, or anyone who can provide child care, even on a short-term basis, so I can study, go to the library, or to a class?

   I can ask _____. Telephone: _____.

   I can ask _____. Telephone: _____.

2. Is there anyone in my family that I can call on short notice to help me with a ride if I need one, last-minute child care, or financial needs?

   I can call _____. Telephone: _____.

   I can call _____. Telephone: _____.

### Friends

Identify those people closest to you that you can count on to help you with child care, studying, or a ride, if you need one. Are there things you can offer to do for them in exchange? Can you offer them child care or other support at times when they need it? Sometimes friends set up an informal child care exchange program. They develop a schedule of support for each other.

I will ask my friend _____ for help with _____.

In exchange, I can offer _____. Telephone: _____.

I will ask my friend _____ for help with _____.

In exchange, I can offer _____. Telephone: _____.

### Neighbors

Do you have one or more neighbors who might consider helping you on short notice if you need it?

A neighbor I might call on for help is _____. Telephone: _____.

A neighbor I might call on for help is _____ Telephone: _____.

### Community

In your community, there are many social services to give you the help you need. These services include child care, transportation, clothing, food, shelter, financial aid, and counseling. Check the Community Service telephone numbers at the front of your telephone directory. Many communities offer

- Health centers
- Family services
- Educational financial aid services

I will check out these Community Services:

_____

_____

_____

_____

_____

_____

Before working with your own barriers, read what Anna has identified as her barriers. See how she plans to overcome some of these barriers with supports.

## Balancing Barriers and Supports Worksheet

| Barriers | Supports |
|---|---|
| **Institutional**<br>Some of my adult classes will be at the new high school. I have never driven there before. So I'm not sure where I go to register. | **Family, Friends, Neighbors, Community**<br>I will ask my friends if they can help me find it. |
| **Circumstantial**<br>I'm not sure I can afford a baby-sitter. I'll need help with my kids while I'm in class. | I will try to get financial aid to help me. I will ask my friends if we can trade baby sitting with each other. |
| **Individual**<br>I'm really afraid that I can't learn how to use a computer. I think I'm too old to start learning. | I want to try for the job. I need to get over my fears. I will talk to my friends and an adult school counselor about this. I have to start thinking more positively about the future. |

As you can see, Anna has some issues that are more easily handled than others. She can try to ask her family and friends to help her with her institutional and circumstantial barriers. She is going to have to really work hard to get over her fear of not being able to succeed in math. That is something for which she must take the major responsibility. Once she gets started, an instructor can help her develop more confidence in herself. Now it is time for you to try this exercise for yourself.

1.  List the institutional, circumstantial, and individual barriers you might face. Use the descriptions in this lesson to help you identify the different barriers. Write these in the spaces provided on the left side of the form below.

2.  Match sources of support that you might use to help you overcome the barriers you have listed. Write these barriers in the right side of the form.

**Balancing Barriers and Supports Worksheet**

| Barriers | Supports |
|---|---|
| Institutional | Family, Friends, Neighbors, Community |
| _____ | _____ |
| _____ | _____ |
| _____ | _____ |
| Circumstantial | |
| _____ | _____ |
| _____ | _____ |
| _____ | _____ |
| Individual | |
| _____ | _____ |
| _____ | _____ |
| _____ | _____ |
| Notes to Myself: | |
| _____ | _____ |
| _____ | _____ |
| _____ | _____ |

## Make Time for Learning

A common complaint of adult learners is that they lack time for studying and other learning activities. This section will help you document and analyze how you currently spend your time. It will also help you develop a plan to include your learning activities. Notice how Anna filled out her calendar: She used an X for fixed activities—working in her case. She used a ◊ for flexible activities that could be scheduled at another time.

Anna filled in her calendar this way:

| | Mon | Tues | Wed | Thurs | Fri | Sat | Sun |
|---|---|---|---|---|---|---|---|
| 7 | XXXX XXXX | XXXX XXXX | XXXX XXXX | XXXX XXXX | XXXX XXXX | | |
| 8 | XXXX XXXX | XXXX XXXX | XXXX XXXX | XXXX XXXX | XXXX XXXX | | |
| 9 | XXXX XXXX | XXXX XXXX | XXXX XXXX | XXXX XXXX | XXXX XXXX | | |
| 10 | XXXX XXXX | XXXX XXXX | XXXX XXXX | XXXX XXXX | XXXX XXXX | | ◊◊◊ ◊◊◊ ◊◊◊ |
| 11 | XXXX XXXX | XXXX XXXX | XXXX XXXX | XXXX XXXX | XXXX XXXX | ◊◊◊ ◊◊◊ | |
| 12 | XXXX XXXX | XXXX XXXX | XXXX XXXX | XXXX XXXX | XXXX XXXX | ◊◊◊ ◊◊◊ | |
| 1 | XXXX XXXX | XXXX XXXX | XXXX XXXX | XXXX XXXX | XXXX XXXX | | |
| 2 | XXXX XXXX | XXXX XXXX | XXXX XXXX | XXXX XXXX | XXXX XXXX | | |
| 3 | XXXX | XXXX | XXXX | XXXX | XXXX | | |
| 4 | ◊ Library with children | | | | | | |
| 5 | | ◊◊◊ | ◊◊◊ | ◊◊◊ | | ◊◊◊ | ◊◊◊ |
| 6 | | ◊◊◊ | ◊◊◊ | ◊◊◊ | | ◊◊◊ | ◊◊◊ |

| | | | | | | |
|---|---|---|---|---|---|---|
| 7 | | ◇ weekly | | | ◇◇◇<br>◇◇◇ | |
| | | ◇ food | | | | |
| | | ◇ shopping | | | | |
| 8 | | ◇◇◇ | | | ◇◇◇ | |
| 8:30 | | | | | ◇◇◇ | |
| 9 | | | | | ◇◇◇<br>◇◇◇ | |
| 10 | | | | | ◇◇◇<br>◇◇◇ | |
| 11 | | | | | | |
| 12 | | | | | | |

**Step One:** Look at this weeklong calendar. Place an X through the times when you know you have activities, such as job hours, family meal times, and other schedules that cannot be changed.

My Weekly Schedule

| Mon | Tues | Wed | Thurs | Fri | Sat | Sun |
|---|---|---|---|---|---|---|
| 6 | | | | | | |
| 7 | | | | | | |
| 8 | | | | | | |
| 9 | | | | | | |
| 10 | | | | | | |
| 11 | | | | | | |
| 12 | | | | | | |
| 1 | | | | | | |
| 2 | | | | | | |
| 3 | | | | | | |

| | | | | | | |
|---|---|---|---|---|---|---|
| 4 | | | | | | |
| 5 | | | | | | |
| 6 | | | | | | |
| 7 | | | | | | |
| 8 | | | | | | |
| 9 | | | | | | |
| 10 | | | | | | |
| 11 | | | | | | |
| 12 | | | | | | |

**Step Two:** You have identified time slots that are NOT available for learning. Now, ask yourself the crucial questions below to help you plan your best times for learning during the week. Use the information you recorded about yourself on the Learning Preference Checklist, in this lesson, to help you.

Here are Anna's responses:

When do I learn best? __Early Morning__

How much time do I need during the day/week to study? __at least 2 hrs a__

Are there any times available when I will be able to study without interruption? _____

Write your conclusions here:

When do I learn best?_____

_____

How much time do I need during the day or week to study?_____

_____

Are there any times available when I will be able to study without interruption? _____

_____

**Step Three:** Use the answers to the questions above to help identify the best times for you to study. If there is a conflict in your schedule, use your Barriers and Supports Worksheet to help you identify your supports. Make time in your schedule for studying by calling on your supports for help with tasks that must be done daily or weekly.

Write these times in on your calendar above and on the lines below:

_____

_____

_____

_____

## LESSON 3  Put It to Work—Here's How

### Create a Personal Learning Plan

Now that you have reflected on your schedule of activities, put all this information to work for you. Complete this learning plan as directed. Next, photocopy it, and put it in a place where you will see it everyday. The refrigerator is a good location.

**My Learning Plan**

Goal/s: _____

_____

_____

Timeline: _____

Supports I need to do to reach my goals:

_____

_____

**My Promises:**

I will study at the times, and in the ways, I learn best.

Write your Learner Preference statement here:



I will refer often to my Barriers and Supports Worksheet.

I will continue to try to find and use the supports I need to overcome obstacles.

I will consult my Weekly Calendar and use the study time I have scheduled.

**I WILL SUCCEED**

# 2 | Reading

## LESSON 1  You Have to Start Somewhere

You met Anna Munoz in Section 1. As you remember, she was ready for a change in her work. The question was whether she was prepared to do the job she chose: a bank teller.

**Words to Know**

| | |
|---|---|
| Counseling | Help with personal matters |
| Reflection | Thoughts about something |
| Process | A series of actions |
| Assessment | A test to evaluate a student's performance |
| Seminar | A group discussion or class |

Anna knew that banking required her to use a computer. She definitely needed help in that area. She also didn't know if her basic math skills would be enough. Anna was lucky that she had a friend, Theresa, who had just taken and passed the TABE test at the adult learning center. Theresa was preparing to go to a community college. To prepare for the TABE tests, Theresa had taken English and math courses. She took one other important step before she took the TABE tests. Theresa started by getting counseling about schools and careers. She advised Anna to do the same.

Anna thought that, after counseling, she would just go to a community college and sign up for a computer class. She had forgotten that Theresa had taken a series of tests first. Before Anna could start classes, she also had to take the TABE tests. Follow Anna through the reflection process at the learning center. Then take the Reading Skills Assessment. You will know much more about your reading skills when you have finished!

First think about your reading habits and skills.

**Reflection: Reading in My Daily Life**

I read approximately _____ hrs a day/_____ hrs a week to keep informed of current events and other issues that concern me.

I read approximately _____ hrs a day/_____ hrs a week ... for workplace tasks

I enjoy reading _____.

I would like to improve my ability to read _____.

**Comprehension**

I am able to understand, analyze and use these types of materials:

| | | | | |
|---|---|---|---|---|
| Newspapers | ___Yes | ___No | ___Need practice | ___I don't know |
| Instructions | ___Yes | ___No | ___Need practice | ___I don't know |
| Maps, Charts and Graphs | ___Yes | ___No | ___Need practice | ___I don't know |
| Stories and Novels | ___Yes | ___No | ___Need practice | ___I don't know |
| Business Letters | ___Yes | ___No | ___Need practice | ___I don't know |
| Manuals, Handbooks | ___Yes | ___No | ___Need practice | ___I don't know |
| Standardized Forms | ___Yes | ___No | ___Need practice | ___I don't know |
| Index, Table of Contents | ___Yes | ___No | ___Need practice | ___I don't know |

**Vocabulary Knowledge**

I know how to figure out the meaning of words from their context (the way they are used in a passage).

      ___Yes ___No ___Need practice ___I don't know

I know how to identify the meaning of words by analyzing their structure (roots, prefixes and suffixes).

      ___Yes ___No ___Need practice ___I don't know

**TEST TIPS**

Before you start this test (and any test):

- Breathe. You probably think that you do this without thinking, and most of the time you do. However, when you are in a stressful situation (as tests sometimes are for Anna), you tend to hold your breath. So, start this test-taking opportunity by taking and releasing four deep breaths. Breathe in through your nose and out through your open mouth.

- Read the directions, including any time limitations.

- Don't linger on any one question. You can always return to it later.

- Use a process of elimination to check multiple-choice answers.

- Use time that is left at the end to check your work.

# Reading Skills Pretest

Here is a small part of a driver license's registration form. Read the form and then do Numbers 1 through 5.

## Application for Driver License or Non-Driver ID Card[PD2]
## Department of Motor Vehicles (DMV)

I Am Applying For (check any that apply):

Learner Permit    □ ID Card  □ Renewal  □ Replacement  □ Change

Voter Registration Questions (Please answer "yes" or "no.")

If you are not registered to vote where you now live, would you like to apply? □ Yes—Fill in Voter Registration Section on page 3

If you are changing your address, would you like the Board of Elections to be notified? □ No—I don't want to register/Already registered

Note: If you don't check either box, you will not be registered to vote.

State Organ and Tissue Donor Registry

□ By checking this box, you allow us to send this information to the Health Department Organ/Tissue Registry. The Health Department will send you more information.

---

Last Name _____ First Name _____ Middle Initial _____

Date of Birth _____ Sex _____ Height _____ Eye Color _____ Social Security Number (SSN) _____

Month/Day/Year Male/Female Feet/Inches  ___/___/___  _____  _____

*You must supply your SSN. Your number will not be given to the public or appear on any other form.

Day Phone NO. (Optional)

Area Code   Number
(  )     ____ ____

Address where you Get Your Mail
Street _____ Apt. No. City/Town _____ Zip Code _____ County _____

Has your name changed? ☐ Yes ☐ No    Has your mailing address changed? ☐ Yes ☐ No
Has the address where you live changed? ☐ Yes ☐ No

If "Yes," print your former name exactly as it appears on your present license or non-driver ID card.
     **Other Change** What is the change? What is the reason for it (new license class, wrong date of birth, etc.)?

_____

Do you now have or have you ever had a license? ☐ Yes ☐ No

If you are under 18 years of age, read this:

Certification by parent(s) or responsible person for minor under 18 years of age:
_____

Signature _____

VOTER REGISTRATION APPLICATION

Are you a U.S. citizen? ☐ Yes ☐ No   I will be 18 years old before election day. ☐ Yes ☐ No
If you answered NO, do not complete this form unless you will be 18 years old by the end of the year.

I swear or affirm that

- I am a citizen of the United States.
- This is my signature.
- The above information is true.


_____     _____
Signature                    Date

**Adapted from several Department of Motor Vehicle (DMV) applications**

**1** Which of these best summarizes the application?

  **A** The application is only for 21-year-old people who have not moved in a year.

  **B** The application can be signed by your teacher.

  **C** The application allows you to do other things in addition to applying for a license.

  **D** The application allows you to register to vote in addition to applying for a license.

**2** If you decide to register to vote, what happens next?

  **A** You do not fill out any other part of the application and you can't get a license.

  **B** You fill out the Voter Registration Application.

  **C** You fill out every other part of the application except the registration part.

  **D** You stop everything and tear up the form.

**3** You must give your social security number. Where does that number go from here?

  **A** It does not go anywhere from here.

  **B** It is immediately erased.

  **C** It goes to your school and work.

  **D** It goes to the public library.

**4** DMV means

  **A** Drivers' Most Valuable

  **B** Department of Motor Vehicles

  **C** Drivers' Many Vehicles

  **D** Department of Medical Vehicles

**5** This form lets you decide if you want to donate something after you die. What can you donate?

  **A** Money

  **B** Your car to a charity that needs it

  **C** Some clothes and shoes to poor people

  **D** Your heart or lungs to someone who is sick

**Here is a story about the 2004 Nobel Prize Winner, Wangari Maathai. Read the story. Then do Numbers 6 through 11.**

The Nobel Peace Prize is one of the highest honors anyone can receive. In 2004, the prize was given to a woman from Kenya. Her name is Wangari Maathai. She is the first woman from Africa to receive the prize. She is 63 years old and a teacher. Maathai fights hard for the environment and to get work for women.

Maathai became famous for fighting to save the forests. Some years ago, people were allowed to cut down forests for fuel and money. Poor women had to cut wood to warm their families.

She said this: "It's a matter of life and death for this country. The Kenyan forests are facing extinction (death). This is a man-made problem."

Although abused and jailed by police, she and other women never gave up their fight for trees.

Maathai founded the Greenbelt Movement in 1977. She and other women began a 30-year fight to reforest the land. They planted just 9 trees. Today about 30 million trees have been planted across Africa. The trees helped stop the land from totally drying out. Caring for living things created food and jobs for women.

How did this happen? Sometimes Maathai says the trees were a lucky happening. When Maathai was chairperson of the National Council of Women of Kenya , many women came to her office. They told her their problems. She heard about their need for fuel. Maathai thought the women, themselves, could do something about it. They had to get involved.

Maathai used the tree as a symbol for change in the people and their lives. To really solve the fuel problem, she said, "If you cut the branches, or you cut a tree, plant two to replace them."

In 1985, the United Nations' encouraged the Greenbelt Movement to share their experience. Greenbelt was a grassroots organization made up of plain people. Each group had up to five members. Every person was from a different household. The groups learned how to organize themselves. Leaders were chosen who would take the members through the process. Each group registered with the Ministry of Culture. They set up 10-step programs for starting a tree nursery. Then they opened a bank account where they could put money to buy the seedlings. They learned from people who knew how to start tree nurseries. But even before all that, they went through an empowerment class or seminar. The seminars helped them understand that their own activities- for example, tree cutting— brought about some of their problems.

6   To really solve the fuel problem, she said, "If you cut the branches, or you cut down a tree, plant two to replace them."

Which of these is the best summary of the statement by Wangari Maathai?

A   When you have five people living in a house, you'll solve the problem of fuel. You will be happier, too.

B   If you have five people in your family, ask the government for work.

C   Start a tree farm on your own. It is very easy to do.

D   You can solve your fuel problem. Always replant as much or more of what you use.

7   What did Wangari Maathai win?

A   Maathai won 3000 seedlings for the farm.

B   Maathai won $500 in 2004.

C   Maathai won the Nobel Peace Prize for 2004.

D   Maathai won the right to lead Green Peace.

8   Which of these statements is an opinion expressed by Maathai?

A   Groups of 18 women were formed.

B   Saving the forests is a matter of life and death for this country.

C   Today about 30 million trees have been planted across Africa.

D   Maathai is a teacher and the first African woman to receive the Nobel Peace Prize.

9   The passage says that Maathai started the "Greenbelt Movement." Greenbelt as it is used here means.

A   Area of natural growth.

**B** The color of Maathai's belt.

**C** The movement to teach children to read.

**D** The movement to start an artist's workshop.

**10** If Maathai had not started the tree planting movement, what might have happened in Kenya?

**A** Families would have had more money to spend on things they really wanted.

**B** People would have had asked her to become president of the country.

**C** The land would have been in much better shape for growing food.

**D** The land might have become so dry that nothing would have grown on it.

**11** Which of these best describes Wangari Maathai?

**A** Caring and persistent

**B** Disloyal and gentle

**C** Impatient and negative

**D** Positive and unsure

**The city of Lakeview is planning several job fairs. Read the newspaper announcement. Then do Numbers 12 through 15.**

**2006 Job Fairs  Your Opportunity to Start a New Career**

Call (000) 000-0000 to register. IT'S FREE!

January 26, 2206 Nursing and Other Healthcare Careers

Lakeview Community Center, 9AM to 6PM.

Repeated on January 28, 2206

Come and talk to healthcare professionals. Hospitals, nursing homes, nurse providers will all be there to talk to you. Bring a resume, including your educational background. GED graduates encouraged to attend.

February 23, 2206 Sales Careers in Retail, Banking, and Insurance

Repeated on February 25, 2006

Lakeview Community Center

Area banks, retail stores, and insurance companies will do on-the-spot interviews. Bring a resume, including your educational background. Some positions require post-high-school or GED courses. We do on-the-job training.

April 6, 2006 Workforce Skills Fair

Repeated on April 8, 2006

Lakeview Community Center

Adult educators, personnel directors, and business school teachers will be on hand. They will discuss the skills needed to succeed in a number of job areas. Small-group discussions will take place. Bring your resume. We'll help you to improve it. Some topics are

- discovering your strengths
- writing a resume and cover letter that sell you to an employer
- preparing for an interview
- quick-checking your writing skills
- keeping up with new technology
- learning to communicate on the job

**12** What is the same about each job-fair meeting?

    **A** The topic and the people leading it

    **B** The dates in January only

    **C** The meeting place is the high school

    **D** The two sessions for each topic

**13** You don't need a college degree to attend these seminars. Which phrase supports that statement?

    **A** Adult educators don't believe in asking you to take courses.

    **B** GED graduates encouraged to attend.

    **C** We do on-the-job training

    **D** Answers B and C

**14** Which of these best summarizes the newspaper announcement?

    **A** Lakeview Community Center celebrates its anniversary with a citywide party.

    **B** Lakeview Community Center has offered adult educators a chance to sign people up for a GED course.

    **C** Lakeview Community Center offers adults important information and opportunities regarding jobs.

    **D** Lakeview Community Center has announced its activity list and calendar for 2006.

**15** According to this job fair announcement, what is an important first step in finding a new job?

    **A** Buying really good clothes to wear to the fair

    **B** Writing a really good resume and cover letter

    **C** Making friends with everyone who attends the fair

    **D** Getting on-the-job training

Henry David Thoreau was born in Massachusetts in 1817. In July

1845, he went to live in a hut on Waldon Pond. He was not far from home. On the pond, he wanted to live simply. He wanted to live in nature. During this time, he wrote the essay *Walking*.

Today, we walk for health and fun. Thoreau, though, had those and other reasons why everyone should walk. Although the language might seem old to us now, the ideas are still very fresh and new.

**Here are a few paragraphs from *Walking* by Henry David Thoreau. Read the paragraphs and answer Numbers 16 through 19.**

I cannot keep my good health and spirits unless I spend four hours a day at least, sauntering through the woods. Sometimes I think of shopkeepers who stay in their shops all day. There they sit all day. You'd think their legs were meant for sitting, not walking. I think they deserve credit for not committing suicide a long time ago.

. . . How women, who are confined to the house even more than men, stand it, I do not know. I have begun to think I do know though. I walk past their houses in the afternoon. Their houses seem to be at rest. My friend whispers, "They've probably all gone to bed." I agree.

The walking of which I speak is not the same as the usual exercise. Don't think of it as taking medicine at certain hours. Walking gives exercise, yes, but more important, it gives you time to think. You have the time to think something through and at length.

Adapted from, *Walking*, by Henry David Thoreau.

**16** Why do you think Thoreau and his friend say, "They've all gone to bed?"

   **A**  It is dark, the dog is inside, and it is late at night.

   **B**  Thoreau's friend is not very smart. Thoreau should know better.

   **C**  Thoreau and his friend think the women are bored because they never go out to walk.

   **D**  At the time, there was a law that said the women had to go to sleep after lunch.

**17** Thoreau says, "I cannot keep my good health and spirits unless I spend four hours a day at least sauntering through the woods." *Sauntering* means about the same as

   **A**  Selling

   **B**  Racing

   **C**  Thinking

   **D**  Walking

**18**  The tone of the passage could best be described as

    **A**  Critical but playful

    **B**  Playful but false

    **C**  Serious but dishonest

    **D**  False but unproven

**19**  According to the passage, walking is

    **A**  More important than anything else in the world

    **B**  Not just for your health

    **C**  Done by every person living on or near Waldon Pond

    **D**  Only for little children.

**Read the letter. Then do Numbers 20 through 22.**

Dear Mr. Manuel,

When I graduated from high school last June, I told you that I would stay in touch with you. You were always so understanding and helpful. At that time, I had no idea what I was going to do. I didn't feel ready for college. I didn't have a job and I didn't know where to get one. After a few months, I remembered what you told me. You said, "Ricardo, what are your favorite things to do? Think about the things that you would love to work at. Then, get the education you need to get a job doing those things. You'll never go wrong doing that."

Mr. Manuel, I cannot ever thank you enough for that advice. It didn't take me long to decide what my interests were. I knew I loved working with cars. I also loved being on my computer. I just didn't know what exactly to do with that information.

A friend of mine, Eduardo, who's working on his GED, suggested that I go to the Lakeview Adult Learning Center to get some advice. The counselor there helped me to find a great program at the Community College. It combines auto mechanics with my computer knowledge.

I have already taken and passed the college entry test: TABE. I'll start classes in September.

Thank you again for being so helpful to me and for believing in me the way that you did. I will stay in touch with you and let you know how I am doing in college.

Sincerely,

Ricardo

**20**  Which of these did Ricardo do after talking to his friend, Eduardo?

    **A**  He took one more year to think about what kind of work he wanted to do.

    **B**  He signed up at the community college to earn his GED degree.

    **C**  He immediately went to look for a full-time job.

    **D**  He went to the Lakeview Adult Learning Center to talk to a counselor.

**21** After reading this letter, Mr. Manuel will probably

    **A** Never help another student.

    **B** Tell all of his students to study computers.

    **C** Write to or call Ricardo to congratulate him on his decisions.

    **D** Call Ricardo's mother to complain about the letter.

**22** The tone of Ricardo's letter could best be described as

    **A** Happy and thankful.

    **B** Depressed and excited.

    **C** Critical and happy.

    **D** Sad and thankful.

**Read this passage about storing medicines. Answer Numbers 23 through 25.**

We hear a lot about house cleaning, but we don't hear enough about one particular task. There is another place in your house that needs cleaning. That is the medicine cabinet. It can be very dangerous if you don't do this important job.

What is the first hint that you need to clean the cabinet? You will suddenly need a bandage or aspirin. You look in the cabinet and neither one is there. You realize that you need supplies. It's time to organize and clean the medicine cabinet.

First, take everything out of the cabinet. Throw away everything whose useful time has expired, or passed. If you can't read the label, then throw the medicine away.

Now you need to buy some medicines. You need medicines for fever and pain, and bandages for cuts, as well as an antibiotic ointment. Add a thermometer and a medicine spoon. Of course you need to buy the special medicines you take. It makes sense to store those where you use them. If you take a medicine at bedtime, store it in the bathroom or in the bedroom. If you have to take the medicine with food, keep it in the kitchen. Finally, follow the instructions about how to store the medicine. Some need to be cold. Others can't be in the humidity. They have to be kept out of the bathroom. Always read directions!

**23** Which of these statements best expressed the main of the passage?

    **A** We should remember to clean out the medicine cabinet once a week.

    **B** You should use a medicine only one time and then throw it away.

    **C** For your safety and convenience, clean out your medicine cabinet at least once a year.

    **D** All medicine cabinets should have childproof locks on them.

**24** Which of these booklists would probably be the best source of information on storing medicines?

    **A** *What Questions to Ask At Your Next Doctor's Appointment*

    **B** *The Best Headache Treatments*

**C**  *Safe Storage for Medicines*

**D**  *Medicine Cabinet Design, 2006*

**25**  Which of these statements is an opinion expressed by the passage?

   **A**  Some medicines need to be cold. Others can't be in the humidity.

**B**  We hear a lot about housecleaning, but we don't hear enough about this particular task.

**C**  Throw away anything whose useful time has expired, or passed.

**D**  If you can't read the label, throw the medicine away.

**Pretest Answer Key**

| | | | | |
|---|---|---|---|---|
| 1. C | 6. D | 11. A | 16. C | 21. C |
| 2. B | 7. C | 12. D | 17. D | 22. A |
| 3. A | 8. B | 13. B | 18. A | 23. C |
| 4. B | 9. A | 14. C | 19. B | 24. C |
| 5. D | 10. D | 15. B | 20. D | 25. B |

**To the Student: After you check your answers, record any incorrect answers in this chart. Then review the lessons that will help you to correct your errors.**

| Item | Answer | Lesson Number (for review) | Reading Skill Category |
|---|---|---|---|
| 1 | | 2 | Summarize |
| 2. | | 2, 3 | Sequence |
| 3. | | 2, 3 | Detail |
| 4. | | 2, 3 | Detail |
| 5. | | 2, 3 | Stated concept |
| 6. | | 2, 3 | Summarize |
| 7. | | 2 | Detail |
| 8. | | 5 | Opinion |
| 9. | | 2 | Synonym |
| 10. | | 4 | Conclusion |
| 11. | | 2 | Character aspect |
| 12. | | 2 | Conclusion |
| 13. | | 4 | Supporting evidence |

| | | | |
|---|---|---|---|
| 14. | | 2 | Summarize |
| 15. | | 2, 3 | Stated concept |
| 16. | | 3 | Conclusion |
| 17. | | 2 | Synonym |
| 18. | | 3 | Style/technique |
| 19 | | 4 | Stated concept |
| 20. | | 4 | Sequence |
| 21. | | 5 | Predict outcomes |
| 22. | | 2 | Style |
| 23. | | 2 | Main idea |
| 24. | | 5 | Reference sources |
| 25. | | 4 | Opinion |

Reading Skills Categories

**Interpret Graphic Information**

Signs

Maps

Dictionary

Index

Reference Sources          24

Graphs

Forms

Consumer Materials

**Words in Context**

Same Meaning          9, 17

Opposite Meaning

Appropriate Word

**Recall Information**

| | |
|---|---|
| Details | 3, 4, 7 |
| Sequence | 2, 20 |
| Stated Concepts | 5, 15, 19 |

**Construct Meaning**

| | |
|---|---|
| Character Aspects` | 11 |
| Main Idea | 23 |
| Summary/Paraphrase | 1, 6, 14 |
| Cause/Effect | |
| Compare/Contrast | |
| Conclusion | 10, 12, 16 |
| Supporting Evidence | 13 |

**Evaluate/Extend Meaning**

| | |
|---|---|
| Fact/Opinion | 8, 25 |
| Predict Outcomes | 21 |
| Apply Passage Elements | |
| Generalizations | |
| Effect/Intention | |
| Author Purpose | |
| Style Techniques | 18, 22 |
| Genre | |

**Note: These broad categories of reading skills are broken down into subskill categories. Question numbers agree with the subskill titles.**

## LESSON 2  Starting Out

In Lesson 2, you will see Anna Munoz take steps to start a new career. As you remember, Anna's friend, Theresa, advised her to talk to someone about the skills she would need to become a bank teller. Anna knew she needed to learn more about her computer and math skills.

Theresa offered to take Anna to the Adult Learning Center in their town. That was where Theresa had taken and passed the TABE Test. Now she had started classes at the community college. Even though she had passed the TABE Tests, Theresa wasn't satisfied with her English score. At the community college, Theresa was taking an English course to improve her skills. Theresa said that Anna needed more information before she took any courses at the community college. The Adult Learning Center in their town was a great place to start.

**Words to Know**

| | |
|---|---|
| Currency | Money |
| Deposit and withdrawal | Pay in and take out |
| Verifies | Makes sure |
| Transactions | Business dealings |

## Information, Please

Anna made an appointment with the director of the adult learning center. When they met, Ms. Allen asked Anna many questions about her job. Together they talked about her computer skills and math skills, and the skills she would need to work in a bank. Ms. Allen showed Anna some of the information the learning center received from the Department of Labor. Later in her training, Anna would learn to find this information, and much more, on the computer. Anna read about the teller's job.

Tellers have many responsibilities. The teller is the person most people think of when they think about a bank. Tellers make up about one-fourth of bank employees. They carry out most of a bank's routine transactions, such as:

- Cashing checks
- Accepting deposits and loan payments
- Processing withdrawals.

In addition, tellers may:

- Sell savings bonds
- Accept payment for customers' utility bills and charge cards
- Sell travelers' checks

*Based on information from this Web site: www.bls.gov*

## TARGET: Reading for Main Ideas and Reading for Details

*Reading for Main Ideas:* What is the first thing you do to get meaning from what you read? You probably know the answer to that question. You look for the main idea in the reading. In the example above, Anna read about a teller's job. What do you think the main idea is in that reading? Another way of saying that is, what is the main idea that the writer wanted you to know?

Write your answer here:

_____

If you said that the writer wanted you to learn that a teller's job includes many responsibilities, you were right.

Read the paragraph again. In what sentence did the writer place the main idea? In this reading, it was easy to find. The main idea was in the first sentence. Is that always the way a paragraph is constructed, or written? Look at the next paragraph for the answer to that question:

Before cashing a check, a teller must verify the date, the name of the bank, and the person receiving the money. The teller also decides if the check is legal. A teller must make sure that the written amount and numbers agree. Of course, the account must have enough money to cover the check. The teller then must carefully count cash to avoid errors. Doing the teller's job requires a great deal of attention to detail.

You can see that the writer gave you all the details first. Then, the paragraph ends with the main idea sentence. In this kind of paragraph, the details seem to "add up to," or support, the main idea. The details are stepping-stones to the main idea. Always ask yourself, "Which sentence is the sum of all the supporting details?"

Stop for a minute to think about the details. In the above paragraph, what are they? List them here.

1.

2.

3.

4.

5.

Write the main idea sentence here: _____.

Read the next paragraph. As you read, ask yourself what the main idea is. Find the sentence in which the main idea is stated. Search for the details that tell you more about the main idea.

Before starting their shifts, tellers receive cash to work with that day. Usually, the head teller verifies the amount. Tellers use this cash for payments during the day. They are responsible for handling the cash safely and accurately. Then, before leaving the bank, tellers count the cash on hand. They also need to list the currency on a balance sheet. Their accounts must balance.

You can tell from the first sentence that this paragraph is about *cash*.

What details are there about the *cash*? Look back to sentences 2 through 7 to find the answer to this question. Write the details in the order in which the teller does them:

2.

3.

4.

5.

6.

7.

### STUDY TIP: WARM UP FOR READING
### MAIN IDEAS AND DETAILS

*Always warm up for the event. Have you heard about that before? A reader should always prepare for reading, just as an athlete would do for sports. Runners warm up before a race. Athletes warm up before practice. A reader needs to warm up before reading. Your warm-up means getting your brain "warmed up" to the subject. How do you do that?*

- If the reading has a title, think about it. Does it give clues about the main idea?

- Look for a chapter title, if there is one.

- Does the reading have more than one paragraph? To find the main idea, read the first sentences of a few paragraphs. Then read the entire *last* paragraph. This may be a summary of main ideas. Any of the above may hold strong main idea clues.

- Ask yourself, before you read the entire article, whether you already know something about the topic. You may be able to predict what it is about.

- Ask yourself what you can expect to learn from the reading. After you finish reading, go back and check to see if you were right.

- Look for graphic information and pictures for clues to the main idea before you start reading.

- As you read, *actively* look for the main idea.

This warm-up will take very little time. The more often you practice this skill, the faster you will finish the warm-up step. The time spent is well worth it. At the end of a reading, you won't hear yourself saying, "I just read two pages, and I have no idea what they were about!"

When you read for a main idea, you actively look for the most important thought in the passage. You ask yourself what idea the writer wanted you to know after reading the passage. Ms. Allen showed Anna more information about the teller's job. She said, "This information will tell you that you were right. As a teller, you will need to know how to do simple tasks on a computer. Later, you may use a computer to write a letter to a customer." Anna read the paragraph below:

Before you read it, here are more words about banking.

- Technology—equipment, such as a computer or the program to run it

- Computer terminals—Computer workstation

- Accounts—Records
- Bank product—An item or service offered by the bank

Technology plays a role in a teller's job. In most banks, for example, tellers use computer terminals. On the terminals, they record deposits and withdrawals. These terminals give tellers quick information on customer accounts. Tellers can use this information to help the customer. They can recommend the right bank product or service to the customer.
*Based on information from Sovereign Bank, RI*

Ms. Allen said to Anna, "When you read this information, you knew you were right about the computer. You'll definitely have to learn more about using a computer."

In the bank information, where did Anna find the main idea sentence? Write your answer here: _____. If you said that Anna found the main idea in the first sentence, you were right. Now, what would you say all the detail sentences added to the main idea? Write your answer here: _____.

Did you notice that the rest of the sentences were about *technology*? Each sentence supports the main idea in one of two ways:
The sentence either talks about a kind of technology.
or
The sentence tells what that technology can do for the teller and the bank.

## More About Supporting Details

Everything that you read has both main ideas and supporting details. Supporting details are descriptions, facts, or ideas. They support the main idea by telling more about it. Details may answer the questions who? what? when? where? why? and how?

Read one of the paragraphs in a company's shipping instructions. Find the main idea first. Then look for the details that support the main idea.

**Cable Systems**
**Shipping Instructions**

We need all of the following information in order to ship your package. In addition to your name and address, include the name of the person who will receive the package. Put your company's reference number on the package. Sign the form. Be sure to insure any items worth more than $100.

What is the main idea in the above paragraph? You probably found it in the first sentence. Write it here:

_____

List all of the details that support the main idea:

1.

2.

3.

4.

5.

These details tell you what information is needed in order to ship a package: (1) your name and address, (2) the name of the person who will receive it, (3) your company's reference number, (4) your signature, (5) amount of insurance

When you read a story, you find main ideas. Many times the main ideas are followed by details that describe. Read this paragraph about Jason. Then look for the details that tell more about him.

When Jason was young, he always entered a classroom in fear, and he felt the same way about doing his homework. In school, he was always afraid that the teacher would call on him to read. At home, he knew he would have trouble with so many pages of reading. Soon he would become bored and angry. Finally, he would get up and walk away from his homework. Fortunately, Jason found a teacher who helped him by using a computer.

You read the main idea in the first sentence. What details describe Jason? Write your answers here.

1.

2.

3.

4.

5.

Compare your answers with the ones in this list:

(1) Jason was afraid the teacher would call on him to read, (2) At home he had trouble with many pages of reading, (3) He became bored and angry, (4) He walked away from his homework, (5) Finally, he met a teacher who helped him.

## Target Practice: Reading for Main Ideas and Supporting Details

Sometimes you need to read charts or graphs. Even though they aren't paragraphs, you will still find main ideas in them. As you read the following chart, look actively for the main idea. Then look for details that support the main idea. Where will you look first?

**Chart 1**

Sample Employment in Banking/Tellers

| Company | Location | Salary/Hr. | Date Posted |
|---|---|---|---|
| Tri-Cities Bank | Miami, FL | $10–$12.5/hr | 1/3/05 |
| First Bank | Baltimore, MD | $7.5–$12.5/hr | 1/3/05 |
| 2nd City Bank | Pico, CA | $10–$12.5/hr | 1/10/05 |

1. What is the main idea or topic of this chart?
   A. All teller jobs in the United States
   B. All teller jobs available in January, 2005
   C. A small sample of teller jobs in January, 2005
   D. The salary paid to all tellers in all banks in 2005

2. In this chart, where is the lowest starting salary being offered?
   A. Miami, FL
   B. Pico, CA
   C. Boston, MA
   D. Baltimore, MD

3. What does the term /hr. mean?
   A. The time the bus leaves
   B. The hours the bank is open
   C. Per hour
   D. Per day

4. *Date Posted* means
   A. The day the bank opened for business
   B. The day the job was listed
   C. The hours you need to work
   D. The day the mail went out

Ms. Allen wanted Anna to look at more than one type of job. Anna might not find a job in banking. Or she might decide that she really didn't like the teller's job.

Ms. Allen gave Anna this reading material below. She also told her to look at the education or training for each job. Did Anna want on-the-job training? Would she rather go to the community college and earn an associate degree?

## Chart 2

*Adapted from Department of Labor News*

The Fastest Growing Occupations, 2002-2012

| Occupation | Employment | | Education or Training |
|---|---|---|---|
| | 2002 | 2012 | |
| Medical Assistants | 365,000 | 579,000 | Moderate On-the-job Training |
| Network Systems | 186,000 | 292,000 | Bachelor's Degree |
| Physician Assistants | 63,000 | 94,000 | Bachelor's Degree |
| Social Service Assistants | 305,000 | 454,000 | On-the-job |
| Home Health Aides | 580,000 | 859,000 | Short-term On-the-job Training |
| Medical Records/Health Info. | 147,000 | 216,000 | Associate's Degree |
| Physical Therapist Assistant | 50,000 | 73,000 | Associate's Degree |

1. *Occupation* is another word for
   A. Being busy
   B. Job
   C. Home
   D. Associate

2. Where did you find the main idea of this chart?
   A. In the line beginning, "Medical Records. . ."
   B. In the date, 2012
   C. In the Education or Training column
   D. In the title, "The Fastest Growing Occupations, 2002-2012"

3. Which of the following is one of the most important details on this chart?
   A. These occupations will grow from 2002–2012
   B. A social service assistant needs a Bachelor's Degree
   C. Medical Assistant is the same as Medical Records technician
   D. All the occupations are the same

**4.** You can conclude that the "assistant" jobs are for people who
   **A.** Want to be in total charge of the office
   **B.** Must have a Bachelor's Degree
   **C.** Want to be aides or supporters
   **D.** Want to work only on the computer

**5.** Some training is short-term and on-the-job, while other training is
   **A.** For physicians only
   **B.** Only for employees who have worked for 5 years or more
   **C.** Given in 2006–2007 only
   **D.** Moderate-term and on-the-job

Ms. Allen told Anna that she could read many other job charts on the Internet. Anna said that she would do that as soon as she learned how to use a computer!

### STUDY TIP: SKIMMING AND SCANNING FOR DETAILS

When a question asks you to find a detail, how do you do it? Do you reread every word in the paragraph or passage? There is a better, faster way to find the answer. First decide exactly what you're looking for. Then scan all the material for that word, number, or phrase. How do you do that? You run your eyes down the middle of the passage. Look only for the word, number, or phrase. You are not reading for the meaning. You are looking for one or two words. When you see the detail, stop and read the words around it. You have to be sure you've found the right detail.

Now answer these detail questions.

**1.** The chart above shows the fastest growing occupations for which years?
   **A.** 2002–2010
   **B.** 2002–2012
   **C.** 2011–2012
   **D.** 2001–2012

You knew from the question that you should be scanning for years (numbers). When you scanned the title, you found the numbers immediately. The chart tells about the years 2002 to 2012. Answer B is correct.

**2.** The chart says that in 2012, there will be
   **A.** 365,000 medical assistants
   **B.** 94,000 medical assistants
   **C.** 579,000 medical assistants
   **D.** 859,000 medical assistants

To find the answer, you scanned for two details: *2012* and *medical assistants*. You knew that occupations were listed in the left-hand column. You ran your eyes down the column and found *medical assistant*. Then you needed to find the right year. You scanned across to 2012 and found Answer C, 579,000 medical assistants.

## Answer Key: Section 2, Lesson 2

### Think About the Supporting Details

1. The teller must verify the date, the name of the bank, and the person receiving the money.
2. The teller decides if the check is legal.
3. The teller makes sure that the written amount and numbers agree.
4. The teller must make sure the account has enough money to cover the check.
5. The teller must carefully count the cash.

Main idea sentence: Doing the teller's job requires a great deal of attention to detail.

### Details About Cash

2. The head teller verifies the amount of money.
3. The tellers use this cash for payments during the day.
4. Tellers are responsible to handle cash safely and accurately.
5. At the end of the day, tellers count the cash on hand.
6. They also list the currency on a balance sheet.
7. Tellers' accounts must balance.

### Target Practice: Reading for Main Ideas and Supporting Details

Chart 1

1. C
2. D
3. C
4. B

Chart 2

1. B
2. D
3. A
4. C
5. D

## LESSON 3 Moving On

In Lesson 3, Anna will learn much more about what she needs to do to start a new career. Anna was very lucky to have a good friend, Theresa, to help her along the way. Now she also needed to use some ideas that Ms. Allen gave her. Ms. Allen told her two things. First, Anna should prepare to take the

TABE tests. The community college would ask for these scores. Next, Anna should read about the computer courses given at the Community College. To do that, she went to the library with Theresa, who said she would help her. Theresa had found the Community College catalogs at their local library. She had used the information to sign up at the college for her first course.

Anna was excited to look at some courses given by the community college. She needed to find out if she could take just one or two courses. Anna wanted to convince herself that she could learn how to use a computer. That would help her in banking. It would also help her if she decided to train for a different job.

In the back of her mind, Anna had this thought: She still had to prepare for the TABE tests!

**Words to Know**

| Home Page | The first page of an Internet Web site |
| (E) Electronic Research | Looking for answers on a computer |
| Web Site Address | A group of Web pages |
| Prerequisite | Something required |
| Word Processing | Typing or creating text on a computer |

Before she even looked at the community college courses with Anna, Theresa showed her how to use the new library catalog. Anna remembered—when she was a child—going to find book titles in special drawers. The index cards in those drawers looked something like this:

HF

3200        Webster, Lillian

W543        The History of Small Towns, 1800-1850

2001        244 p.

HF  W3200  W  632        2001

Library of Congress

*

*The above is a model only.

Now, the information about books was in the library's computer. Theresa showed Anna that the computer was always on and ready to use. Anna just needed to tell the computer what she wanted to know. Look at the screen below. This is the library's Home Page. Theresa showed Anna that it was a good place to start. Can you see why?

North Kingstown Free Library

100 Boone St., North Kingstown, RI

Phone: (000) 000-0000

NKFL Home Page

About the Library

E-Research

Local History

Library Programs

Books & Reading

Just for Kids

Teen Zone

Contact Us

## TARGET: Reading to Get the Meaning—Drawing Conclusions

In Lesson 2, you practiced reading for main ideas and details. In this lesson, you will use the main ideas and details to draw conclusions about what you have read. Drawing conclusions takes special attention. Drawing conclusions means making decisions based on facts. In other words, to draw a conclusion, you take two steps. You use the facts you are given and the facts you already know.

Example: Most states have laws about what home health aides can and cannot do. The paragraph below is from instructions given by a home health care company. Notice the difference in meaning between the words *giving* and *assisting*.

In our state, home health aides cannot give medicine. There is a difference between giving someone medicine and assisting. A nurse on our staff will tell you what medicines the patient takes. You will know the times they should be taken.

What conclusion can you draw from the above paragraph?

A. You can make sure that the medicine is kept out of the patient's house.

B. You can remind the patient when it is time to take the medicine.

C. You can decide which medicine will work better for the patient.

D. The home health care company cannot give you any information.

Write your answer here. _____

Explanation: The state says an aide may not give medicine. Answer A is an incorrect conclusion. An aide cannot make a decision about where the medicine should be kept. Answer C is an incorrect conclusion. Because the aide cannot give medicine, the aide certainly can't decide which medicine will work better. Answer D is an incorrect conclusion. The information comes from the home health care company. Answer B is the correct conclusion. The aide assists the patient. One way to assist is to remind the patient when to take the medicine.

You might have to read a story or passage (or Home Page) more than once in order to draw a conclusion.

You can even draw a conclusion about the North Kingstown Library just from reading their Home Page above.

1. What can you conclude about the people who use this library?
   A. They are adults only.
   B. They are in college so they need to do research.
   C. They are children over six years old.
   D. They are people of all ages.

If you read the library's home page carefully, you saw that all ages use this library. Look at the details in the left-hand column. What conclusion can you draw from them? Notice that Teen Zone, Just for Kids, and E-Research are for people of different ages. The correct conclusion based on the details is found in Answer D.

The librarian, Mr. Lania, helped Anna find the community college Web site. She looked at the list of computer courses. Read the information Anna found with Mr. Lania's help.

**Community College**

**School of Technology**

Course Title: Computer Basics for Beginners

Catalog Number: CB 123

Credit Hours: 4

Professor: Amelia Suarez

Prerequisite(s): None (Familiarity with a keyboard and word processing are pluses.)

Course Description: The student will learn about computer equipment and procedures found in the workplace. Students have hands-on use of word processing, presentation software, and the Internet.

1. Anna wanted to convince herself that she could use a computer. From the information above, is she going in the right direction?
   A. No, she isn't going in the right direction. This course is for people who know all about computers.
   B. Yes, she's going in the right direction. She's taken many other courses, so this will be very easy for her.
   C. No, she's going in the wrong direction. She knows for sure that Ms. Suarez is a very hard teacher.
   D. Yes, she's going in the right direction. This is Computer Basics for Beginners with no prerequisites.

Remember that you are looking for an idea or details that lead to a conclusion. Are there any details that say that the course is for people who know all about computers? No. Answer A is incorrect. Did you read that Anna had taken many other courses? No, she hasn't taken any. Answer B is also incorrect. Anna doesn't know anything about the teachers. Answer C is incorrect. Answer D finally gets to the truth. Anna is a beginner. The course is called Computer Basics for Beginners.

Read another course description. Look for conclusions you can draw.

---

**Community College**

**School of Technology**

Course Title: Introduction to Microsoft Word

Catalog Number: CB 124

Credit Hours: 4

Prerequisite(s): None         (Typing skills a plus.)

Course Description: The student will learn about the most popular word-processing program. Students will learn the main parts of the Microsoft Word window. Also included:

1. How to use toolbars and menus 2. How to scroll, insert, and delete text

---

1. Anna knows that she needs to learn word processing for the bank job. What can she conclude from the course description above?
   A. This course will fill that requirement.
   B. The work is unknown to Anna; she won't be able to learn it.
   C. The course description includes no words that are unknown to Anna at this time.
   D. This course has nothing to do with working in a bank.

When Anna read about the teller's job, Ms. Allen told her that she might have to write a letter to a customer. Tellers in many banks are being cross-trained. They learn to perform customer service tasks. Taking this course will help her do that. We know that Anna does not know word processing. We cannot say that she won't be able to learn it. Answer B is not a conclusion that you can draw. Almost all the words are used in a different way in this course description. Anna probably doesn't know all the words. She never used these: scroll, insert, or delete text. They have to do with word processing. Answer C is incorrect. Word processing is a required skill in a bank. Answer D is incorrect. The correct answer is A. The course will teach Anna something she needs to know for a bank job.

## Practice: Reading to Draw Conclusions

Read the next two paragraphs. What conclusion can you draw about Theresa?

While Anna was looking for computer courses, Theresa searched for information she could use in the paper she was writing for her English class. Mr. Dana, her teacher, said each student could choose a subject. But the paper had to be on some topic of health improvement.
Theresa was interested in learning more about diets. She had heard about so many different diets and she had tried them all. She didn't lose weight on any of them, and she wanted to know why. Theresa used the library's online catalog to search for information.

1. What conclusion can you draw about how Theresa feels about this assignment?
   A. She probably thinks it's a lot of work for a little bit of information.
   B. She's probably completely bored with the idea of reading about diets.
   C. She's probably been looking for a good diet for a long time.
   D. She's probably going to do as little as possible on this assignment.

   In the second paragraph, the first three sentences talk about how much Theresa wants a good diet. Answer A is incorrect because she's ready to do the work. Answer B is not right. The first sentence says she's interested in "learning more about diets." Answer D is incorrect because she's so interested in the topic. Which answer gives you the right conclusion? If you chose answer C, you were correct because Theresa had heard about so many diets. She had tried many diets and she didn't lose weight.
   You can conclude that all of the above has taken quite a while, and that is what Answer C says.

## Practice: Reading for the Main Idea, Details, and to Draw Conclusions

Theresa found the following article. As you read it, look for the main idea and details. Try to draw conclusions from the information.

Finding a way to eat healthfully requires time, effort, and patience. How do you know the correct way to eat? All the wrong information we hear and read makes it difficult to know. We hear about fad diets all the time. They do not work. Have you ever tried to eat mostly protein or just grapefruit all day? People can't give up the foods they love forever. No wonder diets fail 95 percent of the time.

Balance is the key to a successful eating plan. You need to combine three things:

- Complex Carbohydrates—Fruits, Vegetables, 100 percent Whole Grain Breads, Cereals (oatmeal and others), Starchy Vegetables (potatoes, yams)

- Lean Proteins—Fish and Shellfish, Lean Cuts of Meat (beef, lamb, pork, veal), Poultry (chicken, turkey), Eggs or Egg Whites, Tofu or Soy products, Low Fat Dairy products (lower-fat cheeses, skim milk), Beans (black beans, kidney beans, chick peas), Nuts and Seeds

- Good Fats—Vegetable Oils (olive, canola, and flaxseed) Fish (salmon, herring, albacore tuna contain Omega 3 fatty acids), Nuts and Seeds

Then you can add the things you like. You still have to keep it all in control. That's called moderation.

What are some other rules to follow? First, think about serving sizes. We all eat very large portions without any thought. Cut them down. For example, if you're having meat, have about 3 ounces of cooked meat. A baking or sweet potato should be small. You should have 1 cup of pasta or rice.

Plan to exercise. Believe it or not, exercise is also a part of a good eating plan. Exercise helps to take the weight off and keep it off. It allows you to have an ice cream cone once in a while. Finally, be consistent!

Used with permission of Kelly Leddy, Certified Nutritional Specialist, NSCA Certified Personal Trainer

1. You can conclude that a clue to the meaning of "moderation" is the word
   A. Portion
   B. Grapefruit
   C. Control
   D. Fad

2. You can conclude that if you eat very large portions of proteins, carbohydrates, and good fats,
   A. You will lose all the weight you need to.
   B. You will never gain weight.
   C. You won't ever be hungry.
   D. You won't lose the weight you want to.

3. You can conclude that a diet means
   A. Controlling what and how much you eat.
   B. Never eating anything you like.
   C. Always eating everything you like.
   D. Choosing two of the three food groups mentioned.

4. What is the main idea of the passage?
   A. Exercise allows you to have ice cream.
   B. Serving size is the only important part of a diet.
   C. Finding a healthful way to eat requires time, effort, and patience.
   D. All fad diets work well for most people.

5. A good size serving of protein would be
   A. 5 ounces of chocolate
   B. 3 ounces of cooked meat
   C. 2 nuts
   D. 7 small potatoes

## More Practice: Drawing Conclusions

You can draw conclusions from many kinds of reading material. Read the advertisement below. As you do, actively try to draw some conclusions from the details.

NEWEST TECHNOLOGY Dish TV

Over $500 Value Free when you sign up for TecTV

NOW only $24.95 per month for the first 6 months

Must sign up for 1 year of programming (35.99 per month). New customers only. Hardware sold separately.

Satellite dish, receivers & remotes included.

Call now to sign up!

1 888 123-4567

1. There is a reason that $24.95 is in larger print. You can conclude that the company
   A. Will always charge the customer this amount.
   B. Wanted the reader's eye to be caught by the low price.
   C. Has decided that $24.95 is the fair and only price.
   D. Will promise this price to their old customers as well.

2. Which of these important details does the small print hold?
   A. New customers only will pay the lower price—and only for 6 months.
   B. Hardware is sold separately.
   C. You must sign up for 1 year and the price will be $35.99 per month.
   D. Answers A, B, and C.

**3.** You can conclude that careful shoppers
   **A.** Read both the large and small print in an ad before they buy.
   **B.** Call the 888 number quickly so they won't lose a good deal.
   **C.** Believe everything they read in ads.
   **D.** Never believe even one word of any ad they read.

## Answer Key: Section 2, Lesson 3

Practice: Reading for the Main Idea, Details, and to Draw Conclusions

1. C    2. D    3. A    4. C    5. B

More Practice: Drawing Conclusions

1. B    2. D    3. A

## LESSON 4    Making Progress

Anna and Theresa were talking on the phone one day. Theresa asked Anna if she had signed up at the Adult Learning Center. Anna replied, "Yes, I have. I've already started to learn about test-taking skills. I'm also sharpening my reading skills. There's a lot to learn." "I know how you must feel," Theresa said. It was hard for me." She continued, "Still, I think you're lucky. You know what you want to do after you learn how to use a computer. I'm still not sure what I'll do after I finish at the community college."

Anna surprised Theresa with her answer. "I know I said I wanted to be a bank teller. But since you showed me how to use the computer to look for other careers, I'm just not sure. I found some interesting jobs in food service, too." Theresa asked, "Do you mean in a restaurant?" Anna quickly said, "No. There are other places such as hospitals and big companies that need people in food service. The other career that interests me is administrative assistant. I can see myself in someone's office, filing papers, or organizing a calendar. Can't you see me at a beautiful desk, answering the telephone and using the computer?" Theresa laughed and said, "Good luck with your search. Find something for me, too!"

**Words to Know**

| | |
|---|---|
| Thesaurus | A book that lists words related to each other in meaning. Usually gives synonyms and antonyms |
| Synonym | A word that means the same or almost the same as another word |
| Antonym | A word that means the opposite of another word |
| Context | The words and phrases around an unknown word that help to explain it |

# TARGET: Understanding Words in Context

Do you always understand all the words you read or hear? No one does. If you are at home or in school, you can use a dictionary. You can find the definition, or meaning, in a dictionary. Or you can use a Thesaurus to find synonyms and antonyms. (More about that book later.) But when you cannot use those books, you need to use other reading skills.

**TEST TIP:**

What happens when you don't have a dictionary with you when you take a test? There are other ways to figure out the meanings of unknown words. First, you need to use *context clues*. Context clues are found in the word itself and in the ideas around it. Then, you can study the parts of the word for clues to its meaning. Here are some ways to understand unknown words.

- The writer may give you the definition of the unknown word.

    Example: The teacher wrote my name on a copy of the *syllabus*, or outline of topics.

- The writer supplies the meaning of *syllabus* after the comma. *Syllabus* means an outline of topics.

- You may read a word that you have used before, but the word is used differently in this new context. Use your experience to unlock the meaning in the new context.

---

Example: A COURSE ABOUT THE INTERNET

If you know how to use a <u>mouse</u>, you can use the Internet. This class also teaches you to use a <u>browser</u>.

---

The sentences above could be in a catalog of courses. The underlined words are not very difficult. You know both of them <u>in different contexts</u>.

The long-tailed <u>mouse</u> ran under the sofa.

In this case, the <u>mouse</u> is a rodent that we don't want running around in the house.

In the catalog, the <u>mouse</u> has to do with a computer. It's the pushbutton that gives instructions to the computer.

You can see that the context in which you find the word is very important to the meaning.

The same is true for the word <u>browser</u>. It is used in a computer class description. You know that it has to do with a computer. After that, you will ask yourself a question. Which part of the word seems familiar to you? You probably know the word <u>browse</u>. You've used the word to say that you would go to the mall just to <u>browse</u>—to look through stores slowly. Or, you may browse quickly through a book to see if you like it. Either way, you are looking for or at something. When you use a <u>browser</u>, you are searching for information on the World Wide Web.

Look at the next sentence:

This class will teach you to go to a specific <u>address</u> on the Internet. You will use a <u>search engine</u> to research a topic or send <u>email</u>.

Again, the words look familiar. You know what <u>address </u>means. You now have to look at how it's used differently. It is in a different context—the Internet. The same is true for the term <u>search engine</u>. An engine is something that supplies energy. You know what it means to search. You know what an engine is. But what is it in this context? The words around the term give you the answer: it is a "force" or system you use to research or send email. You can see that simple words are used in many different contexts.

Another Example: Molten rock *percolates* beneath the earth and rises up through solid rock.

Use your experience. You are a coffee drinker. You *percolate* coffee every day. How does your experience help you to unlock the meaning of *percolates* in the example sentence? You know that hot water *percolates*, or boils up through the coffee. Apply that to the example. Now you can see that molten rock is so hot, it is thought of as boiling up and rising through solid rock.

- You need to look for clues that surround the unknown word. All of the words around the unknown word will help you to define it.

Example: My children always tried to do things they weren't supposed to do. We said they needed to be home after school to do their homework. They offered excuses about why they couldn't be there. As parents, we had to overcome their *resistance* to the rules.

How do the words and ideas in the paragraph help you to understand *resistance*? You read that the children always tried to do things they weren't supposed to do. Clearly, these parents had to *struggle*, or *resist* as the children pulled in a different direction. The children resisted, or quarreled with rules.

Another example: Look back at the conversation between Anna and Theresa at the beginning of this lesson. Find the word *administrative*. You might not have known the meaning of it. The context will help you. That means all of the words around the unknown word will help you to define *administrative*. Think about the context in which you find the word.

What does Anna say about the job?

"I can see myself in an office, filing papers, or organizing a calendar. Can't you see me at a beautiful desk, answering the telephone and using the computer?"

Anna sees herself overseeing office tasks for someone. She is organizing the calendar and handling phone messages. She is using a computer to complete tasks. She is assisting in a business by *overseeing* the tasks. And that is what the words *administrative assistant* means: a person who helps by overseeing the work of a business.

- You should look at all of the parts of the unknown word. The word may seem very long and difficult to understand. Take another look. You may know the root of the word. You may know the prefix (the letters at the beginning of the word). You may understand the suffix (the syllable at the end of the word). When you put it all together, you have the meaning.

Example: The thought of losing my friend was *unimaginable*.

Take the word *unimaginable* apart. You have the root, *imagine*. That means to see or picture in your mind's eye. What does the prefix un- add to the meaning? Think of words that start with the prefix un-: untie, undo, unleash are just a few. Un- means not. Now we have *not -see- able, or not able to be seen or pictured in your mind's eye.*

## Target Practice: Understanding Words in Context

Read these paragraphs.

Anna found this article when she researched for other jobs. If there are words you don't know, use context clues to figure them out.

What are <u>transferable</u> skills? Some of them are problem solving, organizing, communicating, and giving customer service. They can be used in a <u>new</u> field. Of course, you should research the field you want to get into. Does the job you want use your <u>transferable skills</u>?

Idea from *"Transferable" Skills are Key to New Job or Career*, by Carol Kleiman, *Chicago Tribune*, July 4, 2004.

1. Look at the word itself and the context it is in to figure out the meaning of transferable. What does transferable mean?
   A. Able to use your bus ticket.
   B. Paid
   C. Needs totally different skills.
   D. Moveable from one job to another.

In this paragraph, you will need to read—very carefully—the words around the unknown words. They will help you define the underlined words..

Do you think of yourself as an <u>underemployed</u> worker? You may think that you should have a better job. Perhaps you feel that you are not working up to your <u>potential</u>. If that is the case, stop and do this: Evaluate your skills in reading, writing, and math before your next job interview. Find out if your skills are good enough for the job you want.

As a reader, you can choose how you want to work out a word. Look at its parts. Look at the words around it in the sentence and the paragraph.

2. In the above paragraph, <u>underemployed</u> can be understood by looking at its parts. Write the two meaningful parts here.

3. <u>Underemployed</u> is defined in another sentence. Write that sentence here.

4. After reading the entire paragraph, do you understand the meaning of the word <u>potential</u>? Choose one.
   A. Ability for future achievement
   B. Lack of skills for the job
   C. A possible job offer
   D. The desire to pass the TABE Tests

Read the paragraphs. Pay special attention to the words in italics. Answer the questions that follow.

Sovereign is an equal opportunity employer. Sovereign does <u>not</u> *discriminate* in hiring or employment on the basis or race, color, religious creed, national origin, sex, sexual preference, ancestry, age, veteran or marital status, or the presence of a non-job related *disability*. No question on this application is intended to secure information to be used for such discrimination.

5. Anna found that the bank application started with an important statement. In the longest sentence (above) she read the word *discriminate*. In this context, the word means
   A. Disappoint the job seeker
   B. Decide for the disabled
   C. decide for or against
   D. Develop an attitude about

6. The first sentence of the paragraph helps you to understand the word *discriminate*. How does the bank treat job seekers?
   A. With the same rules
   B. Very impolitely
   C. To lunch on their first day on the job
   D. Very well until they start working

7. The last word in the same sentence is *disability*. Think of any word you know that helps you to define it. In this context, what does *disability* mean?
   A. Unskilled for the job
   B. An inability to do some tasks
   C. Disappointed in the job
   D. Not hired for the job

Theresa was still working on finding a good eating plan. She found this information:

What you eat is not the only *consideration* in a diet plan. Exercise must be a part of your daily routine. Choose an activity you like. You can run if you are able to do that. We know now that walking is just as *effective* an exercise. Pick up the pace a little bit and you'll give your body a workout. Remember. Exercise plus a healthful diet equals weight loss!

Used with permission of Kelly Leddy

8. What is the main idea of this paragraph?
   A. Running is the only good way to exercise.
   B. Exercise without a good diet works better.
   C. Walking has never been a good choice for exercise.
   D. Exercise plus a healthful diet equals weight loss.

9. *Consideration* in this context means
   A. A question you ask of everyone you know.
   B. A quicker walking pace.
   C. Something taken into account before a decision is made.
   D. Whether or not you should have dessert.

10. In this paragraph, what does the word *effective* mean?
    A. Actual
    B. Can be practiced
    C. Successful
    D. Memorable

 **SKILL TIP**

Which books can you use to find the meanings of unknown words?
   Dictionary—for pronunciation, definitions, history of the word, synonym, and sometimes the antonym.

Example: Reference book, noun

   1. A book that is meant to be used for looking up facts, definitions, or other information.

Example: Antonym, noun

   1. A word that means the opposite of another word...

Thesaurus—a book that lists words related to each other in meaning, usually giving synonyms

Example: Part, noun

   1. A section of something...

   2. A division of something such as a book or report...

   3. The line in a hairstyle...

The dictionary and Thesaurus are both reference books. You can refer to, or look at, these reference books when you have questions about words. In addition, there are other reference books that you use all the time. Your telephone book is one. The *Atlas of World Maps* is another. These books hold large amounts of information written in very short entries. Encyclopedias are included in this list too.

## Answer Key

### Section 2, Lesson 4 Understanding Words in Context

1. D
2. *under + employed*
3. You may think that you should have a better job.
4. A
5. C
6. A
7. B
8. D
9. C
10. C

## LESSON 5  Back to School

In this lesson, follow Anna as she finally starts classes at the Adult Learning Center. As you know, Anna needs to take (and pass) the TABE tests so that she can take courses at the community college. She has been to her first class to prepare for the reading skills test. Now she has returned home. She is thinking about the reading she did in class. She enjoyed sharpening her reading skills, as you also will do in the next section.

**Words to Know**

| | |
|---|---|
| Figurative language | Words used in an unusual way, but for an effect Example: His words came out *like the hiss of a snake*. |
| Metaphor | A symbol used to achieve an effect |
| Simile | Compares two things, using "like" or "as" |
| empathizes | Identifies with |

In this lesson, you will have an opportunity to practice the reading skills you learned in Lessons 1 through 4. You will continue to read to find main ideas and details. You also will draw conclusions and use your skill to figure out words in context. Then you will need to apply those skills in stories, essays, and other information about people.

Anna found that she needed to pay closer attention to the way an author described people and situations. Sometimes the writer used figurative language to express creative ideas.

Example: We drove all through the dark night. Looking at the oncoming cars was like staring at the sun.

Explanation: Is the driver really staring at the sun? No. The figurative language, though, gives the reader a clear picture. The reader experiences the drive through the writer's words.

Look at Words to Know above. Is the example you read a simile or metaphor? Write your answer here.

_____

If you said that the example is a simile, you were right. The word *like* compares two unlike things: car lights and the sun's light.

The American author, Washington Irving, wrote about the Catskill Mountains in his story, *Rip Van Winkle*. How does he describe the mountains?

"...When the weather is fair and settled, they are clothed in blue and purple, and print their bold outlines on the clear evening sky..."

Do you usually think of mountains as wearing clothes? No, but here the mountains take on a human quality. With words, Irving paints them in colorful clothes. The mountains are "clothed in blue and purple." This is figurative language—a metaphor.

Now read this:

"Rip Van Winkle was a simple, good-natured man. He was, also, a kind neighbor and an obedient, hen-pecked husband."

Adapted from the original.

Did you already know the meaning of *hen-pecked*? If not, what word would help you to define it in context?

- **A.** Neighborly
- **B.** Simple
- **C.** Loving
- **D.** Obedient

If you chose D., *obedient*, you were right. Rip's wife told him what to do and he obeyed.

## Target Practice: Read to Understand Figurative Language, to Find Main Ideas and Details, and to Draw Conclusions

More about Rip Van Winkle:

1. "Rip Van Winkle was one of those happy, foolish people, of *well-oiled* nature, who take the world easy and would rather starve than work."

*Well-oiled* seems to compare Rip's nature to
A. His wife
B. His dog
C. An enemy
D. An engine

The great error in Rip's makeup was his aversion, his great dislike of profitable work. He would hold a heavy fishing rod all day without a single nibble. He would carry a heavy gun all day to shoot a few squirrels. He would never refuse to help a neighbor even in the hardest work. The women of the village, too, used him to run their errands and do odd jobs. In short, he would attend to anybody's business but his own.

2. What is the synonym in the first sentence that gives you the meaning of the word *aversion*?
A. Happy
B. Error
C. Dislike
D. Profitable

3. The main idea of the paragraph is where?
A. In both the first and last sentences
B. In the words *heavy fishing rod*
C. In the words *run the errands*
D. In the words *refuse to help*

Anna and her classmates learned about a new way some companies are hiring people. It's a good thing that Anna is learning to use a computer. Why? For many companies, meeting a computer is like meeting a manager. In one supermarket, people are encouraged and invited to apply for a job. A computer is placed near customer service. The computer gathers information about the person. The computer asks for your name, address, and social security number. It also asks many other questions that gather information. The answers tell the company if the person might do a good job and stay a while.

4. In sentence 4, the computer "meets" the person before a manager does. What is that an example of?
A. Poor judgment
B. Figurative language/simile
C. Poor writing
D. Customer service

5. Where does one store place the computer that greets job seekers?
A. Out in the open, near Customer Service
B. Hidden behind the Customer Service counter

**C.** At the bagging area

**D.** In the parking lot

6. You can conclude that the computer
   **A.** Can't be very helpful to the company because the information is old
   **B.** Gathers only false information
   **C.** Can't recognize people who haven't learned the simplest computer skills
   **D.** Saves the hiring company money and time by weeding out people who probably won't work out

7. Why does the paragraph say, "It's a good thing that Anna is learning to use a computer"?
   **A.** She'll need to know how to use the computer at this supermarket only.
   **B.** More and more companies believe that people have and need computer skills.
   **C.** More and more companies think that computers are too difficult to use.
   **D.** A company would never, ever teach an employee to use their computer system.

 **SKILL TIP**

When you read a personal piece of writing, you'll find figures of speech. If you read carefully, you'll also be able to recognize the mood and tone of the article. A writer carefully chooses words that set the mood and tone of the passage.

Think about the changes in your own moods. Sometimes you are sad, even gloomy. Other times you might be playful or sarcastic (mocking) or afraid. Do any of these words explain the mood of these writers?

What tone does each writer take? The way they use words to make their thinking understood is the tone.

Example:

Dear Bob,

As my best friend, I want you to know that I've decided to leave this dead-end job. I'm going back to school and I'm going to do what I've always wanted to do!

The tone that this letter will take is clear. The writer uses the word *dead-end*. Bob will have no trouble understanding the writer's feelings about the job. The decision is clear, and it is exciting: He's going to do what he's always wanted to do!

As you read the two passages below, look for the words that tell you the writers' mood. A student wrote the first one. A famous comedian wrote the other. Both writers used the same metaphor, a figure of speech, or symbol for *life*. Read carefully to answer this question: What symbol did both writers use for *life*?

**Essay #1**

I find that life can be compared to a gigantic roller coaster. The roller coaster is on a never-ending track with extremely dangerous curves. Sometimes I am moving so fast that it feels like the brakes have been torn out from under me. When it starts in a downward motion, the roller coaster car can be hard to steer on your own.

But sometimes in the roller coaster nightmare, I am going so fast that it becomes difficult to get off. I begin to feel like there is nobody who is willing or capable of helping me slow down that roller coaster car. No one can help me get around those tight and narrow turns.

Sometimes there are other people's roller coaster cars that are more skilled at traveling that track. They are so concerned about reaching the end of their journey that they forget about other people's roller coaster cars. When I am traveling that track, my body and soul become worn down. Finally, I end up falling off on one of those tight and narrow turns.

Is there anybody on that track who is willing to slow down and help me travel that twisty, windy path? I hope that someone exists on our track of life today, for you and me.

If this individual does exist, I hope I can find him or her before I hit the wall and end up burning in a ball of flames. I hope we're all able to realize the importance of the gifts these helpers offer us.

Adapted from Cindy Hedrick, *The Roller Coaster Voices:* New Writers for New Readers Issue 10 Volume 4, Number 1 Fall 1991

**Essay #2**

Life is truly a ride. We're all strapped in and no one can stop it. When the doctor slaps your behind, he's ripping your ticket and away you go. As you make each passage from youth to adulthood to maturity, sometimes you put your arms up and scream; sometimes you just hang on to that bar in front of you. But the ride is the thing. I think the most you can hope for at the end of life is that your hair's messed, you're out of breath, and you didn't throw up.

—Jerry Seinfeld Excerpt from *SeinLanguage* p. 153

## Target Practice: Reading to Recognize Literary Techniques

You can see that two very different people wrote the passages. Still, they both have used the same technique. Both used a metaphor, or symbol, for *life*. What is that symbol? Write your answer here. _____

_____

You probably realized that both writers used a ride or *roller coaster* as a symbol for what happens in life. The reader easily empathizes with the picture of the rider hurled through space. You know or can easily imagine the feeling of being flung through space (life) as you hang on with all your strength.

What else can you tell about the two writers from these passages? Can you tell something about their moods? What is the overall tone, that is, the outlook or feelings of each author?

Answer the following questions to explore the writers' tone, and meaning.

8. The conclusion that Jerry Seinfeld has reached is that
   A. If you don't want to ride, just get off.
   B. Everyone knows exactly what life will bring to them.
   C. The ride is the important thing.
   D. You're a baby if you scream.

9. The tone of the first passage tells you that the writer's life has been
   A. Really easy and predictable
   B. Easily steered, especially the tight turns
   C. As frantic and scary as a roller coaster ride
   D. All of the above

10. The student's essay ends
    A. In complete despair
    B. On a hopeful note
    C. With no hope
    D. In negotiation

11. In the Seinfeld article, what does the final sentence mean?
    A. Don't go on the roller coaster if you don't like getting your hair messed up in the wind.
    B. Don't go on the roller coaster if you're afraid of throwing up and if you have a hard time breathing.
    C. Don't go on the roller coaster if you do have a cold and have a hard time breathing,
    D. If your hair's messed, you're out of breath, and you didn't throw up, you've probably taken part in and succeeded in life.

12. Cindy's second and third paragraphs express
    A. A real cry for help
    B. Her despair because she is worn down in body and soul
    C. The fear that she will fall off the track
    D. All of the above

13. What is Cindy's hope for society?
    A. Society will realize the importance of people who help others.
    B. Everyone will leave her alone so that she can get on with her life.
    C. She can get her children to school on time with the help of others.
    D. Answers A and B above

**14.** Compare the two passages. Which of the following statements is true about the passages?
  **A.** Seinfeld's is true for everyone, while Cindy's is true for no one.
  **B.** Seinfeld's is prepared to accept, but positive, while Cindy's is fearful but willing to go forward.
  **C.** Seinfeld's is without humor, while Cindy's is humorous throughout.
  **D.** Cindy writes about other people's lives, while Seinfeld writes only about himself.

 **SKILL TIP**

As you read a newspaper article, evaluate what you read. Form your own opinion on the subject.

This newspaper article contains an important idea for job seekers.

Read the article to find the main idea. See if you agree with the writer about applying for a job.

Don't make this mistake! You find a great job advertisement in the newspaper. You may have found it on the Internet. Of course, you want to make sure that you get the job. You dash off a letter to make an appointment for an interview. Without rereading it or making corrections, you put it in the mail. What is the end result of your effort? You never hear from the company.

Consider this a serious warning. If you are asked to send a letter, the first rule of a job search is to send a really well written letter. Otherwise, the employer will probably throw your letter aside. Why is this important? You've made a terrible first impression. And you probably won't get a chance to talk about your excellent work record. A carelessly written letter turns off an employer. Spelling and grammar do count!

This writer has strong opinions about applying for a job. How do you think the writer would feel if you answered a job ad that included the manager's name, Mr. Sparzo. You started your letter with, "Dear Ms. Sparzo."

**15.** This writer would warn you to
  **A.** Arrive at the interview on time.
  **B.** Write a second letter to Ms. Sparzo.
  **C.** Get the manager's name right.
  **D.** Forget spelling; just put it in the mail.

**16.** According to this writer, the first rule of a job search is to
  **A.** Find the letter the employer threw aside.
  **B.** Buy all new clothes whether or not you have the money.
  **C.** Stop reading the newspaper.
  **D.** Know how to write a really well written letter.

**17.** What effect is this article meant to have on the reader?
- **A.** The reader will probably stop and wonder if his or her letter writing needs improvement.
- **B.** The reader will probably say that the writer should mind his or her business.
- **C.** This article will have no effect because it is all wrong.
- **D.** The reader will probably say that the writer hasn't said anything important.

## Answer Key Section 2, Lesson 5

| | | | | | |
|---|---|---|---|---|---|
| 1. D | 4. B | 7. B | 10. B | 13. A | 16. D |
| 2. C | 5. A | 8. C | 11. D | 14. B | 17. A |
| 3. A | 6. D | 9. C | 12. D | 15. C | |

# SECTION 3

# Mathematics

The math section of the TABE has two parts. On the first part (Mathematics Computation), you will have to add, subtract, multiply, and divide whole numbers, fractions, and decimals. This part has 40 multiple-choice questions with 4 answer choices and a fifth choice, "None of these." You can't use a calculator on this part. The second part of the test (Applied Mathematics) covers math topics that are used in day-to-day life, such as percents, measurement, geometry, averages, and reading charts and graphs. There are 50 multiple-choice questions with 4 answer choices, but you can use a calculator on this part.

This section is also divided into these two main parts. Each of these is further subdivided into topics made up by the TABE D test writers. There are six topics in the Mathematics Computation section:

- Multiplying Whole Numbers
- Dividing Whole Numbers
- Fractions
- Decimals
- Percents
- Integers

  There are eight topics in the Applied Mathematics section:

- Numeration
- Number Theory
- Data Interpretation
- Pre-Algebra and Algebra
- Measurement
- Geometry
- Computation in Context
- Estimation

Don't worry if you aren't sure of the meaning of all these topics. They will be explained in the chapter. Don't worry if you had trouble with math in school. You are now older, with more life experience, and you'll probably find that the math you might have found hard before now seems easy!

There will be things in math you've forgotten or need to brush up on. You need to start by learning what your weaknesses are. The best way to do this is to take the Math Skills Pretests that follow. These tests have sample problems like the ones on the actual TABE D tests, except they are shorter. After you check the answer keys, you can determine the types of problems you got wrong and study these parts of the section first.

# Math Skills Pretest
## PART I: Mathematics Computation
## Note: No calculator permitted

Date: _____   Start Time: _____

1
$$467$$
$$\times\ 8$$

   A   3286

   B   3736

   C   3656

   D   3284

   E   None of these

2   $12\overline{)480}$

   A   4

   B   30

   C   40

   D   44

   E   None of these

3   $\$6.48 - \$3.61 =$

   A   $3.87

   B   $3.27

   C   $2.87

   D   $3.13

   E   None of these

4   $\dfrac{-50}{10} =$

   A   $-5$

   B   5

   C   $\dfrac{-1}{5}$

   D   $\dfrac{1}{5}$

   E   None of these

5   $84 \div 6 =$

   A   10 R 2

   B   16

   C   14

   D   12 R 2

   E   None of these

6   $\dfrac{5}{7} - \dfrac{2}{7} =$

   A   $\dfrac{3}{7}$

   B   $\dfrac{3}{14}$

   C   $\dfrac{3}{0}$

   D   $\dfrac{7}{14}$

   E   None of these

7   $0.5 + 0.8 =$

   A   0.13

   B   1.3

   C   13

   D   0.013

   E   None of these

8   6% of 50 =

   A   30

   B   3

   C   12

   D   6

   E   None of these

**9**    $-4 + 9 =$

     **A**    $-13$

     **B**    13

     **C**    $-5$

     **D**    5

     **E**    None of these

**10**    $41 \times 263 =$

     **A**    10,783

     **B**    1315

     **C**    10,683

     **D**    9783

     **E**    None of these

**11**    $4 \times \dfrac{3}{5} =$

     **A**    $\dfrac{15}{20}$

     **B**    $\dfrac{12}{5}$

     **C**    $\dfrac{3}{20}$

     **D**    $\dfrac{7}{5}$

     **E**    None of these

**12**    $\dfrac{2}{3} \div \dfrac{1}{2} =$

     **A**    $\dfrac{1}{3}$

     **B**    $\dfrac{4}{3}$

     **C**    $\dfrac{3}{4}$

     **D**    $\dfrac{3}{5}$

     **E**    None of these

**13**    18 is 30% of what number?

     **A**    6

     **B**    5.4

     **C**    60

     **D**    54

     **E**    None of these

**14**    $4\overline{)4.04}$

     **A**    1.1

     **B**    1.01

     **C**    .01

     **D**    1.11

     **E**    None of these

**15**    $-66 \div 3 =$

     **A**    22

     **B**    $-11$

     **C**    10

     **D**    $-22$

     **E**    None of these

**16**    $-8 - 12 =$

     **A**    20

     **B**    $-20$

     **C**    4

     **D**    $-4$

     **E**    None of these

**17**    $27 \div 1.8 =$

     **A**    1.5

     **B**    0.15

     **C**    15

     **D**    0.015

     **E**    None of these

**18**
$$428 \\ \times 287$$

   **A**  122,836

   **B**  7276

   **C**  12,970

   **D**  120,836

   **E**  None of these

**19**  $6\dfrac{3}{10} + 1\dfrac{1}{100} =$

   **A**  7.31

   **B**  7.3

   **C**  8.31

   **D**  8.4

   **E**  None of these

**20**  $22\overline{)418}$

   **A**  24

   **B**  18

   **C**  19

   **D**  28

   **E**  None of these

**21**  What percent of 80 is 16?

   **A**  50%

   **B**  20%

   **C**  500%

   **D**  12.8%

   **E**  None of these

**22**  $.012 \times .023 =$

   **A**  0.00276

   **B**  0.000276

   **C**  0.0276

   **D**  0.0000276

   **E**  None of these

**23**  $-4 - 1 =$

   **A**  5

   **B**  3

   **C**  $-3$

   **D**  $-5$

   **E**  None of these

**24**  $\dfrac{3}{4} \times 12 =$

   **A**  8

   **B**  9

   **C**  10

   **D**  $2\dfrac{1}{4}$

   **E**  None of these

**25**  18% of $30.00

   **A**  $44.00

   **B**  $4.40

   **C**  $5.00

   **D**  $5.40

   **E**  None of these

# Part II: Applied Mathematics
## Note: Calculator Permitted

Date: _____     Start Time: _____

**1** Which of these is another way to write $4^3$?

    **A**   $4 + 4 + 4$

    **B**   $4 \times 3$

    **C**   $4 \times 4 \times 4$

    **D**   $3 \times 3 \times 3 \times 3$

**2** Which fraction is greater than $\frac{1}{3}$ but less than $\frac{2}{3}$?

    **A**   $\frac{1}{4}$

    **B**   $\frac{1}{2}$

    **C**   $\frac{1}{5}$

    **D**   $\frac{7}{9}$

**3** A map has a scale of 1 inch equals 3 miles. How far apart are two places if they are 3 inches apart on the map?

    **A**   9 miles

    **B**   5 miles

    **C**   6 miles

    **D**   1 mile

**4** You and your friends spend $42.00 at a restaurant for dinner. A 15% tip will be

    **A**   $4.35

    **B**   $15.00

    **C**   $6.30

    **D**   $7.50

**5** Which of these figures is a trapezoid?

**6** Which symbol goes in the space to make the number sentence true?

88 _____ 3 < 30

    **A**   $+$

    **B**   $-$

    **C**   $\times$

    **D**   $\div$

**7** George's telephone plan charges $10.00 for the first 400 minutes. Each minute over 400 costs $.05. George made 500 minutes of phone calls last month. How much was his bill?

    **A**   $11.00

    **B**   $10.50

    **C**   $15.00

    **D**   $12.50

**8** A construction crew started working at 6:45 a.m. on Monday. They worked for four hours. Then they took a 45-minute lunch break. They worked for four-and-a-half more hours. What time did they finish work?

    **A**   4:15 p.m.

    **B**   4:30 p.m.

    **C**   4:00 p.m.

    **D**   3:34 p.m.

**9** Jim is making phone calls for a fund-raiser. He expects about 5% of the people he calls to make a donation. He made 39 calls Monday morning. About how many of these calls should result in donations?

A 2

B 4

C 6

D 8

**The yard at Linda's house has the shape and dimensions shown in the diagram. Use this diagram to do numbers 10 and 11.**

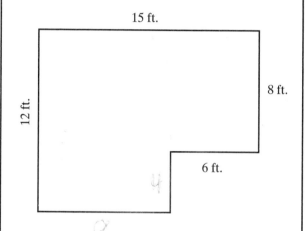

15 ft.

8 ft.

12 ft.

6 ft.

**10** Linda wants to plant some grass seed. How much area would she have to cover?

A 224 sq ft

B 208 sq ft

C 216 sq ft

D 156 sq ft

**11** Linda wants to fence in her whole yard. How much fencing would she need?

A 41 ft

B 54 ft

C 60 ft

D 64 ft

**12** How many of the numbers below round to 85.2?

85.29   85.24   85.14   85.19   85.28

A 0

B 1

C 2

D 3

**A survey organization published a graph showing men's favorite sport to watch on TV. Use the graph to answer numbers 13, 14, and 15.**

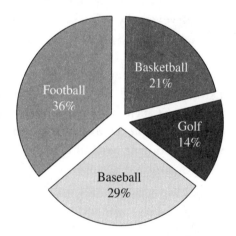

**13** What percent chose football or baseball as their favorite?

A 55%

B 57%

C 65%

D 67%

**14** Which was the least popular sport?

    **A** basketball

    **B** football

    **C** baseball

    **D** golf

**15** According to the graph, which of the statements is true?

    **A** Over half of chose baseball or basketball as their favorite TV sport.

    **B** More chose baseball than football as their favorite TV sport.

    **C** Half chose football or golf as their favorite TV sport.

    **D** The smallest number of those surveyed chose basketball as the favorite TV sport.

**16** Jim flies to Denver from Boston with a stop in Chicago. Flying time from Boston to Chicago is three hours, and from Chicago to Denver is four hours. What fraction of total time is the part from Boston to Chicago?

    **A** $\dfrac{3}{4}$

    **B** $\dfrac{3}{7}$

    **C** $\dfrac{4}{7}$

    **D** $\dfrac{1}{2}$

**The following table shows the number of people who know a rumor at various times. Use the table to answer number 17.**

THE SPREAD OF A RUMOR

| Time | Number of People |
| --- | --- |
| 9:00 a.m. | 2 |
| 10:00 a.m. | 4 |
| 11:00 a.m. | 8 |
| 12:00 noon | 16 |

**17** If the pattern continues, how many people will know the rumor by 3:00 p.m.?

    **A** 22

    **B** 24

    **C** 32

    **D** 128

**18** The regular price of a washing machine is $550. It is on sale at a discount of 20%. What is the sale price?

    **A** $440

    **B** $530

    **C** $495

    **D** $110

**19** Which triangle appears to be congruent to the shaded triangle?

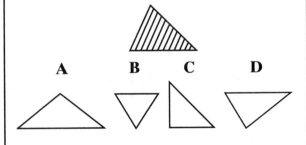

**20** Between them, Megan and Melissa sold 240 boxes of Girl Scout cookies. If $x$ represents the number of boxes sold by Megan, which represents the number of boxes sold by Melissa?

**A** $120 + x$

**B** $2x$

**C** $240 - x$

**D** $x - 240$

**21** Which of these figures could have two pairs of parallel sides?

**A** right triangle

**B** rectangle

**C** trapezoid

**D** pentagon

**A survey was taken to find out how people spend their leisure time. Study the results of the survey. Then do numbers 22, 23, and 24.**

HOW PEOPLE SPEND THEIR LEISURE TIME

| Activity | Percent of People |
|---|---|
| Watching TV | 55% |
| Reading | 15% |
| Playing Sports | 10% |
| Gardening | 8% |
| Taking Day Trips | 7% |
| Listening to Music | 5% |

**22** What is the ratio of the percent of people who spend their leisure time watching TV to the percent that spend their leisure time playing sports?

**A** 11 to 2

**B** 11 to 13

**C** 2 to 11

**D** 2 to 13

**23** What is the probability that a person from the survey spends leisure time gardening?

**A** $\dfrac{1}{8}$

**B** $\dfrac{1}{80}$

**C** $\dfrac{2}{25}$

**D** $\dfrac{8}{25}$

**24** Based on information in the table, which statement is true?

**A** More than half of those surveyed watch TV.

**B** One out of three people read.

**C** If 200 people were surveyed, only 7 took day trips.

**D** One-fifth of those surveyed either read or played sports.

**25** Michael made 16 of 20 free throws so far this basketball season. At this rate, how many free throws would he make if he had 50 tries?

**A** 32

**B** 46

**C** 40

**D** 38

**To the student. Check your answers and circle the question numbers you get wrong. Then go to the lesson for that type of question and try to find out why you got the wrong answer. Double the number you got right to get your percent score.**

# Pretest Answer Key, Lesson Key, and Problem Type
## Part I: Mathematics Computation

| Question | Answer | Lesson | Type of Problem |
|---|---|---|---|
| 1 | B | 1 | Multiplying Whole Numbers |
| 2 | C | 2 | Dividing Whole Numbers |
| 3 | C | 4 | Decimals |
| 4 | A | 6 | Integers |
| 5 | C | 2 | Dividing Whole Numbers |
| 6 | A | 3 | Fractions |
| 7 | B | 4 | Decimals |
| 8 | B | 5 | Percents |
| 9 | D | 6 | Integers |
| 10 | A | 1 | Multiplying Whole Numbers |
| 11 | B | 3 | Fractions |
| 12 | B | 3 | Fractions |
| 13 | C | 5 | Percents |
| 14 | B | 4 | Decimals |
| 15 | D | 6 | Integers |
| 16 | B | 6 | Integers |
| 17 | C | 4 | Decimals |
| 18 | A | 1 | Multiplying Whole Numbers |
| 19 | A | 3 | Fractions |
| 20 | C | 2 | Dividing Whole Numbers |
| 21 | B | 5 | Percents |
| 22 | B | 4 | Decimals |
| 23 | D | 6 | Integers |
| 24 | B | 3 | Fractions |
| 25 | D | 5 | Percents |

# Part II: Applied Mathematics

| Question | Answer | Lesson | Type of Problem |
|---|---|---|---|
| 1 | C | 7 | Numeration |
| 2 | B | 8 | Number Theory |
| 3 | A | 8 | Number Theory |
| 4 | C | 13 | Computation in Context |
| 5 | C | 12 | Geometry |
| 6 | D | 10 | Pre-Algebra and Algebra |
| 7 | C | 10 | Pre-Algebra and Algebra |
| 8 | C | 11 | Measurement |
| 9 | A | 14 | Estimation |
| 10 | D | 11 | Measurement |
| 11 | B | 11 | Measurement |
| 12 | C | 14 | Estimation |
| 13 | C | 9 | Data Interpretation |
| 14 | D | 9 | Data Interpretation |
| 15 | C | 9 | Data Interpretation |
| 16 | B | 8 | Number Theory |
| 17 | D | 10 | Pre-Algebra and Algebra |
| 18 | A | 13 | Computation in Context |
| 19 | D | 12 | Geometry |
| 20 | C | 10 | Pre-Algebra and Algebra |
| 21 | B | 12 | Geometry |
| 22 | A | 8 | Number Theory |
| 23 | C | 13 | Computation in Context |
| 24 | A | 9 | Data Interpretation |
| 25 | C | 13 | Computation in Context |

## LESSON 1   Multiplying Whole Numbers

Bill is deciding whether to buy or lease a car. If he leases for the amount of money advertised, he would have to stay under 15,000 miles per year. He plans to use the car for commuting, and his commute is 60 miles per day. Bill works 230 days each year. Bill needs to multiply 60 by 230 to find out if he will stay under the 15,000-mile limit. This is an example of a calculation that you might have to do by hand on the TABE D.

The answer to a multiplication problem is called the *product*. The numbers being multiplied are called *factors*. Multiplying whole numbers is really nothing more than a shortcut to repeated addition. In the example above, 230 × 60 means 60 + 60 + . . . + 60 (230 times). You would get the same answer if you multiplied 60 × 230.

In order to multiply accurately and easily, you need to know the multiplication table for the numbers 1 through 9. This is shown in the figure below. *You need to memorize it.*

## Multiplication Table

|   | 1 | 2 | 3 | 4 | 5 | 6 | 7 | 8 | 9 |
|---|---|---|---|---|---|---|---|---|---|
| 1 | 1 | 2 | 3 | 4 | 5 | 6 | 7 | 8 | 9 |
| 2 | 2 | 4 | 6 | 8 | 10 | 12 | 14 | 16 | 18 |
| 3 | 3 | 6 | 9 | 12 | 15 | 18 | 21 | 24 | 27 |
| 4 | 4 | 8 | 12 | 16 | 20 | 24 | 28 | 32 | 36 |
| 5 | 5 | 10 | 15 | 20 | 25 | 30 | 35 | 40 | 45 |
| 6 | 6 | 12 | 18 | 24 | 30 | 36 | 42 | 48 | 54 |
| 7 | 7 | 14 | 21 | 28 | 35 | 42 | 49 | 56 | 63 |
| 8 | 8 | 16 | 24 | 32 | 40 | 48 | 56 | 64 | 72 |
| 9 | 9 | 18 | 27 | 36 | 45 | 54 | 63 | 72 | 81 |

Note. Zero times any number is zero.

When you multiply two numbers that have more than one digit you have to pay close attention to place value. This means you have to "carry" an amount to the next place value.

## 1 Digit by 2 Digits

```
   58
 ×  6
 ----
  348
```

Work from right to left: first multiply 6 times 8 to get 48.

Write the 8 under the 6 and carry the 4. Then multiply 6 times 5 and add the 4 you carried, getting 34.

Write the 34 to the left of the 8, to get the final answer 348.

## 2 Digits by 2 Digits

```
     53
 ×   36
 ------
    318
   159
 ------
   1908
```

Work from right to left, just as above, multiplying by 6.

Then do the same thing with the 3, except move the work over one place to the left.

Add the two lines to get the answer.

## 2 Digits by 3 Digits

```
   329
 ×  84
  1316
 2632
 27636
```

Work from right to left: first multiply by 4 times 9 to get 36.

Write the 6 under the 4 and carry the 3.

Multiply 4 times 2, getting 8 and add the 3 you carried, getting 11.

Write the 1 to the left of the 6.

Multiply 4 times 3 and add the 1 you carried, getting 13.

This gives you the first line of 1316.

Then do the same thing with 8, except move the work over one place to the left.

Add the two lines to get the answer.

You could multiply two numbers of any sizes by following this process. If the two numbers you are multiplying have different numbers of digits, you can always write the smaller number under the larger one and follow the pattern.

## Practice Multiplying Whole Numbers

These problems are *not* in multiple-choice format, so that you won't be tempted to guess the answer. This is true of all the practice problems in the Math Computation part of this book. The problems have been written horizontally to save space. You should rewrite the problems on a piece of paper vertically to work them.

| | | | |
|---|---|---|---|
| 1. $4 \times 36$ | 2. $7 \times 83$ | 3. $5 \times 67$ | 4. $6 \times 91$ |
| 5. $21 \times 35$ | 6. $17 \times 18$ | 7. $64 \times 36$ | 8. $79 \times 54$ |
| 9. $6 \times 235$ | 10. $2 \times 189$ | 11. $5 \times 450$ | 12. $9 \times 754$ |
| 13. $13 \times 427$ | 14. $71 \times 765$ | 15. $46 \times 917$ | 16. $68 \times 872$ |

## LESSON 2 Dividing Whole Numbers

Dividing is the reverse of multiplying. When you divide 20 by 5 you get 4, and 4 times 5 is 20. You have to be carefully when you say (or write) a division problem. You can also say, "Divide 5 into 20." This changes the order of naming the two numbers. It does not mean the same as "Divide 5 by 20." For example, if you have $20 to be divided among 4 people, each person gets $5. But if you have $5 to be divided among 20 people, each person only gets a quarter ($0.25).

The answer to a division problem is called the *quotient*. In 20 divided by 5, 20 is called the *dividend*, 5 is called the *divisor*, and 4 is called the *quotient*.

There are two main ways of writing a division problem. You can write the problem 20 divided by 5 equals 4 as $20 \div 5 = 4$ or as $5\overline{)20}$ with 4 above. The second form is usually the one used if you can't do the problem in your head. The division problems on TABE D have divisors with one or two digits.

You can think of whole number division as a way of separating a number of objects (dividend) into equal groups. The divisor is the number of groups, and the quotient is the number objects in each group. If there are some objects left over after they are divided equally, this number is called the *remainder*.

Let's look at some examples.

## One-Digit Divisor

Example A.  $5\overline{)783}$

First divide 5 into the 7. It doesn't go evenly, but it does go 1 time, so put 1 above the line, multiply 1 times 5 and put the answer 5 below the 7.

Then subtract 5 from 7 to get 2, and bring down the 8.

$$
\begin{array}{r}
1\phantom{00} \\
5\overline{)783} \\
5\phantom{00} \\
\hline
28\phantom{0}
\end{array}
$$

Repeat the process, this time dividing 5 into 28.

This goes 5 times, so put the 5 above the 8, multiply 5 times 5, and put the answer (25) under the 28.

Then subtract 25 from 28 to get 3, and bring down the 3.

$$
\begin{array}{r}
15\phantom{0} \\
5\overline{)783} \\
5\phantom{00} \\
\hline
28\phantom{0} \\
25\phantom{0} \\
\hline
33
\end{array}
$$

Repeat the process again, this time divide 5 into 33.

This goes 6 times, so put the 6 above the 3, multiply 6 times 5, and put the answer (30) under the 33.

Then subtract 30 from 33 to get 3, the remainder.

$$\begin{array}{r} 156 \leftarrow \text{Quotient} \\ 5\overline{)783} \\ \underline{5\phantom{00}} \\ 28\phantom{0} \\ \underline{25\phantom{0}} \\ 33 \\ \underline{30} \\ 3 \leftarrow \text{Remainder} \end{array}$$

The remainders (after the subtraction step) must always be smaller than the divisor.

Example B.    $5\overline{)135}$

In this problem, 5 doesn't divide into the first digit 1, so divide 5 into the first two digits 13.

This goes 2 times, so put the 2 above the 3, multiply 2 times 5, and put the answer (10) under the 13.

The subtract 10 from 13 to get 3 and bring down the 5.

$$\begin{array}{r} 2\phantom{0} \\ 5\overline{)135} \\ \underline{10\phantom{0}} \\ 35 \end{array}$$

Repeat the process, this time dividing 5 into 35.

This goes 7 times, so put the above the 5, multiply 7 times 5, and put the answer (35) under the 35.

When you subtract, you get 0, so there is no remainder (5 goes into 135 evenly).

$$\begin{array}{r} 27 \leftarrow \text{Quotient} \\ 5\overline{)135} \\ \underline{10\phantom{0}} \\ 35 \\ \underline{35} \\ 0 \leftarrow \text{Remainder} \end{array}$$

## Two-Digit Divisor

As the next problem shows, division with a two-digit divisor is a little harder.

Example C.    $23\overline{)385}$

The first digit of 23 (2) is less than the first digit of 38 (3), so you can just divide 2 into 3 and get 1.

Multiply 1 times 23, put the answer (23) under the 38, and subtract to get 15.

$$\begin{array}{r} 1\phantom{00} \\ 23\overline{)385} \\ \underline{23}\phantom{0} \\ 155 \end{array}$$

Bring down the 5, and repeat by dividing 23 into 155.

Unfortunately, the first digit of 23 (2) doesn't go into the first digit of 155 (1), so you try 2 into the first two digits of 155 (15).

The 2 goes into 15 7 times, but when you multiply 7 times 23, you get 161, which is bigger than 155, so you have to reduce the 7 to a 6.

Then 6 times 23 is 138, so write that below the 155 and subtract to get a remainder of 17.

$$\begin{array}{r} 16 \quad \longleftarrow \text{Quotient} \\ 23\overline{)385} \\ \underline{23}\phantom{0} \\ 155 \\ \underline{138} \\ 17 \quad \longleftarrow \text{Remainder} \end{array}$$

In summary, the quotient is 16 with a remainder of 17.

## Practice Dividing Whole Numbers

The horizontal form (using ÷) of division is used to save space. You should write these problems using the $\overline{)}$ form on a piece of paper and work them out there.

| | | | |
|---|---|---|---|
| 1. 16 ÷ 2 | 2. 48 ÷ 4 | 3. 84 ÷ 6 | 4. 85 ÷ 5 |
| 5. 108 ÷ 6 | 6. 136 ÷ 8 | 7. 272 ÷ 4 | 8. 322 ÷ 7 |
| 9. 96 ÷ 12 | 10. 312 ÷ 12 | 11. 425 ÷ 17 | 12. 506 ÷ 22 |

## LESSON 3  Fractions

A *proper fraction* is part of a whole. For example, the fraction $\frac{5}{8}$ is 5 out of 8. In baseball, this could mean 5 hits out of 8 times at bat. Or it could mean 5 slices of a pizza that is cut into 8 slices. The top number is called the *numerator*, and the bottom number is called the *denominator*. The numerator of a proper fraction is smaller than the denominator.

An *improper* fraction has a numerator that's larger than its denominator. Improper fractions are bigger than 1. Usually an improper fraction is changed to a *mixed number*. A mixed number such as $2\frac{1}{2}$ is a number that falls between two whole numbers. It has a whole number part (2 in this example) and a fractional part $\left(\dfrac{1}{2} \text{ in this example}\right)$.

For the TABE D, you need to know how to add, subtract, multiply, divide, and reduce fractions. You also need to be able to work with mixed numbers. In this section, we'll first describe how to add, subtract, and reduce proper fractions. Then we'll see how to work with improper fractions and mixed numbers.

## Reducing Fractions

You can reduce a fraction by finding a number that divides evenly into both the numerator and denominator. For example, you reduce the fraction $\dfrac{16}{24}$ to $\dfrac{8}{12}$ by dividing the numerator and denominator by 2. You can divide by 2 again to reduce further to $\dfrac{4}{6}$, and again by 2 to reduce to $\dfrac{2}{3}$. This is as far as you can go. The original $\dfrac{16}{24}$ has now been reduced to *lowest terms* $\dfrac{2}{3}$. If you had divided numerator and denominator by 8 to begin with, you would have reduced to lowest terms in one step instead of three. Although you can use this method to reduce both proper and improper fractions, only proper fractions need to be reduced on the TABE D.

A reduced fraction is in the same proportion as the original fraction. If you get 16 problems right on a 24-problem test, you would expect to get 8 right on a 12-problem test, 4 right on a 6-problem test, or 2 right on a 3-problem test. We'll return to this point when we look at percents, and again in the Applied Mathematics Section.

## Practice Reducing Fractions

Reduce each fraction to lowest terms.

1. $\dfrac{6}{8}$    2. $\dfrac{6}{9}$    3. $\dfrac{5}{15}$    4. $\dfrac{7}{21}$    5. $\dfrac{4}{12}$

6. $\dfrac{6}{16}$    7. $\dfrac{5}{10}$    8. $\dfrac{8}{12}$    9. $\dfrac{9}{27}$    10. $\dfrac{14}{21}$

## Adding and Subtracting Fractions with the Same Denominators

You can only add or subtract fractions that have the same denominators. The denominator of your answer is the same as the common denominator of the two fractions you add. Then you simply add the numerators to get the numerator of your answer. The same idea applies to subtracting fractions, except that you subtract the numerators instead of adding them.

Examples:

$$\frac{1}{5} + \frac{2}{5} = \frac{3}{5} \qquad \frac{6}{7} + \frac{2}{7} = \frac{8}{7}$$

You can write a problem that adds or subtracts fractions in horizontal form (as done here) or in vertical form, such as $\begin{array}{r} \frac{1}{5} \\ + \frac{2}{5} \end{array}$. To save space, all fraction problems in this book and on the TABE D are in horizontal form.

If you can reduce a fraction after adding, be sure to do so. For example $\frac{1}{8} + \frac{3}{8} = \frac{4}{8}$, and $\frac{4}{8}$ reduces to $\frac{1}{2}$.

## Practice Adding and Subtracting Fractions with the Same Denominators

Add or subtract as indicated, and reduce the answer to lowest terms if possible.

1. $\frac{2}{5} - \frac{1}{5}$     2. $\frac{5}{8} + \frac{1}{8}$     3. $\frac{7}{10} - \frac{3}{10}$

4. $\frac{8}{15} + \frac{2}{15}$     5. $\frac{5}{12} - \frac{1}{12}$     6. $\frac{2}{7} + \frac{4}{7}$

## Adding and Subtracting Fractions with Different Denominators

Fractions with different denominators can't be added or subtracted directly. You first have to find a common denominator. This is a denominator that the two different denominators both divide into evenly. For example, two fractions that have denominators of 2 and 3 have 6 as a common denominator because 2 and 3 both divide evenly into 6. Once you have a common denominator, you have to get new numerators.

For example, suppose you have to subtract $\frac{2}{3} - \frac{1}{2}$.

The denominators 3 and 2 both go evenly into 6, so 6 is a common denominator. Write $\frac{\phantom{0}}{6} - \frac{\phantom{0}}{6}$.

The first fraction is $\frac{2}{3}$. Divide the denominator 3 into 6 and multiply by the answer (2) by the numerator 2. This answer is 4, and it goes in the numerator of the first fraction: $\frac{4}{6} - \frac{\phantom{0}}{6}$.

Do the same for the other fraction. Divide the 2 into 6 and multiply by the 1. The answer is 3. Put this in the numerator of the second fraction: $\dfrac{4}{6} - \dfrac{3}{6}$.

Now you can subtract the fractions: $\dfrac{4}{6} - \dfrac{3}{6} = \dfrac{1}{6}$.

## Practice Adding and Subtracting Fractions with Different Denominators

Add or subtract as indicated, and reduce if possible.

1. $\dfrac{3}{4} - \dfrac{1}{3}$       2. $\dfrac{1}{6} + \dfrac{1}{3}$       3. $\dfrac{5}{8} - \dfrac{1}{4}$

4. $\dfrac{2}{3} + \dfrac{1}{5}$       5. $\dfrac{7}{8} - \dfrac{3}{4}$       6. $\dfrac{2}{5} + \dfrac{3}{10}$

## Changing Improper Fractions to Mixed Numbers

So far, we've talked about adding and subtracting proper fractions with the same and different denominators. In all the sample problems, answers were also proper fractions. Two proper fractions might add to an improper fraction, such as $\dfrac{3}{4} + \dfrac{1}{2}$, which add to $\dfrac{3}{4} + \dfrac{2}{4} = \dfrac{5}{4}$. Usually, you change the improper fraction to a mixed number.

To change $\dfrac{5}{4}$ to a mixed number, divide 5 by 4, and get 1 with a remainder of 1. The remainder can be written as the numerator of a fraction. The denominator of this fraction is the divisor. This gives you the mixed number $1\dfrac{1}{4}$. Before moving on, you should practice changing improper fractions to mixed numbers.

## Practice Changing Improper Fractions to Mixed Numbers

Change each improper fraction to a mixed number.

1. $\dfrac{3}{2}$       2. $\dfrac{7}{4}$       3. $\dfrac{11}{7}$

4. $\dfrac{9}{2}$       5. $\dfrac{19}{8}$       6. $\dfrac{7}{5}$

## Adding and Subtracting Mixed Numbers, Fractions, and Whole Numbers

Before looking at these problems, you need to know how to change mixed numbers to improper fractions. Multiply the denominator by the whole number and add the numerator. Then put this answer over the denominator. Example: $2\frac{1}{3} = \frac{7}{3}$. Multiply 3 by 2 and add 1, to get 7, so $2\frac{1}{3} = \frac{7}{3}$.

*To add or subtract mixed numbers,* follow these steps:

1. Change each mixed number to an improper fraction.

2. Add or subtract the improper fractions just as you would proper fractions.

3. Change the answer back to a mixed number.

**Example A.** $2\frac{1}{3} + 1\frac{5}{6}$

1. Change to improper fractions. $\frac{7}{3} + \frac{11}{6}$

2. Get a common denominator and add. $\frac{14}{6} + \frac{11}{6} = \frac{25}{6}$

3. Change to a mixed number. $\frac{25}{6} = 4\frac{1}{6}$

**Example B.** $5\frac{1}{2} - 2\frac{2}{3}$

1. Change to improper fractions. $\frac{11}{2} - \frac{8}{3}$

2. Get a common denominator and subtract. $\frac{33}{6} - \frac{16}{6} = \frac{17}{6}$

3. Change to a mixed number. $\frac{17}{6} = 2\frac{5}{6}$

To *add a fraction and a whole number,* just put the fraction next to the whole number to make a mixed number.

**Example C.** $\frac{4}{5} + 7 = 7\frac{4}{5}$

To *add a whole number and a mixed number,* just add the whole number parts and leave the fractional part with the answer.

**Example D.** $2 + 3\frac{1}{3} = 5\frac{1}{3}$

To *subtract a fraction or a mixed number from a whole number,* follow these steps:

1. Write the whole number as an improper fraction with a denominator of 1.

2. Write the mixed number as an improper fraction.

3. Subtract as you would with two fractions.

Example E.   $7 - 2\dfrac{5}{8}$

1. Change 7 to $\dfrac{7}{1}$

2. Change $2\dfrac{5}{8}$ to $\dfrac{21}{8}$

3. Do the subtraction $\dfrac{7}{1} - \dfrac{21}{8} = \dfrac{56}{8} - \dfrac{21}{8} = \dfrac{35}{8} = 4\dfrac{3}{8}$

## Practice Adding and Subtracting Mixed Numbers, Fractions, and Whole Numbers

1. $1\dfrac{2}{3} + 4\dfrac{2}{3}$    2. $3\dfrac{4}{5} - 1\dfrac{3}{5}$    3. $3 + \dfrac{3}{5}$

4. $8\dfrac{1}{9} - 3\dfrac{4}{9}$    5. $6 - \dfrac{3}{5}$    6. $10\dfrac{2}{3} - 5\dfrac{1}{3}$

7. $7\dfrac{3}{8} + 2\dfrac{5}{8}$    8. $1\dfrac{3}{4} + 3\dfrac{3}{4}$    9. $4 - 1\dfrac{2}{3}$

10. $3\dfrac{3}{7} - 1$    11. $4 - 2\dfrac{1}{2}$    12. $3 + 3\dfrac{2}{3}$

## Multiplying Fractions

Multiplying fractions is easier than adding or subtracting them. When you multiply two proper fractions, the answer is a proper fraction. Multiply the two numerators to get the numerator of the answer. Do the same thing with the denominators.

Example F.   $\dfrac{2}{3} \times \dfrac{4}{5}$. $2 \times 4 = 8$ and $3 \times 5 = 15$. The answer is $\dfrac{8}{15}$.

Sometimes it is possible to reduce the answer.

Example  G.   $\dfrac{2}{3} \times \dfrac{3}{4}$. $2 \times 3 = 6$ and $3 \times 4 = 12$.  The  answer  is  $\dfrac{6}{12}$, but

this can be reduced to $\dfrac{1}{2}$ by dividing the numerator and denominator by 6.

## Multiplying a Whole Number and a Fraction

To multiply a whole number and a fraction, multiply the numerator by the whole number, and leave the denominator alone.

Example H.    $3 \times \dfrac{1}{5} = \dfrac{3}{5}$

You might get an improper fraction as an answer. In a multiple-choice question, the correct answer choice might be the improper fraction or the equivalent mixed number.

Example I.    $\dfrac{2}{7} \times 4 = \dfrac{8}{7} = 1\dfrac{1}{7}$

## Dividing Fractions

To divide fractions, you turn the second fraction (the divisor) upside down and multiply.

Example J.    $\dfrac{3}{4} \div \dfrac{1}{3} = \dfrac{3}{4} \times \dfrac{3}{1} = \dfrac{9}{4}$    $\left( \dfrac{1}{3} \text{ is changed to } \dfrac{3}{1} \right)$. This is the same

as the mixed number $2\dfrac{1}{4}$. Either one could be the correct answer choice.

## Practice Multiplying and Dividing Fractions

Multiply or divide as indicated. Reduce answers and change improper fractions to mixed numbers.

1. $\dfrac{2}{3} \times \dfrac{1}{4}$    2. $\dfrac{3}{5} \times \dfrac{2}{5}$    3. $\dfrac{5}{8} \times \dfrac{3}{4}$    4. $2 \times \dfrac{2}{3}$

5. $\dfrac{4}{5} \div \dfrac{1}{2}$    6. $\dfrac{7}{2} \div \dfrac{2}{3}$    7. $\dfrac{1}{2} \div \dfrac{5}{3}$    8. $\dfrac{2}{3} \div \dfrac{2}{1}$

## Mixed Practice on Fractions

1. $\dfrac{1}{4} + \dfrac{3}{4}$    2. $\dfrac{2}{3} \times \dfrac{3}{4}$    3. $\dfrac{1}{2} - \dfrac{1}{6}$    4. $\dfrac{2}{3} \div 2$    5. $\dfrac{5}{6} \times \dfrac{3}{7}$    6. $2 - \dfrac{1}{3}$

7. $\dfrac{1}{2} \times \dfrac{2}{5}$    8. $\dfrac{3}{5} + \dfrac{2}{3}$    9. $5 + \dfrac{3}{8}$    10. $\dfrac{1}{3} - \dfrac{1}{5}$    11. $\dfrac{1}{3} \times \dfrac{1}{5}$    12. $\dfrac{1}{3} \div \dfrac{1}{5}$

## LESSON 4  Decimals

Decimals are like fractions. They are a way of representing part of a whole. For example, the decimal number 6.2 is equal to the mixed number $6\dfrac{2}{10}$ (six and two-tenths). The decimal number 3.14 is equal to the mixed number $3\frac{14}{100}$ (three and fourteen hundredths). Digits to the left of the decimal point make up the whole number part. Digits to the right of the decimal point make up the fractional part.

In decimals, the denominators of the fractional parts are always 10, 100, 1000, etc. Whole numbers are decimals with zeros to the right of the decimal point. For example, the decimal numbers 4.0, 4.00, 4.000, etc. are all the same number as the whole number 4.

Money is written in decimal form. The digits to the left of the decimal give you the dollars. The two digits to the right of the decimal give you the cents. Cents represent parts of a dollar. For example, $3.25 is 3 dollars and 25 cents, or $3\frac{25}{100} = 3\frac{1}{4}$ dollars.

On the TABE D you will be expected to be able to add, subtract, multiply, and divide decimals.

## Adding and Subtracting Decimals

If a problem adding or subtracting decimals is written in vertical form, all you have to do is make sure the decimal points are lined up, and then add or subtract as you would with whole numbers.

Examples:
$$\begin{array}{r} 4.28 \\ + \ 5.16 \\ \hline 9.44 \end{array} \qquad \begin{array}{r} 6.42 \\ - \ 2.08 \\ \hline 4.34 \end{array}$$

If one decimal has more places to the right than the other, just fill in the blanks with zeros.

Examples:
$$\begin{array}{r} 3.2 \\ + \ 4.93 \end{array} \Rightarrow \begin{array}{r} 3.20 \\ + \ 4.93 \\ \hline 8.13 \end{array} \Rightarrow \begin{array}{r} 4.3 \\ - \ 1.75 \end{array} \Rightarrow \begin{array}{r} 4.30 \\ - \ 1.75 \\ \hline 2.55 \end{array}$$

In this book, and in most of the TABE D problems, decimals problems are written in horizontal form to save space: 1.23 + 4.56 instead of
$$\begin{array}{r} 1.23 \\ + \ 4.56 \end{array}$$

You should rewrite all problems in vertical form and line up the decimal point before adding or subtracting. Write one number above the other. If you're adding, it doesn't matter which number is on top. If you're subtracting, the number that is being subtracted (the smaller one) goes on the bottom.

## Practice Adding and Subtracting Decimals

1. 1.8 + 2.6
2. 6.75 − 3.38
3. 12.32 + 3.41
4. 17.24 − 8.58
5. 5.2 + 3.11
6. 7.1 − 6.06

## Multiplying Decimals

Multiply decimals the same way you would whole numbers. Then count the total number of places to the right of the decimal point in *both* numbers. Count that many spaces from the right side of the answer and place a decimal point there.

Examples:

$$\begin{array}{r} 2.34 \\ \times\phantom{0}\phantom{0}8 \\ \hline 18.72 \end{array} \qquad \begin{array}{r} 4.6 \\ \times 1.5 \\ \hline 230 \\ 46\phantom{0} \\ \hline 6.90 = 6.9 \end{array} \qquad \begin{array}{r} 15 \\ \times\phantom{0}.2 \\ \hline 3.0 = 3 \end{array}$$

Multiplication problems are also written in horizontal form on the TABE-D and in this book. As before, you should re-write them in vertical form before attempting to do the calculations.

## Practice Multiplying Decimals

1. 8 × 3.21
2. 2.7 × 3.6
3. .503 × 1.2
4. 18.6 × 8.5
5. 1.03 × 26
6. 17 × .124

## Dividing Decimals

The *dividend* of a division problem is the number being divided up. The *divisor* is the number that does the dividing. The answer is called the *quotient*. For example, in the division problem 10 ÷ 5 = 2, 10 is the dividend, 5 is the divisor, and 2 is the quotient. This problem can also be written $5\overline{)10}$, or $\frac{10}{5} = 2$.

All three forms could appear on the TABE D. *You should always rewrite the problem in $\overline{)\phantom{0}}$ form before you work it out.*

When dividing decimals, it doesn't matter what kind of number the dividend is. You need to look at two cases for the divisor.

**Case 1. The divisor is not a decimal.** In this case, divide as you would with whole numbers, but place a decimal in the quotient in the same location as it is in the dividend.

Examples:

$$2\overline{)10.4}^{\,5.2} \qquad 2\overline{)1.04}^{\,.52} \qquad 15\overline{)3.45}^{\,.23} \qquad 8\overline{).016}^{\,.002}$$

**Case 2. The divisor is a decimal.** In this case, move the decimal to the right to make the divisor a whole number. Then move the decimal in the dividend the same number of places to the right. If the dividend is a whole number, or if it has fewer places to the right of the decimal point, write in zeros until you have the correct number of places.

Examples: $.4\overline{)7.6} \Rightarrow 4\overline{)76.}^{\,19.}$    $3.1\overline{)93} \Rightarrow 31\overline{)930.}^{\,30.}$    $.06\overline{).102} \Rightarrow 6\overline{)10.2}^{\,1.7}$

## Practice Dividing Decimals

1. $3\overline{)1.05}$    2. $9\overline{)145.8}$    3. $4\overline{).052}$

4. $11.5 \div 2.3$    5. $18.72 \div 3.6$    6. $1539 \div 2.7$

7. $\dfrac{22.82}{7}$    8. $\dfrac{3.45}{1.15}$    9. $\dfrac{12}{2.4}$

## LESSON 5  Percents

Percents are all around us. A department store has a 15% off sale. You can finance a car for 5% interest. A basketball player has a 46% shooting average. You score 80% on your test. In all these examples, percent is a way of measuring *part* of a *whole*. The department store sale saves you part of the whole cost of what you buy. The interest is the part of the total amount of money you borrow that you have to pay back (in addition to repaying the borrowed money!) The free throw average is the part of all the free throws the player takes. The test score is part of all the questions that you got right.

Percents give you an idea of how much of the whole the part is, regardless of how many things there are or what they are. A score of 80% on a test could be 8 correct answers out of 10 questions or 20 correct out of 25 questions. A 46% shooting average could be 46 shots made out of 100 taken, or 23 made out of 50 taken. The 15% off sale could mean that you save $4.50 on a $30 jacket or $75 on a $500 TV set. This is because the part is *standardized* to a whole of 100.

There are three types of percent problems in this section of the TABE D.

- The problem tells you the whole and the part, and you have to find the %.
- The problem tells you the whole and the %, and you have to find the part.
- The problem tells you the part and the %, and you have to find the whole.

In other words, you are told 2 of the 3 amounts, and you have to find the third. There is a formula for each of these:

$\% = Part \div Whole \times 100$    To get the %, divide the part by the whole, and then multiply by 100 (move the decimal point 2 places to the right).

$Part = \% \times Whole \div 100$     To get the part, multiply the % by the Whole, and then divide by 100 (move the decimal point two places to the left).

$Whole = Part \div \% \times 100$     To get the whole, divide the part by the %, and then multiply by 100 (move the decimal point two places to the right).

Once you've memorized these formulas, you need to be to determine which 2 numbers a problem tells you. This isn't too hard. The number that is in front of the % sign is the %. The number that comes after the word "of" is the whole. The number that comes after the word "is" or "=" is the part. Let's look at an example of each of these.

Example A.    What is 20% of 50?

The problem tells you the % and the whole, so use the formula for the part:

$Part = 20 \times 50 \div 100 = 1000 = 10.$    20% of 50 is *10*.

Example B.    What percent of 30 is 12?

The problem tells you the whole and the part, so use the formula for the %:

$\% = Part \div Whole \times 100 = 12 \div 30 \times 100 = 40.$    12 is *40%* of 30.

Example C.    3 is 30% of what number?

The problem tells you the part and the %, so use the formula for the whole:

$Whole = Part \div \% \times 100 = 3 \div 30 \times 100 = 10.$    3 is 30% of *10*.

## Practice Percent Problems

1. Find 12% of 50.
2. What percent of 20 is 9?
3. 10 is 25% of what number?
4. What percent of 10 is 7?
5. 15% of what number is 9?
6. 8% of 300 = ?
7. What percent of 18 is 9?
8. 12 is 20% of what number?
9. 7 is 25% of what number?
10. Find 90% of 150.

## LESSON 6   Integers

Whole numbers are 0,1,2,3,. . . on forever. Their opposites are −1,−2,−3,. . . (negative 1, negative 2, negative 3, and so forth), on forever. These whole numbers and their opposites are called *integers*. Most of the numbers you use in day-to-day life are positive. However, negative numbers have an important place in real life as well. When someone owes you money, it is a positive amount. When you owe someone else money, it is a negative amount. When a football team gains yards, it is positive yardage. When the team loses yards, it is negative yardage. There are temperatures above zero and below zero. Land may be above sea level (positive) or below sea level (negative).

It is useful to think of integers as the marks on an outdoor thermometer held sideways. Zero is in the middle. Positive integers go right and negative integers go left.

An integer and its opposite are the same distance from zero. They just go in opposite directions. For example 3 and −3 are both 3 away from 0.

You need to be able to add, subtract, multiply, and divide integers on the TABE D. When adding or subtracting integers, it might not be clear whether the − sign is part of a negative number or a subtraction. There are certain rules for writing positive and negative numbers:

1. If a number is positive, it doesn't need a + sign in front of it.

2. If a number is negative, it must have a − sign in front of it.

3. If a negative number comes first in a problem, it doesn't need to be in parentheses, such as −3 + 7.

4. If a negative number doesn't come first in a problem it must be in parentheses, such as 7 + (−3).

Let's see how to read some examples.

Example A.   −1 + 5: 1 *add* 5

Example B.   −7 + (−6): −7 *add* −6

Example C.   4 + (−3): 4 *add* −3

Example D.   5 − 8: 5 *subtract* 8

Example E.   −3 − 9: −3 *subtract* 9

Example F.   2 − (−6): 2 *subtract* −6

Example G.   −3 − (−7): −3 *subtract* −7

This is part of the language of math. You need to make sure you know how to read math correctly.

## Adding Integers

If two integers are both positive, just add them like whole numbers. If they are negative, ignore the sign, add them, and put a negative sign in front of the answer. For example, $6 + 2 = 8$ (6 *add* 2 = 8) and $-6 + (-2) = -8$ (−6 *add* −2 = −8). If two integers have different signs, follow these steps:

1. Ignore the signs

2. Subtract the smaller number from the larger number.

3. Attach the minus sign to the answer if that number is larger.

   Example A.   $8 + (-3)$ (8 *add* −3)

1. Ignore the signs: 8, 3.

2. Subtract the smaller number from the larger number: $8 - 3 = 5$.

3. Since 8 is larger than 3, the answer is 5.

   Example B.   $-12 + 3$ (−12 *add* 3)

1. Ignore the signs: 12, 3.

2. Subtract the smaller number from the larger number: $12 - 3 = 9$.

3. Attach the negative sign, because 12 is larger than 3. The answer is −9.

## Practice Adding Integers

1. $-4 + 8$        2. $5 + (-8)$        3. $-6 + (-14)$

4. $7 + (-5)$      5. $-3 + 1$          6. $-7 + (-4)$

## Subtracting Integers

The word "subtract" means "add the opposite." For example $5 - 7$ (5 *subtract* 7) means $5 + (-7)$ (5 *add* −7). So you change a subtract problem to an add problem (add the opposite).

Example A.   $-6 - 2 = -6 + (-2)$: −6 *subtract* 2 means −6 *add* −2 = −8

Example B.   $4 - (-10) = 4 + 10$: 4 *subtract* −10 means 4 *add* 10 = 14

Example C.   $9 - 12 = 9 + (-12)$: 9 *subtract* 12 means 9 *add* −12 = −3

Example D.   $15 - 8 = 15 + (-8)$: 15 *subtract* 8 means 15 *add* −8 = 7

You could do Example D just like a regular whole number subtraction problem because both 15 and 8 are positive and 8 is smaller than 15.

## Practice Subtracting Integers

1. $8 - (-3)$     2. $-4 - 13$     3. $-1 - (-8)$     4. $12 - (-1)$

5. $10 - 12$      6. $-11 - 4$

## Multiplying and Dividing Integers

Multiplying and dividing integers is easy. Just multiply or divide as you would with whole numbers. If the numbers have the same sign (both positive or both negative), the answer is positive. If the numbers have different signs, the answer is negative.

Example A. $-6 \times 4 = -24$

Example B. $3 \times (-15) = -45$

Example C. $-2 \times (-4) = 8$

Example D. $18 \div -3 = -6$

Example E. $25 \div -5 = -5$

Example F. $-12 \div (-2) = 6$

### Practice Multiplying and Dividing Integers

1. $-7 \times 4$
2. $15 \div -3$
3. $9 \times -22$
4. $-63 \div 7$

5. $-13 \times (-4)$
6. $-66 \div 11$
7. $3 \times -9$
8. $-54 \div (-6)$

### Mixed Practice on Integers

1. $21 - (-8)$
2. $-35 \div 7$
3. $-19 + (-6)$
4. $-20 \div (-5)$

5. $-32 - (-8)$
6. $-3 \times -7$
7. $-9 + (-13)$
8. $42 \times (-1)$

9. $-1 + (-1)$
10. $-15 \div (-3)$
11. $12 \div (-2)$
12. $6 - (-5)$

13. $-7 \div (-1)$
14. $8 + (-17)$
15. $-4 \times (-4)$
16. $-3 - 4$

17. $-3 \times -12$
18. $20 \div (-10)$
19. $-17 + (-3)$
20. $7 - 2$

## LESSON 7  Numeration

There are three kinds of numeration problems on the TABE D. The first kind is about *place value*. For example, the number 371 has the same digits as the number 317. How and why are they different? The second kind is about *comparing* numbers. Which number is bigger? The third kind is about *fractional parts* of a whole amount (like what part of your day is spent watching TV). Lets look at these one at a time.

## Place Value

In order to understand place value, you need to know about exponents. An exponent is a way of showing a number multiplied by itself. For example, you can write $2 \times 2 \times 2$ as $2^3$. The *raised* number is called an *exponent*. The other number is called the base. In this example, 2 is the base, and 3 is the exponent. The exponent shows how many times the base is multiplied. Since $2 \times 2 = 4$, and $4 \times 2 = 8$, $2 \times 2 \times 2 = 8$, or $2^3 = 8$. Exponents are sometimes called powers. For example, you read $2^3$ as 2 to the power 3.

The number 10 is used as the base for writing numbers. Each place value is a power of 10. The units place stands alone. The tens place is 10 to the power 1 ($10 = 10^1$). The hundreds place is 10 to the power 2 ($100 = 10^2$). The thousands place is 10 to the power 3 ($1000 = 10^3$). And so forth. You can break a number such as 2836 down into its place values:

$$2836 = 2000 + 800 + 30 + 6$$
$$= 2 \times 1000 + 8 \times 100 + 3 \times 10 + 6$$
$$= 2 \times 10^3 + 8 \times 10^2 + 3 \times 10^1 + 6$$

Decimal numbers such as .253 can be broken down the same way, except the powers of ten are negative numbers. The place value just to the right of the decimal is tenths. The tenths place is 10 to the power $-1 (10^{-1})$. The hundredths place is 10 to the power $-2 (10^{-2})$. The thousandths place is 10 to the power $-3 (10^{-3})$. You can break the number .253 breaks down into its place values:

$$.253 = .2 + .05 + .003$$
$$= 2 \times .1 + 5 \times .01 + 3 \times .001$$
$$= 2 \times 10^{-1} + 5 \times 10^{-2} + 3 \times 10^{-3}$$

Be careful to pay attention to the difference between tens and tenths, hundreds and hundredths, thousands and thousandths, and so forth.

The chart below shows place values to the right and left of the decimal point. Each column in this chart shows a place value. Place values get larger as you move from right to left.

| Whole Numbers | | | | | | | | | | | Decimals | | | |
|---|---|---|---|---|---|---|---|---|---|---|---|---|---|---|
| Billions | | | Millions | | | Thousands | | | Units | | | ____ths | | |
| Hundred Billions | Ten Billions | Billions | Hundred Millions | Ten Millions | Millions | Hundred Thousands | Ten Thousands | Thousands | Hundreds | Tens | Ones | Tenths | Hundredths | Thousandths | Ten Thousandths | Hundred Thousandths |

## Comparing Numbers

The words "larger than" and "smaller than" are used to compare numbers. For example, 6 is larger than 5, and 2 is smaller than 10. The symbol abbreviation for "larger than" is >, and the symbol abbreviation for "smaller than" is <. In math, 6 > 5 means 6 is larger than 5, and 2 < 10 means 2 is less than 10. Notice that *the symbol always points to the smaller number.*

## Comparing Fractions

If two fractions have the same denominator (bottom number), just compare the top number. For example $\frac{3}{5} < \frac{4}{5}$ because the bottoms are the same and 3 < 4. Suppose two fractions have different denominators, such as $\frac{2}{3}$ and $\frac{3}{4}$. Find a common denominator (a number than both 3 and 4 divide evenly into). Then change the two fractions to two fractions with the same denominator: $\frac{2}{3} = \frac{8}{12}$ and $\frac{3}{4} = \frac{9}{12}$. Now compare $\frac{8}{12}$ and $\frac{9}{12}$. Since 8 < 9, $\frac{8}{12} < \frac{9}{12}$. Therefore, $\frac{2}{3} < \frac{3}{4}$.

## Comparing Decimals

When you compare two decimals, look at one place value at a time, starting from the left. When you compare .3 and .4 you conclude that .4 is larger because 4 is larger than 3, and the two numbers have the same place value (tenths). If you compare .3 and .04 you would conclude that .3 is larger because you compare the numbers in the tenths place value (3 and the 0), and 3 > 0. If the digits are tied in a position, you move to the next position and compare. For example, when comparing .56 and .57 you conclude that .57 is larger because the 5s are tied and 7 > 6.

## Comparing Decimals to Fractions

If one number is a fraction and the other is a decimal, it's generally easiest to change the fraction to a decimal. Then compare the two decimals. Use a calculator to change the fraction to a decimal. Divide the numerator by the denominator (numerator ÷ denominator). For example, if you compare $\frac{3}{4}$ with .72, divide 3 by 4 on a calculator (3 ÷ 4) and get the answer .75. Then compare .72 and .75, and conclude that .75 > .72.

## Finding Part of a Whole

Remember that a proper fraction is one way of representing part of a whole. For example, the fraction $\frac{5}{8}$ represents 5 slices of a pizza that has been cut into 8 slices. Suppose you had a party and ordered 16 pizzas. If you only ate $\frac{5}{8}$ of the 16 pizzas, how many pizzas did you have left? To find $\frac{5}{8}$ of 16, multiply $\frac{5}{8} \times 16$. On a calculator, this would be $5 \div 8 \times 16$, which equals 10. Because 10 pizzas were eaten, 6 $(16 - 10)$ were left.

To find a fractional part of a number, *multiply* the fraction by the number. Be careful to read the problem carefully to answer the right question.

They say, "A picture is worth a thousand words." Nowhere is this more true than in math. Numbers (including whole numbers, fractions, and decimals) are pictured on a horizontal line. Because there is no largest or smallest number, the line extends forever in both directions. Arrowheads at both ends indicate this. A typical portion of a number line is shown below.

Zero is in the center. Positive numbers extend out to the right. Negative numbers extend out to the left. The numbers get larger as you move from left to right anywhere on the number between two labeled numbers. Points on the line represent numbers. The numbers $-3$ and 4 are labeled A and B.

A problem might ask you to locate a number that is between two labeled numbers. For example, look at the problem below. Which point—A, B, C, or D—represents the number 4.3? There are 10 tick marks (the short vertical lines) from 4 to 5. Each of these is one-tenth (.1). The number 4.3 is the third tick mark to the right of 4. The answer is B.

## Numeration Practice

Name the place value of the underlined digit in each number.

1. 30<u>2</u>,425

2. 74.6<u>5</u>3

3. 84,<u>4</u>57,059.02

4. 3,241.341<u>1</u>2

5. 23.<u>0</u>6

6. Which number is eighty-three thousand, fifty nine?
   a. 80,359
   b. 83,059
   c. 803,059
   d. 8,003,059

7. Which number is seven hundred five million, forty-one thousand, four hundred eight?
   a. 70,541,408
   b. 700,541,408
   c. 705,041,408
   d. 7,005,541,408

8. Which of the following is another way to show the number 30,000 + 1000 + 600 + 70 + 9?
   a. 31,070
   b. 31,670
   c. 31,670
   d. 31,679

9. Which of these is another way to write 2407?
   a. $2 \times 10^2 + 4 \times 10^1 + 7$
   b. $2 \times 10^3 + 4 \times 10^2 + 7 \times 10^1$
   c. $2 \times 10^3 + 4 \times 10^2 + 7$
   d. $2 \times 10^4 + 4 \times 10^3 + 7$

10. Which of these is another way to write 4,396,302?
    a. $4 \times 10^5 + 3 \times 10^4 + 9 \times 10^3 + 6 \times 10^2 + 3 \times 10^1 + 2$
    b. $4 \times 10^6 + 3 \times 10^5 + 9 \times 10^4 + 6 \times 10^3 + 3 \times 10^2 + 2$
    c. $4 \times 10^6 + 3 \times 10^5 + 9 \times 10^4 + 6 \times 10^3 + 3 \times 10^2 + 2 \times 10^1$
    d. $4 \times 10^7 + 3 \times 10^6 + 9 \times 10^5 + 6 \times 10^4 + 3 \times 10^3 + 2$

11. Which of these is another way to write .534?
    a. $5 \times 10^{-2} + 3 \times 10^{-1} + 4$
    b. $5 \times 10^{-1} + 3 \times 10^{-2} + 4 \times 10^{-3}$
    c. $5 \times 10^2 + 3 \times 10^1 + 4$
    d. $5 \times 10^{-2} + 3 \times 10^{-3} + 4 \times 10^{-4}$

12. Which of these is another way to write .9021?
    a. $9 \times 10^0 + 2 \times 10^{-1} + 1 \times 10^{-2}$
    b. $9 \times 10^{-1} + 2 \times 10^{-2} + 1 \times 10^{-3}$
    c. $9 \times 10^{-1} + 2 \times 10^{-2} + 1 \times 10^{-4}$
    d. $9 \times 10^{-1} + 2 \times 10^{-3} + 1 \times 10^{-4}$

13. Bill plans to walk 12 miles in a walk-a-thon. What is $\frac{1}{3}$ of this distance?
    a. 4 miles
    b. 6 miles
    c. 8 miles
    d. 3 miles

**14.** Ladds Clothing is having a $\frac{1}{2}$ off sale on every item in the store. Crescent Clothing is taking $\frac{3}{5}$ off every item. Roberts is taking 35% off all items. Which store is reducing its prices by more?
  **a.** Ladds
  **b.** Crescent
  **c.** Roberts
  **d.** All equal

**15.** The Johnston family is planning a vacation. They will spend 3 days in New York City, 2 days in Niagara Falls, 1 day in Cooperstown, and 4 days camping in the Adirondack Mountains. What fraction of their vacation will be spent in Niagara Falls?

  **a.** $\frac{2}{9}$

  **b.** $\frac{1}{5}$

  **c.** $\frac{1}{10}$

  **d.** $\frac{1}{3}$

**16.** What number is represented by Point A on the number line?
  **a.** −6.8
  **b.** −6.2
  **c.** −5.8
  **d.** −5.2

## LESSON 8   Number Theory

Number theory problems are about ratio, proportion, and percent. A *ratio* is one way of comparing two numbers. For example, the ratio of the width of a rug to its length may be 3 to 5. The width of the rug is $\frac{3}{5}$ of its length. A *proportion* says two ratios are equal. For example, $\frac{3}{5} = \frac{9}{15}$ is a proportion. This would say that a 3-by-5 rug is in the same proportion as a 9-by-15 rug. The two rugs are proportional in size. Their shapes are the same. A *percent* is a ratio where one of the numbers is 100. A 60-by-100 rug would have the same shape as a 3-by-5 rug or a 9-by-15 rug because $\dfrac{3}{5}$, $\dfrac{9}{15}$, and $\dfrac{60}{100}$ are all equal.

Percents are used as ratios because they give a standard of comparison. For example, if you wanted to know which is more square, a 3-by-5 rug or a 4-by-8 rug? You would calculate the width as a percent of the length in each case. If the width is 100% of the length, the rug is square. For the 3-by-5 rug you would say that the width is 60% of the length. For the 4-by-8 rug the width would only be 50% of the length. Therefore, the 3-by-5 rug is more square.

Most proportion problems ask you to find a number that makes two ratios equal. There are 4 numbers in a proportion, two numerators and two denominators. These problems tell you 3 of the numbers, and you have to find the fourth number.

In the percent problems you have to be able to convert between percents, fractions, and decimals. You also have to calculate percent increases and decreases. Examples are used to show you how to solve problem like these.

## Change a Fraction to a Percent

To change a fraction to a percent, divide the numerator by the denominator and move the decimal point two places right (multiply by 100). This is just like finding the percent if you know the part and the whole.

Example A.   What percent of the square is shaded?

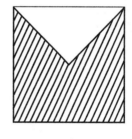

   **a.** 3%      **b.** 30%        **c.** 60%        **d.** 75%

The square is divided into 4 equal sections. Three parts are shaded, so the fraction that is shaded is $\dfrac{3}{4}$. Divide 3 by 4 and move the decimal point two places to the right. The correct answer is d, 75%.

Example B.   A health club manager determines that 2 of 5 people who try out the club eventually join. What percent is this?

   **a.** 25%      **b.** 30%      **c.** 35%      **d.** 40%

Because 2 of 5 eventually join, the fraction that joins is $\dfrac{2}{5}$. Divide 2 by 5 and move the decimal two places to the right. The correct answer is d, 40%.

Example C.    A large package of raisins contains 16 oz. A small package of raisings contains 4 oz. What percent of the large package is in the small package?

    **a.** 10%    **b.** 25%    **c.** 30%    **d.** 40%

The small package contains $\frac{4}{16}$ of the amount of raisins in the large package. Divide 4 by 16 and move the decimal point two places to the right. The correct answer is b, 25%.

## Change a Decimal to a Fraction

To change a decimal to a fraction, identify the place value of the digit farthest to the right. This tells you what the denominator of the fraction will be. Then write the digits in the decimal in the numerator.

Example D.    A can of soda contains .85 liters. Which of these is another way to show the amount of soda in a can of this size?

    **a.** $\frac{3}{4}$ liter    **b.** $\frac{8}{10}$ liter    **c.** $\frac{17}{20}$ liter    **d.** $\frac{18}{20}$ liter

The digit farthest to the right is 5, and it is in the hundredths place. This makes the denominator 100. Therefore, the decimal .85 equals the fraction $\frac{85}{100}$. You can reduce this to $\frac{17}{20}$ by dividing the numerator and denominator by 5. The correct answer is c, $\frac{17}{20}$.

Example E.    The average number of children in a certain U.S. city is 2.3. Which of these is another way to show the average number of children in this city?

    **a.** $2\frac{3}{4}$    **b.** $2\frac{3}{5}$    **c.** $2\frac{3}{8}$    **d.** $2\frac{3}{10}$

The whole number part is 2. The digit farthest to the right is 3, and it is in the tenths place. This makes the denominator of the fractional part 10. Therefore, the decimal 2.3 equals the mixed number $2\frac{3}{10}$. The correct answer is d.

## Percent Problems

These are word problems that ask you to find the part, whole, or %. You learned how to do this in Lesson 5.

- To find the %, divide the part by the whole and move the decimal point 2 places to the right.

- To find the part, multiply the % by the whole, and move the decimal point 2 places to the left.
- To find the whole, divide the part by the percent, and move the decimal point 2 places to the right.

Example F.    A small New England town has 5000 registered voters. During a recent election, 2700 voted. What percent of registered voters actually voted in that election?

  **a.** 54%  **b.** 52%  **c.** 45%  **d.** 27%

The problem asks for %. The part is 2700, and the whole is 5000. Use the formula and a calculator to get $2700 \div 5000 = .54 \Rightarrow 54\%$.

Example G.    Suzanne spent $19.55 for dinner at a restaurant. She wants to leave a 15% tip. Which of the following is a way to calculating 15% of $19.55?

  **a.** $19.55 $\times$ .15   **b.** $19.55 $\times$ 1.5

  **c.** $19.55 $\div$ .15   **d.** $19.55 $\div$ 1.5

In this problem, the tip is the part, the cost of dinner is the whole , and 15 is %. According to the formula the part is $19.55 \times 15$ with the decimal point moved two places to the left. The decimal point is after the 5 in the number 15. If you move that decimal point 2 places to the left, you get .15. The correct answer is a.

Example H.    George took a test with 20 questions on it. Four of his answers were wrong. What percent did he get right?

  **a.** 96%  **b.** 86%  **c.** 80%  **d.** 75%

If 4 of his answers were wrong, 16 were right. The part is 16, and the whole is 20. Use the formula and a calculator to get $16 \div 20 = .8 \Rightarrow 80\%$. The correct answer is c.

Example I.    The retail price of a shirt is $30. The store will add 7% sales tax. How much will the shirt cost with tax?

  **a.** $30.70  **b.** $37.00  **c.** $32.10  **d.** $31.70

First find the amount of tax. This is the part. The whole is 30, and the % is 7. To calculator the part, multiply 7 times 30, and move the decimal point two places to the left. The amount of tax is $2.10. Add this to the $30.00 to get the total price $32.10, answer c.

Example J.    During the last six months, the price of gasoline went from $1.75 to $2.10. What was the percent increase in the price of gasoline?

  **a.** 17%  **b.** 20%  **c.** 35%  **d.** 83%

The amount of the increase is $.35 ($2.10 − $1.75). The part is .35, and the whole is 1.75 (the starting amount). Use the formula and a calculator to get $.35 \div 1.75 = .2 \Rightarrow 20\%$. The correct answer is b, 20%.

Example K.    Michelle paid $15 for a coffee pot that was on sale at 20% off. What was the original price?

**a.** $18.00    **b.** $12.00    **c.** $18.75    **d.** $3.00

This is a tricky problem. You first have to realize that if the Michelle got 20% off the cost of the pot, she paid 80%. So the % is 80, not 20, the part is 15, and the problem asks you to find the whole. Use the formula and a calculator to get $15 \div 80 = .1875 \Rightarrow 18.75$.

## Solve a Proportion

Percent problems are proportions where the denominator of one fraction is 100: $\dfrac{Part}{Whole} = \dfrac{\%}{100}$. In a proportion that is not a percent, other numbers replace the % and 100. These other two numbers are another part and whole. In a proportion problem 3 of the 4 numbers are known, and you have to find the fourth number. An example will help here. In the proportion problem $\dfrac{3}{4} = \dfrac{x}{8}$, you have to determine what number $x$ is. In this example, you know the 2 denominators. Divide the larger one (8) by the smaller one (4). Then multiply the numerator (3) by the answer (2), and that's the other numerator ($x = 6$). In the example, $8 \div 4 = 2$, and $2 \times 3 = 6$. If you knew the two numerators and only one denominator instead, the procedure would be exactly the same. Let's look at some specific examples.

Example L.    Michael made 6 free throws in 8 tries. How many would you expect him to make in 24 tries?

**a.**  12    **b.** 16    **c.** 18    **d.** 20

Let $x$ stand for the answer (number of free throws made in 24 tries). Then $\dfrac{6}{8} = \dfrac{x}{24}$ are the two equal fractions. First divide 24 by 8 and get 3. Then multiply 3 by 6 to get 18.

Example M.    The ratio of red tulips to yellow tulips in Cherie's garden is 5:2. This year Cherie has 20 yellow tulips in her garden. How many red tulips does she have?

**a.**  23    **b.** 25    **c.** 50    **d.** 60

The proportion in this problem is $\dfrac{5}{2} = \dfrac{x}{20}$. Twenty divided by 2 is 10, and 10 times 5 is 50.

The hair color of 500 members of the high school senior class was classified as brunette, blonde, or redhead. The results are shown in the table below.

| Hair Color | Number of Students |
| --- | --- |
| Brunette | 230 |
| Blonde | 180 |

| | |
|---|---|
| Redhead | 90 |
| Total | 500 |

**Example N.** If there are 2000 students in the high school, how many brunettes would you expect to find?

Set up the proportion $\dfrac{230}{500} = \dfrac{x}{2000}$, where $x$ is the number of brunettes in the school. Then $2000 \div 500 = 4$ and $4 \times 230 = 920$. You would expect to find 920 brunettes in a school with 2000 students.

## Number Theory Practice

1. A map has a scale of 1 inch = 5 miles. How far is it Barnesville from Carlton if the map distance between them is 3 inches?
   a. 15 miles
   b. 7 miles
   c. 9 miles
   d. 8 miles

2. A 12-ounce can of soda costs $1.25. How much would you expect a 15-ounce bottle to cost?
   a. $1.40
   b. $1.56
   c. $1.62
   d. $1.75

3. Josh got 35% of the vote in a Student Council election at a school with 1500 students. If everyone at the school voted, how many votes did Josh receive?
   a. 500
   b. 525
   c. 540
   d. 550

4. The cost of chicken wings at the local supermarket increased from $1.29 a pound to $1.59 a pound in the last month. About what percent increase is this?
   a. 19%
   b. 68%
   c. 30%
   d. 23%

5. Debra is planning to paint a picture of a photograph that is 4 inches wide by 6 inches high. If her painting must be 16 inches wide, how high should it be?
   a. 18 inches
   b. 20 inches
   c. 24 inches
   d. 28 inches

6. A large order of French fries costs $2.00. A super size order has 30% more fries. How much should a super size order of fries cost?
   a. $2.30
   b. $2.60
   c. $3.00
   d. $3.30

7. George took a 20-question math test, and he got 16 problems right. How many problems could he expect to get right on a 50-question test covering the same topics?
   a. 46
   b. 40
   c. 38
   d. 32

8. A 16-ounce package of frozen vegetables costs $2.10. How much would you expect an 8-ounce package to cost?
   a. $1.75
   b. $1.45
   c. $1.25
   d. $1.05

9. A small package of 30 colored candies contained 10 red pieces. How many red pieces would you expect to find in a large package containing 45 pieces?
   a. 15
   b. 20
   c. 25
   d. 30

10. Five of eight cameras sold in the Camera Mart Store are digital cameras. Last week Camera Mart sold 72 cameras. How many digital cameras did they sell?
    a. 36
    b. 40
    c. 45
    d. 50

## LESSON 9 Data Interpretation

In a data interpretation problem you have to draw conclusions from looking at diagram, chart, or table of numbers. You see these in newspapers and magazines all the time. Unfortunately, there is no set way to interpret one of these figures. You have to read the titles and labels on them carefully in order to understand what is being presented.

The examples below illustrate the various types of figures you will see on the TABE D.

## Venn Diagrams

A Venn diagram is a picture that helps you count objects that may be in two overlapping groups.

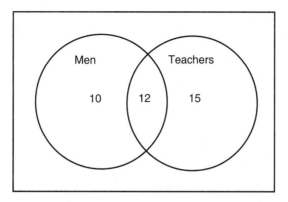

Example A.   One circle represents a group of men. The other circle represents a group of teachers. The space where the two circles overlap represents people who are both teachers and men. In this picture, there are 12 male teachers, 10 men who aren't teachers, and 15 teachers who aren't men. If you were asked how many teachers there are, you would add 12 and 15 and get the answer 27. If you were asked how many men there are, you would add 12 and 10 and get the answer 22.

## Graphs

A graph is a figure that shows how two quantities are related. A graph has a horizontal axis and a vertical axis. Each of the two quantities is measured along one axis.

Example B.   The graph below describes a car trip. The horizontal axis measures the amount of time that has passed since the people left home. The vertical axis measures distance traveled. Point A shows a distance of 100 miles in 2 hours. Point B indicates that the travelers stopped for an hour after traveling the first 100 miles (because they had still only traveled 100 miles after 3 hours).

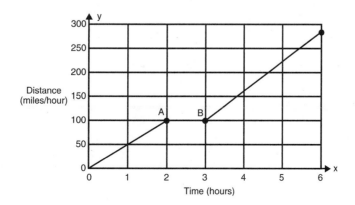

## Bar Graphs

A bar graph is like a graph, except one of the axes represents categories instead of a quantity.

Example C. The bar graph below shows the average rainfall for the months. You can tell quickly that March, April, and May are the rainiest months, and that August is the driest month.

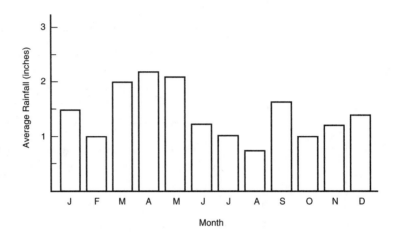

## Circle Graphs

Circle graphs are good way of showing how a total breaks down into parts. You can think of the circle as a pie and the parts as pieces of pie. The size of each piece corresponds to the percent of the total.

Example D. This circle graph shows the breakdown of favorite summer nonalcoholic drinks. The graph shows that people like soda, water, and iced tea about equally. A smaller percentage of people like fruit drinks.

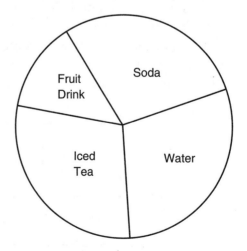

Favorite Summer Nonalcoholic Beverages

## Tables

Tables are another way of showing how two quantities are related. Tables are often used to show how some quantity changes over time.

**Example E.** The table below shows the population of some town at the end of each year indicated. The population increased gradually between 1950 and 1990. Then it went down between 1990 and 2000.

Annual Population   Anytown, U.S.A.

| Year | Population |
|------|-----------|
| 1950 | 11,486 |
| 1960 | 13,052 |
| 1970 | 15,955 |
| 1980 | 19,821 |
| 1990 | 22,006 |
| 2000 | 19,955 |

There are two other concepts in data interpretation.

- Find the *mean* of a set of numbers.

  To find the mean, add the numbers and divide by the number of numbers. This is usually just called the average. For example, the mean of 4, 8, 3, 5, and 10 is 6 (30 ÷ 5)

- Find the *median* of a set of numbers.

  To find the median, arrange the numbers in order from smallest to largest. There are two cases:

  (a) The number of numbers is odd. In this case there is a middle number, and that's the median. For example, the median of the five numbers, 4, 8, 13, 25, and 37 is 13.

  (b) The number of numbers is even. In this case there are two "middle" numbers. The median is their average. For example, suppose there are six numbers: 4, 8, 13, 25, 37, and 38. The two middle numbers are 13 and 25.

  The median is (13 + 25) ÷ 2 = 19, the average of 13 and 25.

## Data Interpretation Practice

1. The circle graph shows the market share of four major cable TV companies. Which company, if any, has more than half the market share?
   a. CabCo
   b. TV4U
   c. Media Monster
   d. None

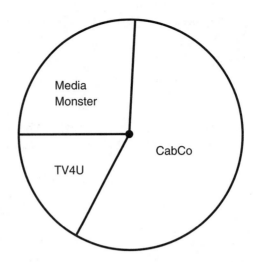

A radar gun was aimed at 5 cars on the interstate highway. Their speeds were 70 mph, 63 mph, 72 mph, 65 mph, and 60 mph. Use this information to answer questions 2 and 3.

**2.** What was the median speed?
   **a.** 72 mph
   **b.** 65 mph
   **c.** 66 mph
   **d.** 60 mph

**3.** What was the mean speed?
   **a.** 72 mph
   **b.** 65 mph
   **c.** 66 mph
   **d.** 60 mph

A jug is being filled with water. The graph shows how much water there is in the jug over time after the filling starts. Use this graph to answer questions 4 and 5.

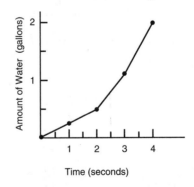

**4.** How long did it take to fill the jug with $\frac{1}{2}$ gallon?
   **a.** 1 sec
   **b.** 2 sec
   **c.** 3 sec
   **d.** 4 sec

**5.** How much of the jug was filled after 2.5 seconds?

    **a.** 1 gal

    **b.** 1.5 gal

    **c.** 2 gal

    **d.** 2.5 gal

A standard die with 6 faces was rolled a hundred times. The outcomes are summarized in the table. Use this table to answer questions 6 and 7.

| OUTCOME | FREQUENCY |
|---------|-----------|
| 1 | 14 |
| 2 | 20 |
| 3 | 9 |
| 4 | 15 |
| 5 | 25 |
| 6 | 18 |

**6.** Which face turned up least frequently?

    **a.** 1

    **b.** 3

    **c.** 18

    **d.** 24

**7.** What percent of the time did 6 turn up?

    **a.** 6%

    **b.** 10%

    **c.** 18%

    **d.** 24%

**8.** Middlesex Community College kept track of how many students enrolled in math and English courses. The numbers of students taking math, English, and both types of courses are shown in the Venn diagram. How many students enrolled in math courses?

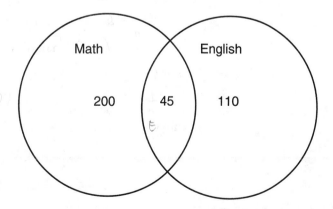

a. 245

b. 200

c. 155

d. 45

Average high and low temperatures in a certain city were measured in the months of January, April, July, and October. These are shown in the bar graph. Use this graph to do problems 9 and 10.

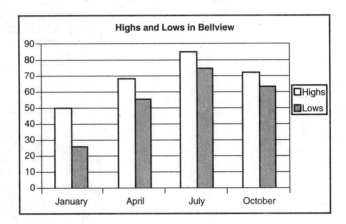

9. When was the difference between the average high and the average low temperatures the greatest?

a. January

b. April

c. July

d. October

10. Which of these is the best estimate of the average high temperature for the 4 months shown in the graph?

a. 65°F

b. 75°F

c. 80°F

d. 85°F

## LESSON 10  Pre-algebra and Algebra

The word "algebra" can sound pretty scary. It has been said that algebra is the "gateway" to mathematics. In algebra you learn the language of math—the symbols and many vocabulary words. Algebra also shows how math can describe patterns. These could be patterns in science and nature or patterns of production and manufacturing. Using math to describe patterns is called mathematical modeling.

You will only need to know fundamental concepts of algebra for the TABE D. There are five types of problems in this section.

## Recognize Patterns

These problems require you to recognize number or picture patterns and either continue them or fill in the missing number or picture.

**Example A.** Find the next number in the pattern 5, 8, 11, 14, . . . .

In this pattern, each number is 3 more than the one before it, so add 3 to 14, and the next number is 17.

**Example B.** Find the missing number in the pattern 75, 70, _____, 60, 55, 50, . . . .

In this pattern, the numbers decrease by 5, so the missing number must be 65.

An example of a picture pattern is shown below.

**Example C.** Find the next row of the tile pattern.

Because the number of dots goes up by 1 each time, the next row should have 5 dots.

## Write an Algebra Expression

An algebra expression is numbers, letters, and symbols that represent a situation.

**Example D.** The Math Department at Central High School ordered lined paper and graph paper. They ordered 50 more reams of graph paper than lined paper. If $x$ represents the number of reams of lined paper, which of the following expressions gives the number of reams of graph paper?

    **a.** $x \div 50$     **b.** $x + 50$     **c.** $x - 50$     **d.** $50x$ (50 times $x$)

To find 50 more than a number, you add 50 to the number. The correct answer is b, $x + 50$.

## Fill in a Blank with a Number or a Symbol

**Example E.** What symbol goes in the box to make the following number sentence true? $3.7 + 1.05$ _____ $4.1$

    **a.** $<$      **b.** $>$    **c.** $=$    **d.** $\leq$

You need to add the two decimals: $3.7 + 1.05 = 4.75$, which is more than 4.1. The symbol for "more than" is $>$, so the correct answer is b.

Example F.   What symbol goes in the box to make the number sentence true? 27_____ 9 < 4

**a.**  +     **b.**  −     **c.**  ×     **d.**  ÷

You can do this problem by trying each answer choice. Only ÷ makes the number sentence true because $27 ÷ 9 = 3$ and $3 < 4$.

## Interpret an Input-Output Table

This is similar to finding a pattern. You are given several pairs of numbers. Each pair consists of an input and an output. You have to find the math rule (formula) that you follow to change to input numbers to output numbers. The same rule must be used for all pairs.

Example G.

| Input | Output |
|-------|--------|
| 0 | 1 |
| 1 | 3 |
| 3 | 7 |
| 6 | 13 |
| 8 | 17 |

If you multiply the input number by 2 and add 1, you'll get the output number:

$$2 × 0 + 1 = 1$$
$$2 × 1 + 1 = 3$$
$$2 × 3 + 1 = 7$$
$$2 × 6 + 1 = 13$$
$$2 × 8 + 1 = 17$$

This example is difficult because the rule has two parts: multiply by 2 and add 1.

If a problem asks you to find the output for an input of 10, you multiply 10 by 2 and add 1 to get 21.

Although there is no set method for doing these, there are some things you can try. If the input numbers follow a sequence, such as 1, 2, 3, etc. or 2, 4, 6, etc. see if you can find a sequence for the output numbers. This doesn't work in the example above because the input numbers 1, 3, 6, and 8, don't follow a sequence. It does, however, work for the example below:

Example H.   Use the input/output table below to find the output for an input of 11.

| Input | Output |
|-------|--------|
| 1 | 5 |
| 3 | 10 |
| 5 | 15 |
| 7 | 20 |
| 9 | 25 |

The number 11 follows the input pattern 1, 3, 5, 7, 9. The output numbers also follow the pattern of counting by 5s. The next output number (that goes with 11) is 30.

## Solve Equations

You are given a number sentence with a letter in it. You have to determine what number to replace the letter with to make the number sentence true. For example, what number can you put in place of $x$ to make $3x - 2 = 4$ a true sentence? ($3x$ means 3 times $x$). In the TABE D, you should *guess* numbers to replace and *check* to see if they work. If you replace $x$ with the number 1, the sentence would say $3 \times 1 - 2 = 4$, or $3 - 2 = 4$, which is false because $3 - 2 = 1$. If you replace $x$ with the number 2, the equation would say $3 \times 2 - 2 = 4$, or $6 - 2 = 4$, which is true. Therefore, 2 is the solution to the equation.

## Pre-Algebra and Algebra Practice

**1.** What symbol goes in the space to make the number sentence true?
8_____ 3 > 20
**a.** +
**b.** −
**c.** ×
**d.** ÷

A bicycle rental shop charges $20 for the rental and $15 for each hour the bike is used. The table below shows the total charges based on the amount of time a bike is rented. Study the table. Then do problems 2 through 4.

| Hours Rented | Total Charge |
|--------------|--------------|
| 1 | $35 |
| 2 | $50 |
| 3 | $65 |
| 4 | $80 |

**2.** What would the total charges be if the bike is rented for 5 hours?
   **a.** $75
   **b.** $85
   **c.** $95
   **d.** $105

**3.** $C$ = total cost of a rental

   $h$ = the number of hours a bike is rented

   Which equation shows the relationship of $C$ to $h$?
   **a.** $C = 20h$
   **b.** $C = 20 + h$
   **c.** $C = 15 + 20h$
   **d.** $C = 20 + 15h$

**4.** It cost Cheryl $110 to rent a bike. How long did she rent it?
   **a.** 6 hour
   **b.** 7 hours
   **c.** 8 hours
   **d.** 9 hours

**5.** Steven cut $\frac{3}{4}$ of the grass in his yard before being interrupted by a salesman. Which expression shows the fraction of the lawn that still had to be cut?

   **a.** $1 + \frac{3}{4}$

   **b.** $1 - \frac{3}{4}$

   **c.** $1 \times \frac{3}{4}$

   **d.** $1 \div \frac{3}{4}$

**6.** Three friends share a rumor. The number of people who know the rumor doubles every hour. If this pattern continues, how many people will know the rumor after 4 hours?
   **a.** 36
   **b.** 48
   **c.** 54
   **d.** 60

**7.** If $y = 8x - 3$, what is the value of $y$ when $x = 3$?
   **a.** 2
   **b.** 8
   **c.** 15
   **d.** 21

**8.** The table below shows input numbers that have been changed by a certain rule to get output numbers. What is the output number if the input number is 10?

| Input | Output |
|-------|--------|
| 0 | 1 |
| 1 | 3 |
| 2 | 5 |
| 3 | 7 |
| 4 | 9 |
| 5 | 11 |

  **a.** 21
  **b.** 20
  **c.** 16
  **d.** 13

**9.** Which of these expressions gives the perimeter of the rectangle?

$x$ [rectangle]

$3x + 1$

  **a.** $4x + 1$
  **b.** $8x + 2$
  **c.** $3x^2 + 1$
  **d.** $3x^2 + x$

**10.** What symbol goes in the blank space to make the number sentence true?

$$\frac{1}{2} + \frac{1}{3} \underline{\hspace{1cm}} 1$$

  **a.** $=$
  **b.** $>$
  **c.** $<$
  **d.** $\geq$

## LESSON 11   Measurement

Measurement problems are about length, weight, temperature, time, and money. Two measurement systems for length, weight, and temperature are used in the United States. One is the *metric* system. The other is called the *customary* system. For TABE D problems you will use one system or the other. You will not have to know how to convert between these two systems.

Temperature is measured in degrees Fahrenheit in the customary system or degrees Celsius in the metric system. There is one set of units for time (seconds, minutes, hours, days, weeks, months, years). In the United States, money is measured in dollars and cents.

Before describing the types of measurement problems on the TABE D, let's briefly review the relationships between the units within each system.

## Units of Time

The *second* is the smallest time unit. After this,

60 seconds make 1 *minute*

60 minutes make 1 *hour*

24 hours make 1 *day*

7 days make 1 *week*

4 weeks make 1 *month* (actually, a fraction more than 4)

52 weeks make 1 *year*

12 months make 1 *year*

10 years make 1 *decade*

10 decades (100 years) make 1 *century*

## Units of Money

The penny is the smallest money unit. After this,

5 pennies make 1 nickel

2 nickels make a dime

5 nickels make a quarter

10 dimes (20 nickels) make a dollar

There are 50-cent pieces, but these are going out of circulation.

## Units of Length

| Customary | Metric |
|---|---|
| inch is the smallest unit | millimeter is the smallest unit |
| 12 inches make 1 foot | 10 millimeters make 1 centimeter |
| 3 feet make 1 yard | 100 centimeters make 1 meter |
| 1760 yards (5280 feet) make 1 mile | 1000 meters make 1 kilometer |

## Units of Liquid Volume

**Customary**

Pint is the smallest unit

2 pints make 1 quart

4 quarts make 1 gallon

**Metric**

milliliter is the smallest unit

1000 milliliters make 1 liter

## Units of Weight

**Customary**

ounce is the smallest unit

16 ounces make 1 pound

2000 pounds make 1 ton

**Metric**

milligram is the smallest unit

1000 milligrams make 1 gram

1000 grams make 1 kilogram

## Units of Temperature

**Customary**

degrees Fahrenheit

water freezes at 32°F

water boils at 212°F

**Metric**

degrees Celsius

water freezes at 0°C

water boils at 100°C

Units of length are used to measure length, area, and volume. Examples are used to illustrate the various types of measurement problems.

Example A.  The fish tank shown below is 3 feet long, 1 foot wide, and 2 feet deep. How much water can the tank hold (cu ft = cubic feet)?

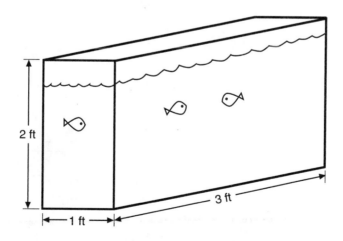

**a.** 5 cu ft     **b.** 6 cu ft     **c.** 8 cu ft     **d.** 12 cu ft

To find the volume, multiply the length times the width times the height: $3 \times 1 \times 2 = 6$. The correct answer is 6 cu ft. (b)

Example B.   Samantha wants to fence in her flower garden shown in the figure below. How much fencing will she need?

   **a.** 23 ft      **b.** 45 ft      **c.** 49 ft      **d.** 69 ft

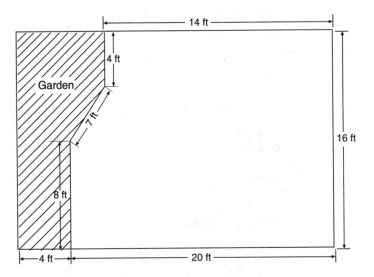

   The amount of fencing needed is the perimeter of the flower garden. Add up lengths that surround the flower garden. You will have to figure out two of them. The top piece is 10 feet (20 + 4 − 14). The left side is 16 feet (same as the right side). The total perimeter of the garden is 49 feet (10 + 16 + 4 + 8 + 7 + 4 = 49). The correct answer is c.

Example C.   A box of grass seed will cover 1500 square feet? How many boxes are needed to seed a rectangular lawn that is 60 feet by 100 feet?

   **a.** 10 boxes      **b.** 6 boxes      **c.** 4 boxes      **d.** 2 boxes

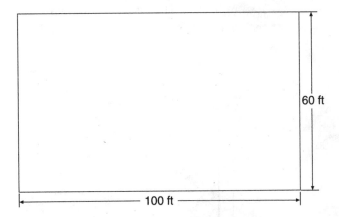

   You need to find the area of the lawn and divide that by 1500. To find the area of the rectangular lawn, multiply the length and width. This gives you 6000 sq ft. Because each box covers 1500 square feet, you will need 6000 ÷ 1500, or 4 boxes. The correct answer is c.

Example D.   A roofing crew started work at 7:45 a.m. and worked for $3\frac{1}{2}$ hours. They took a half-hour lunch break and worked for 4 more hours. What time did they stop working?

   **a.** 3:15 p.m.      **b.** 3:45 p.m.      **c.** 4:15 p.m.      **d.** 4:45 p.m.

   Add the morning hours, lunch, and afternoon hours: $3\frac{1}{2}+\frac{1}{2}+4$. The total time was 8 hours. Quitting time was 3:45 p.m. (b).

Example E.   A cashier needs to make 47 cents in change. What is the smallest possible number of coins that can be used to make exactly 47 cents?

   **a.** 5      **b.** 6      **c.** 7      **d.** 8

   You need a quarter, two dimes, a nickel, and two pennies to make 47 cents. The correct answer is 6 coins (b).

Example F.   How many 9-inch-by-9-inch tiles are needed to cover a floor that is 8 feet by 10 feet?

   **a.** 100      **b.** 128      **c.** 137      **d.** 143

   You need to calculate the area of the floor in square inches. Then divide the answer by 81 (9 × 9). Because 12 inches make 1 foot, you have to multiply 8 by 12 and 9 by 12. The room's size is 96 inches by 120 inches. Multiply 96 by 120 to get an area of 11,520 square inches. Because 11520 ÷ 81 = 142.22···, you will need at least 143 tiles to cover the floor. The correct answer is d.

Example G.   George is reading a map that has a scale of 1 centimeter equals 5 kilometers. The map distance to his destination is 8 centimeters. How far away is his destination?

   **a.** 40 km      **b.** 4 km      **c.** 10 km      **d.** 20 km

   Each centimeter on the map represents 5 kilometers. A map distance of 8 centimeters represents 8 × 5 = 40 kilometers. The correct answer is a.

## Measurement Practice

**1.** A box measures 5 feet long, 2 feet wide, and 1 foot high. How much space in inside the box?
   **a.** 11 cu ft
   **b.** 7 cu ft
   **c.** 10 cu ft
   **d.** 21 cu ft

2. Don picks $\frac{1}{3}$ an acre of blueberries on his farm from 8:00 a.m. to 10:00 a.m. At this rate, what time would he finish the <u>entire acre</u> if he takes an hour for lunch?
   a. 1:00 p.m.
   b. 2:00 p.m.
   c. 3:00 p.m.
   d. 4:00 p.m.

3. When Jack woke up this morning, the temperature outside was 6°F below zero. By the time he got to work, it was 13°F above zero. How many degrees F did the temperature rise?
   a. 7°F
   b. 16°F
   c. 19°F
   d. 21°F

4. Fran saves spare change. She has 64 nickels. How much is this in dollars and cents?
   a. $3.04
   b. $3.20
   c. $3.25
   d. $2.70

5. What is the length of BD?

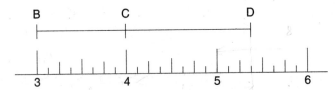

   a. $2\frac{3}{8}$ in

   b. $2\frac{1}{2}$ in

   c. $2\frac{3}{4}$ in

   d. $3\frac{3}{8}$ in

6. A patient in a hospital must receive 20 milliliters of glucose each hour. How many *liters* of glucose will the patient receive in 12 hours?
   a. 240 liters
   b. 24 liters
   c. 2.4 liters
   d. .24 liters

The Conti family is planning to clean their swimming pool. The diagram below shows the measurements of the pool. Study the diagram. Then do problems 7 through 9.

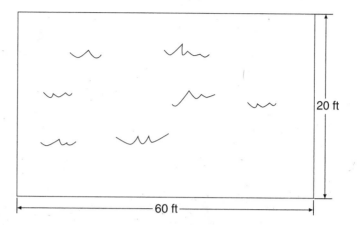

7. What is the length of the pool in yards?
   a. 30
   b. 20
   c. 15
   d. 12

8. If the pool on average is 4 feet deep, how many cubic feet of water will it hold?
   a. 1200
   b. 3600
   c. 4800
   d. 6000

9. The garden hose fills the pool at a rate of 240 cubic feet per hour. At this rate, how many hours will it take to fill the pool?
   a. 2 hours
   b. 10 hours
   c. 20 hours
   d. 40 hours

10. It started to rain at 7:15 a.m. and didn't end until 2:45 p.m. How long did it rain?
    a. 6 hours, 30 minutes
    b. 6 hours, 45 minutes
    c. 7 hours, 30 minutes
    d. 7 hours, 45 minutes

Geometry is the study of shapes. Most TABE D problems are about plane geometry. This is the geometry of flat surfaces, or two dimensions. You will only need to know the names of some solid figures. You see geometry all around you. A yield sign is a triangle. A stop sign is an octagon. The U.S. Department of Defense building in Washington is in the shape of a pentagon. The curbs of a street are parallel lines. The letter "T" consists of perpendicular lines.

You need to understand the "language" of geometry in order to be successful on this part of the TABE D. This means that you have to know definitions of various figures and relationships between them. You must also know what certain symbols mean. In other problems you must recognize geometry patterns. Finally, you will have to apply a few geometry facts to solve some problems. First you need to review a long list of definitions.

## Lines

Parallel lines: a pair of lines that never cross each other, like railroad tracks.

Perpendicular lines: a pair of lines that form a right angle (90°), like the corner of a piece of paper.

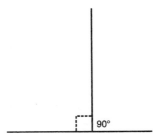

Line: a straight line that extends forever in both directions.

Line segment: a line that stops at *both* ends. Segment $AB$ $(\overline{AB})$ is shown.

Ray: a line with *one* endpoint. Ray $AB$ $(\overrightarrow{AB})$ is shown.

## Angles

Angle: 2 rays with the same endpoint. Angle $A(\angle A)$ is shown. Sometimes you need three letters to name an angle. Look at $\angle BAC$ below. You could not just call this $\angle A$ because you couldn't be sure which angle had that name.

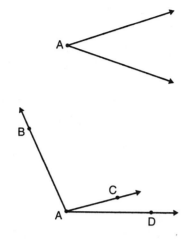

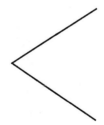

Right angle: 90°

Acute angle: less than 90°

Obtuse angle: more than 90°

# Types of Triangles

Right triangle: 1 right angle

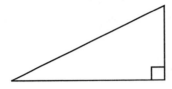

Isosceles triangle: two sides of equal length

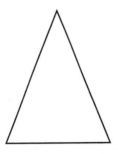

Equilateral triangle: all three sides have equal length

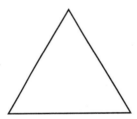

Scalene triangle: all three sides have different lengths

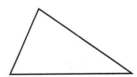

Acute triangle: all three angles are acute (less than 90°)

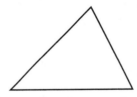

Obtuse triangle: one obtuse angle (more than 90°)

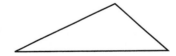

## Types of Quadrilaterals (Four-Sided Shapes)

Rectangle: four-sided figure with four right angles

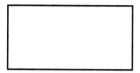

Parallelogram: four-sided figure with both pairs of opposite sides parallel

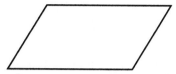

Rhombus: four-sided figure with all sides equal in length

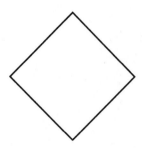

Trapezoid: four-sided figure with one pair of parallel sides and the other pair not parallel

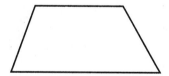

## Names of Other Shapes

Hexagon: six-sided figure

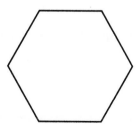

Octagon: eight-sided figure

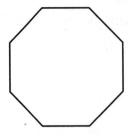

## Solid Figures

Pyramid: solid figure with triangular sides that come to a point

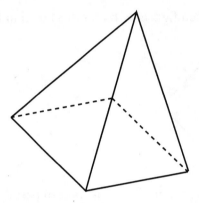

Cylinder: solid figure shaped like a can

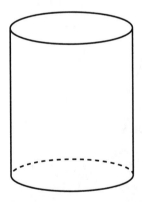

Congruent figures: figures that have the same shape and size

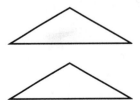

Similar figures: figures that the same shape but different sizes

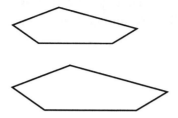

## Circles

Diameter: a line segment that goes through the center of the circle

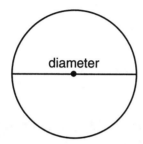

Radius: a line segment from the center of a circle to the circle (half a diameter)

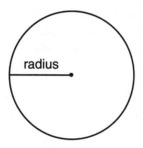

## Important Facts

- The angles of any triangle add up to 180°.

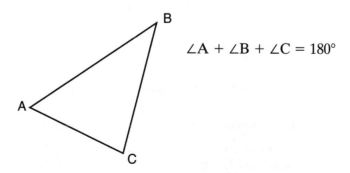

$$\angle A + \angle B + \angle C = 180°$$

- If two figures are similar, the lengths of their corresponding sides are proportional. For example, suppose you know that the two triangles below ($\triangle ABC$ and $\triangle XYZ$) are similar. What is the length of side $\overline{YZ}$?

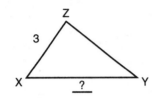

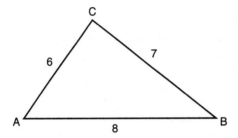

Since $\overline{AB}$ is twice as long as $\overline{XY}$, $\overline{BC}$ must be twice as long as $\overline{YZ}$. This means the length of $\overline{YZ}$ is 4.

- If two sides of a triangle have equal lengths, the angles opposite them are equal. All 3 angles of an equilateral triangle are equal (because all three sides are equal). Combine this with fact (1) to conclude that the angles of an equilateral triangle are all 60° (180 ÷ 3 = 60).

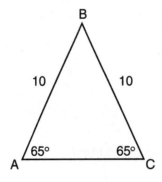

## Geometry Practice

1. Which of these figures could contain two obtuse angles?
   a. right triangle
   b. trapezoid
   c. rectangle
   d. obtuse triangle

**2.** Which of these triangles is congruent to the shaded triangle?

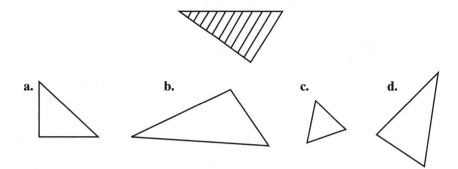

**a.**    **b.**    **c.**    **d.**

**3.** Which two figures are congruent?
   **a.** figures 2 and 3
   **b.** figures 1 and 3
   **c.** figures 2 and 4
   **d.** figures 1 and 2

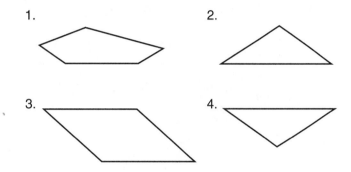

1.    2.

3.    4.

**4.** Which of these best describes $\triangle ABC$?
   **a.** equilateral triangle
   **b.** congruent triangle
   **c.** scalene triangle
   **d.** right triangle

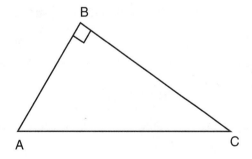

B

A    C

**5.** If the radius of a circle is 20 inches, what is its diameter?

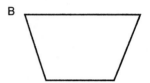

   **a.** 10 inches
   **b.** 30 inches
  √**c.** 40 inches
   **d.** 62.8 inches

**6.** Which of these figures is a rhombus?

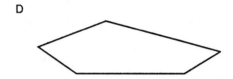

   **a.** A
   **b.** B
   **c.** C
   **d.** D

In the diagram below, $\triangle ABC$ and $\triangle PQR$ are similar. Use this fact to answer questions 7 and 8.

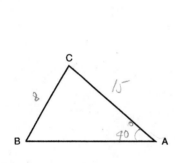
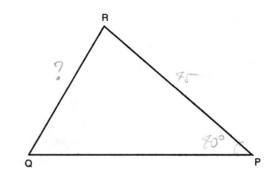

**7.** If $\angle A$ measures 40°, what is the measure of $\angle P$?

   **a.** 25°
  √**b.** 40°
   **c.** 45°
   **d.** 50°

**8.** If $AC = 15$, $PR = 45$, and $BC = 8$, what is the length $RQ$?

   **a.** 38
   **b.** 32
  √**c.** 24
   **d.** 20

**9.** In $\triangle LMN$, $\angle L = 55°$ and $\angle M = 95°$. What is the measure of $\angle N$?

   **a.** 30°
   **b.** 50°
   **c.** 55°
   **d.** 60°

**10.** Billy is making a cylinder out of cardboard. What combination of shapes does he need to cut out?

   **a.** 2 circles and 1 triangle
   **b.** 2 circles and 1 rectangle
   **c.** 1 circle and 2 triangles
   **d.** 1 circle and 2 rectangles

## LESSON 13  Computation in Context

Computation in context means finding the answers to a variety of real-life problems. You may have to add, subtract, multiply, divide, or work with percents to do these problems. There is no set method for doing these problems. You just have to read the problems carefully and make sure you are answering the question. Examples are given below.

Example A.   Suzanne has a monthly budget of $2000. Her monthly rent is $800. What percent of her monthly budget is spent on rent?

   **a.** 20%     **b.** 40%     **c.** 60%     **d.** 80%

Rent is part of the total. Use the formula and method for finding percent from Section 3.1.5: $\dfrac{800}{2000} = \dfrac{percent}{100}$. Therefore, $percent = 800 \times 100 \div 2000 = 40$. The correct answer is b.

The table below shows the weight of the shrimp catch by Gulf Shellfish one weekend. Examples B land C are based on this table.

### Weekend Shrimp Catch

| Day | Weight of Catch |
|---|---|
| Saturday | 24,312 pounds |
| Sunday | 19,848 pounds |

Example B.   What was the total weekend catch?

   **a.** 33,160     **b.** 33,260     **c.** 34,260     **d.** 44,160

You get the total by adding the Saturday and Sunday catches: 24,312 + 19,848 = 44,160. The correct answer is d.

Example C.   How much bigger was Saturday's catch than Sunday's?

  **a.** 4,464     **b.** 4,564     **c.** 5,464     **d.** 5,564

You get the difference by subtracting Sunday's catch from Saturday's: 24,312 − 19,848 = 4,464. The correct answer is a.

Example D.   Jim's pulse count is 17 for fifteen seconds. What is his number of beats per minute?

  **a.** 58     **b.** 68     **c.** 78     **d.** 88

There are 4 fifteen-second periods each minute. Multiply 17 × 4 = 68. The correct answer is b.

Example E.   What is the total length of a walking trail is shown below?

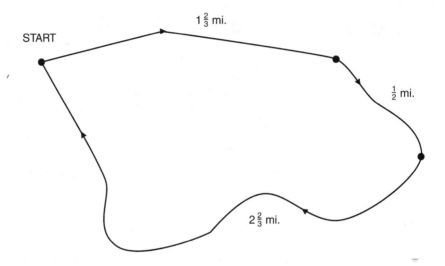

  **a.**  $3\frac{5}{6}$ miles     **b.** 4 miles     **c.**  $4\frac{5}{6}$ miles     **d.** 5 miles

Add the three distances shown:  $1\frac{2}{3} + \frac{1}{2} + 2\frac{2}{3}$  to get  $4\frac{5}{6}$  miles miles (c).

Example F.   Four businesses share a building. They want to build a parking garage at a cost of $9,000,000. They will pay equal amounts. How much would each business have to pay?

  **a.** $225,000     **b.** $250,000     **c.** $2,250,000     **d.** $2,500,000

Divide 9,000,000 by 4 to get $2,250,000.

Example G.   Chicopee Canoe Rental charges $20 plus $5 an hour to rent a canoe. How much would it cost to rent a canoe for 2 hours?

  **a.** $25     **b.** $30     **c.** $35     **d.** $50

# Computation in Context Practice

1. Frank is using a recipe that calls for $\frac{3}{4}$ cup of flour. He only wants to make half of the recipe. How much flour should he use?

   a. $\frac{1}{2}$ cup

   b. $\frac{3}{5}$ cup

   c. $\frac{2}{5}$ cup

   d. $\frac{3}{8}$ cup

Use a restaurant's pizza menu shown below to answer questions 2 and 3.

PIZZA MENU

6-INCH PIZZAS  $9.50   12-INCH PIZZAS  $18.00

EACH TOPPING  $2.25   EACH TOPPING  $3.75

2. How much is a 6″ individual pizza with two toppings?
   a. $11.75
   b. $14.00
   c. $14.50
   d. $17.00

3. How much are two 12″ large pizzas with one topping each?
   a. $43.50
   b. $39.75
   c. $36.00
   d. $25.50

4. The homeowners association gave the local food bank 270 pounds of food. If there are 50 members in the association, and they each gave the same amount of food, how much did each member give?
   a. 4.5 pounds
   b. 4.55 pounds
   c. 5.4 pounds
   d. 5.45 pounds

5. The regular price of a washing machine is $450. It is on sale for 20% off. What is the sale price?
   a. $430
   b. $400
   c. $360
   d. $330

6. In a survey of 2000 people, 45% were opposed to gun control. How many people in the survey opposed gun control?
   a. 450
   b. 600
   c. 800
   d. 900

7. A vinyl strip is used to separate the carpeting from tile flooring. The strip needs to be placed as shown in the diagram below? How long a strip is needed?
   a. 149.4 cm.
   b. 150.4 cm.
   c. 155.4 cm.
   d. 159.4 cm.

48.6 cm.

35.2 cm.

75.6 cm.

8. Three carpenters each work on a job for 4 hours. They each receive $10.50 an hour for their work. What is the cost of this job?
   a. $42.00
   b. $31.50
   c. $94.50
   d. $126.00

9. What is the smallest number of coins that can be used to make 58 cents?
   a. 4
   b. 5
   c. 6
   d. 7

**10.** Fran picks up two packages of ground meat at the grocery store. One weighs 2.45 pounds (lbs.) and the other weighs 3.48 lbs. What is the total weight of the two packages of ground meat?
a. 5.83 lbs.
b. 5.93 lbs.
c. $6.03 lbs.
d. 6.93 lbs.

## Lesson 14 Estimation

When you don't need an exact answer to a computation, you can use estimation to find an approximate answer. Estimation takes advantage of certain math shortcuts to make a calculation quicker and easier. You can also get a better number sense by estimating answers instead of picking up a calculator.

### Rounding to a Place Value

The idea of rounding a number to a place value is best illustrated by examples. Take the number 4736.

- Round 4736 to the nearest thousand. You have to determine if 4736 is closest to 1000 or 2000 or 3000 or 4000, etc. You can quickly narrow the search from 4000 or 5000 because 4736 is between these two. Because it is closer to 5000, *4736 rounded to the nearest thousand is 5000.*

- Round 4736 to the nearest hundred. You can quickly narrow the search from 4700 and 4800 because 4736 is between these two. Because it is closer to 4700, *4736 rounded to the nearest hundred is 4700.*

- Round 4736 to the nearest ten. You can quickly narrow the search from 4730 to 4740 because 4736 is between these two. Because it is closer to 4740, *4736 rounded to the nearest ten is 4740.*

The idea is similar when rounding a decimal number. Take the number .2463 for example.

- Round .2463 to the nearest thousandth. The thousandths place is the third place to the right of the decimal. In this case the digit 6 is in the thousandths place. You can quickly narrow the search from .2460 to .2470 because .2463 is between these two. Because it is closer to .2460, *.2463 rounded to the nearest thousandth is .2460 (=.246).*

- Round .2463 to the nearest hundredth. The hundredths place is the second place to the right of the decimal. In this case the digit 4 is in the hundredths place. You can quickly narrow the search from .2400 to .2500 because .2463 is between these two. Because it is closer to .2500, *.2463 rounded to the nearest hundredth is .2500 (=.25).*

- Round .2643 to the nearest tenth. The tenths place is the first place to the right of the decimal. In this case the digit 2 is in the tenths place. You can quickly narrow the search from .2000 to .3000 because .2643 is between these two. Because it is closer to .3000, *.2643 rounded to the nearest tenth is .3000 (.3)*.

You might be asked to round a decimal number to the nearest unit. Suppose you have to round .2643 to the nearest unit. The units place is the first place to the left of the decimal. In this case the digit 0 is in the units place. Therefore .2643 rounds to either 0 or 1. Because it is closer to 0, *.2643 rounded to the nearest unit is 0*.

Round 38.09 to the nearest unit. The digit 8 is in the units place. You can quickly narrow the search from 38 to 39. Because it is closer to 38, *38.09 rounded to the nearest unit is 38*.

## Rule for Rounding to a Place Value

The rule for rounding was shown in these examples. Call the digit in the place value you are rounding to the "rounding digit." Look at the digit just to the right of the rounding digit. If this digit is less than 5, leave the rounding digit as is and change the remaining digits to the right to 0. If this digit is 5 or more, increase the rounding digit by 1 and change the remaining digits to the right to 0.

Some of the TABE problems just ask you to round numbers. For most of the problems rounding is only part of the problem. Rounded numbers are used in shortcut calculations to answer questions. These shortcuts are illustrated in the following examples.

Example A.   Which of the following is the best estimate of 297.4 ÷ 10.2?

   **a.** 6000     **b.** 3000     **c.** 1000     **d.** 30

Round 297.4 to the nearest hundred—300. Round 10.2 to the nearest ten—10. Multiply 300 by 10 to get 3000 (b).

Example B.   Which of these is the best estimate of 5910.8 ÷ 6?

   **a.** 10     **b.** 100     **c.** 1000     **d.** 10,000

Round 5910.8 to 6000. 6000 ÷ 6 = 1,000. The correct answer is c.

Example C.   One month a contractor earns $563, $612, $890, and $392 on four jobs. About how much did the contractor earn on these four jobs?

   **a.** $2500     **b.** $2400     **c.** $2300     **d.** $2200

Round the numbers to the nearest hundred because the answers are written to that place value. The rounded earnings are $600, $600, $900, and $400.

Because all of these are hundreds, just add 6, 6, 9, and 4 mentally to get 25. The correct answer is $2500 (a).

Example D.    Clair rounded the number 8835 to the nearest 100. Steve rounded this number to the nearest 1000. What was the difference between the two rounded numbers?

  **a.** 35    **b.** 100    **c.** 150    **d.** 200

To the nearest 100, 8835 rounds to 8800. To the nearest 1000, 8835 rounds to 9000. The difference between 9000 and 8800 is 200 (d).

Example E.    A wedding ceremony cost $4985. There were 98 guests at the wedding. The cost per guest was about

  **a.** $10    **b.** $50    **c.** $100    **d.** $150

Round $4985 to $5000. Round 98 guests to 100 guests. Divide $5000 by 100 to get $50 per guest (b)

A shortcut was used in Example A. Move the decimal point one place to the right when multiplying by 10. Because the number 300 is the same as 300.0, you get 3000 when you move the decimal point one place to the right. In general, move the decimal point as many places to the right as there are zeros when multiplying by 10, 100, 1000, etc.

A shortcut used in Example C. Add only the rounding digits. Then attach however many 0s required to get the answer in units.

A shortcut was used in Example E. Move the decimal point two places to the left when dividing by 100. If you move the decimal point two places to the left in $5000, you get $50.00, which is the same as $50. In general, move the decimal point as many places to the left as there are zeros when dividing by 10,100, 1000, etc.

## Estimation Practice

The table below shows the areas of the world's continents rounded to the nearest thousand square miles. Study the table. Then do problems 1 and 2.

| Continent | Area (Thousands of Square Miles) |
|---|---|
| Asia | 17,212 |
| Africa | 11,608 |
| North America | 9,365 |
| South America | 6,880 |
| Antarctica | 5,100 |
| Europe | 3,837 |
| Australia | 2,968 |

1. Which of these is the best estimate of how many times larger North America is than Australia?
   a. 2
   b. 3
   c. 4
   d. 5

2. Which of these is the best estimate of the total area of the world's continents?
   a. between 40 and 50 thousand square miles
   b. between 50 and 60 thousand square miles
   c. between 60 and 70 thousand square miles
   d. between 70 and 80 thousand square miles

3. Kathy bought a desk that was on sale for 30% off. The original price was $399. Which of these is the best estimate of the amount of money she saved by buying the desk on sale?
   a. $12
   b. $16
   c. $120
   d. $160

Richard owns a house-cleaning business. He charges customers $14.50 per hour. Do problems 4, 5, and 6 about Richard's business.

4. A customer would like Richard to do a major spring cleaning. Richard estimates the job will take about 6 hours. Which of these is the most reasonable estimate for the total amount he will charge?
   a. $50
   b. $60
   c. $70
   d. $80

5. One week Richard did four housecleaning jobs with earnings of $32.50, $41, $50.50, and $58. Which of these is the best estimate of Richard's earnings for the four jobs?
   a. $180
   b. $200
   c. $220
   d. $240

6. Eight friends spent $49.20 to throw a party. If they share the cost equally, about how much will each pay (to the nearest dollar)?
   a. $5.00
   b. $6.00
   c. $7.00
   d. $8.00

7. The Kincaid family used 72 gallons of heating oil last December. If heating oil cost $1.99 per gallon, what was this heating cost to the nearest $10?
   a. $70
   b. $100
   c. $140
   d. $150

8. The opening on a wrench is .2875 inches. What is this measurement rounded to the nearest tenth of an inch?
   a. .2
   b. .288
   c. .28
   d. .3

9. A book has 300 pages. Joe counted 202 words on one page. To the nearest 10,000, how many words are in the whole book?
   a. 60,000
   b. 30,000
   c. 20,000
   d. 6,000

10. Carol plans to take a car trip. She will take 3 CDs with her. The playing times for the CDs are shown as minutes:seconds in the table.

   CD 1      62:12

   CD 2      61:45

   CD 3      58:34

   To the nearest 10 minutes, how long will these three CDs last?
   a. 150
   b. 160
   c. 170
   d. 180

## Answers to Practice Questions

### Practice Multiplying Whole Numbers

**1.** 144     **2.** 581     **3.** 335     **4.** 546
**5.** 735     **6.** 306     **7.** 2,304     **8.** 4,266
**9.** 1,410     **10.** 378     **11.** 2,250     **12.** 6,786
**13.** 5,551     **14.** 54,315     **15.** 42,182     **16.** 59,296

### Practice Dividing Whole Numbers

**1.** 8    **2.** 12    **3.** 14    **4.** 17    **5.** 18    **6.** 17
**7.** 68    **8.** 46    **9.** 8    **10.** 26    **11.** 25    **12.** 23

### Practice Reducing Fractions

**1.** $\frac{3}{4}$   **2.** $\frac{2}{3}$   **3.** $\frac{1}{3}$   **4.** $\frac{1}{3}$   **5.** $\frac{1}{3}$   **6.** $\frac{3}{8}$   **7.** $\frac{1}{2}$   **8.** $\frac{2}{3}$   **9.** $\frac{1}{3}$   **10.** $\frac{2}{3}$

### Practice Adding and Subtracting Fractions with the Same Denominators

**1.** $\frac{1}{5}$    **2.** $\frac{3}{4}$    **3.** $\frac{2}{5}$    **4.** $\frac{2}{3}$    **5.** $\frac{1}{3}$    **6.** $\frac{6}{7}$

### Practice Adding and Subtracting Fractions with Different Denominators

**1.** $\frac{5}{12}$    **2.** $\frac{1}{2}$    **3.** $\frac{3}{8}$    **4.** $\frac{13}{15}$    **5.** $\frac{1}{8}$    **6.** $\frac{7}{10}$

### Practice Changing Improper Fractions to Mixed Numbers

**1.** $1\frac{1}{2}$    **2.** $1\frac{3}{4}$    **3.** $1\frac{4}{7}$    **4.** $4\frac{1}{2}$    **5.** $2\frac{3}{8}$    **6.** $1\frac{2}{5}$

### Practice Adding and Subtracting Mixed Numbers, Fractions, and Whole Numbers

**1.** $6\frac{1}{3}$    **2.** $2\frac{1}{5}$    **3.** $3\frac{3}{5}$    **4.** $4\frac{2}{3}$    **5.** $5\frac{2}{5}$    **6.** $5\frac{1}{3}$

**7.** 10    **8.** $5\frac{1}{2}$    **9.** $2\frac{1}{3}$    **10.** $2\frac{3}{7}$    **11.** $1\frac{1}{2}$    **12.** $6\frac{2}{3}$

### Practice Multiplying and Dividing Fractions

**1.** $\frac{1}{6}$    **2.** $\frac{6}{25}$    **3.** $\frac{15}{32}$    **4.** $1\frac{1}{3}$

**5.** $1\frac{3}{5}$    **6.** $5\frac{1}{4}$    **7.** $\frac{3}{10}$    **8.** $\frac{1}{3}$

## Mixed Practice on Fractions

**1.** 1  **2.** $\frac{1}{2}$  **3.** $\frac{1}{3}$  **4.** $\frac{1}{3}$  **5.** $\frac{5}{14}$  **6.** $1\frac{2}{3}$

**7.** $\frac{1}{5}$  **8.** $1\frac{4}{15}$  **9.** $5\frac{3}{8}$  **10.** $\frac{2}{15}$  **11.** $\frac{1}{15}$  **12.** $1\frac{2}{3}$

## Practice Adding and Subtracting Decimals

**1.** 4.4  **2.** 3.37  **3.** 15.73  **4.** 8.66  **5.** 8.31  **6.** 1.04

## Practice Multiplying Decimals

**1.** 25.68  **2.** 9.72  **3.** .6036  **4.** 158.1  **5.** .2678  **6.** 2.108

## Practice Dividing Decimals

**1.** .35  **2.** 16.2  **3.** .013  **4.** 5  **5.** 5.2
**6.** 570  **7.** 3.26  **8.** 3  **9.** 5

## Practice Percent Problems

**1.** 6  **2.** 45%  **3.** 40  **4.** 70%  **5.** 60
**6.** 24  **7.** 50%  **8.** 60  **9.** 28  **10.** 135

## Practice Adding Integers

**1.** 4  **2.** −3  **3.** −20  **4.** 2  **5.** −2  **6.** −11

## Practice Subtracting Integers

**1.** 11  **2.** −17  **3.** 7  **4.** 13  **5.** −2  **6.** −15

## Practice Multiplying and Dividing Integers

**1.** −28  **2.** −5  **3.** −198  **4.** −9
**5.** 52  **6.** −6  **7.** −27  **8.** 9

## Mixed Practice on Integers

**1.** 29  **2.** −5  **3.** −25  **4.** 100
**5.** −24  **6.** 21  **7.** −22  **8.** −42
**9.** −2  **10.** 5  **11.** −6  **12.** 11
**13.** 7  **14.** −9  **15.** 16  **16.** −7
**17.** −36  **18.** −2  **19.** −20  **20.** 5

## Numeration Practice

**1.** thousands  **2.** hundredths  **3.** hundred thousands
**4.** thousandths  **5.** tenths  **6.** b
**7.** c  **8.** d  **9.** c  **10.** b
**11.** b  **12.** d  **13.** a  **14.** b
**15.** b  **16.** d

## Number Theory Practice

| | | | | |
|---|---|---|---|---|
| **1.** a | **2.** b | **3.** b | **4.** d | **5.** c |
| **6.** b | **7.** b | **8.** d | **9.** a | **10.** c |

## Data Interpretation Practice

| | | | | |
|---|---|---|---|---|
| **1.** a | **2.** b | **3.** c | **4.** b | **5.** c |
| **6.** b | **7.** c | **8.** a | **9.** a | **10.** b |

## Pre-Algebra and Algebra Practice

| | | | | |
|---|---|---|---|---|
| **1.** c. | **2.** c | **3.** d | **4.** a | **5.** b |
| **6.** b | **7.** d | **8.** a | **9.** b | **10.** c |

## Measurement Practice

| | | | | |
|---|---|---|---|---|
| **1.** c | **2.** c | **3.** c | **4.** b | **5.** a |
| **6.** d | **7.** b | **8.** c | **9.** c | **10.** c |

## Geometry Practice

| | | | | |
|---|---|---|---|---|
| **1.** b | **2.** d | **3.** c | **4.** d | **5.** c |
| **6.** c | **7.** b | **8.** c | **9.** a | **10.** b |

## Computation in Context Practice

| | | | | |
|---|---|---|---|---|
| **1.** d | **2.** b | **3.** a | **4.** c | **5.** c |
| **6.** d | **7.** d | **8.** d | **9.** c | **10.** b |

## Estimation Practice

| | | | | |
|---|---|---|---|---|
| **1.** b | **2.** b | **3.** c | **4.** d | **5.** a |
| **6.** b | **7.** c | **8.** d | **9.** a | **10.** d |

## LESSON 1  Getting Ready for the Test

When Anna started classes at the Adult Learning Center, she thought she would do a very fast review of English. Then she met a student named Tim. He told her that he been studying the practice material for the English section of the TABE Tests. The test was not as easy as he had thought it would be before he came to the center. Tim had not taken an English class in a long time. Tim said, "Me and my friend Julio didn't do so good on the practice test. We're studying harder now."\* Anna knew that what she heard was incorrect English, but she didn't know why. Both Anna and you will find out why in Section 4 Language.

\*Anna knew that Tim should have said, "My friend Julio and I didn't do so well on the practice test." Tim will know better after he studies this lesson and the ones that follow!

### Words to Know

Standard English     Correct use of grammar, spelling, vocabulary, and punctuation

Odyssey              A long trip or adventure

Proprietor           Owner

Ms. Allen asked the class to think about writing in their daily lives. You, too, should start by filling out the form that follows.

### Reflection: Writing in My Daily Life

I estimate that I write _____ hours a week, including reminder notes or lists for myself and notes or letters to communicate with others.

I estimate that I write _____ hours a week for work-related tasks.

I enjoy writing _____.

I want to improve my ability to write _____ for my personal satisfaction.

I want to improve my ability to write _____ for job or career advancement.

**Composition**

I am able to organize my thoughts and express myself clearly when I need to write:

| | | | | |
|---|---|---|---|---|
| Instructions | ___Yes | ___No | ___Need practice | ___I don't know |
| Business letters | ___Yes | ___No | ___Need practice | ___I don't know |
| Reports | ___Yes | ___No | ___Need practice | ___I don't know |

I understand the meaning of "Standard English" and can recognize it when I read it.

       ___Yes   ___No   ___Need practice   ___I don't know

**Editing**

I am able to correct my own writing:   ___Yes   ___No   ___Need practice   ___I don't know

I know how to check it for:

| | | | | |
|---|---|---|---|---|
| Correct use of words | _____ | _____ | _____ | _____ |
| Complete sentences | _____ | _____ | _____ | _____ |
| Organized paragraphs | _____ | _____ | _____ | _____ |
| Spelling | _____ | _____ | _____ | _____ |
| Punctuation | _____ | _____ | _____ | _____ |
| Capitalization | _____ | _____ | _____ | _____ |

**Spelling**

I am able to identify the correct spelling of a word when I am given more than one choice.

       ___Yes   ___No   ___Need practice   ___I don't know

I can identify the correct spelling of a word by the way it "looks."

       ___Yes   ___No

I can identify the correct spelling of a word by knowing the rules.

       ___Yes   ___No   ___Need to review the rules

I know how to use a spell-checker

       ___Yes   ___No   ___Need practice

# Language Skills Assessment

**For Numbers 1 through 5, decide which punctuation mark, if any, is needed in the sentence.**

**1** Are you a good enough listener to get the directions right.

   **A**    ,

   **B**    ?

   **C**    !

   **D**    None

**2** "I think I'm a very good listener," he replied, and I can follow directions well."

   **A**    "

   **B**    !

   **C**    ;

   **D**    None

**3** In the meantime I think you should you should paint the kitchen.

   **A**    ,

   **B**    ?

   **C**    .

   **D**    None

**4** Julio is the most polite, helpful, and cheerful person in the class.

   **A**    ;

   **B**    ?

   **C**    !

   **D**    None

**5** Mr. Johnson would you like me to work late?

   **A**    ?

   **B**    ,

   **C**    .

   **D**    None

**For Numbers 6 through 9, choose the word or phrase that best completes the sentence.**

**6** In our first class, we _____ about the meaning of learning style.

   **A**    talks

   **B**    will talks

   **C**    talked

   **D**    has talked

**7** The taller twin is also the _____ one.

   **A**    more older

   **B**    the most old

   **C**    older

   **D**    more old

**8** That child has _____ a candy bar more than once.

   **A**    stolen

   **B**    stole

   **C**    been stole

   **D**    stealing

**9** _____ have lunch together every day at work.

   **A**    I and him

   **B**    Me and he

   **C**    He and I

   **D**    I and him

**For Numbers 10 through 14, choose the answer that is written correctly and shows the correct capitalization and punctuation. Be sure the answer you choose is a complete sentence.**

10 A Marco and me always help our mother with the housework.

B All the time found it's easier that way.

C Someday soon, I'm sure she'll tell you and me to do it ourselves.

D We're not looking forward to that day.

11 A We had hardly no time to get to work in the morning.

B Since our car broke down and we couldn't afford to fix it.

C Now, since we lost our jobs, it ain't going to make any difference.

D No one can get to work on time without a car!

12 A We'll leave on Wednesday for vacation and come back on sunday.

B Try going down Smith Street and turning right on Broad street.

C My friend's birthday is in May and mine is in June.

D I go to the gym every Monday and friday.

13 A Julio said, "Don't forget the team meeting at 10 o'clock tomorrow.

B I'll be there for sure" Hector replied, "and I'll be on time".

C "That will be a great surprise to everyone!" Julio joked.

D "Well, youll see," Hector shouted back.

14 A Marcel started by saying that he'd keep the plant open at night as well.

B Complete surprise and it was not a pleasant one either we're upset.

C Ever since May, weve been waiting for the announcement it hasn't happened.

D Don't be surprised if the schedule starts in july that's the earliest.

**For Numbers 15 through 17, read the underlined sentences. Then choose the sentence that best combines those sentences into one.**

15 <u>We could not find the car in the parking lot.</u>

<u>The car had been stolen.</u>

A We could not find the car in the parking lot even though the car had been stolen.

B We could not find the car in the parking lot because the car had been stolen.

C The car had been stolen. We could not find it.

D After we could not find the car in the parking lot, the car had been stolen.

**16**  I have a great new backpack for hiking.
The backpack is green.

   **A**   My backpack for hiking is new and my back pack is green.

   **B**   I hike and backpack and carry a new green bag.

   **C**   I have a great new backpack for hiking although it is green.

   **D**   I have a great new green backpack for hiking.

**17**  The park looks beautiful this spring.
We didn't have much rain.

   **A**   The park looks beautiful this spring and then we didn't have much rain.

   **B**   The park looks beautiful this spring; therefore we didn't have much rain.

   **C**   The park looks beautiful this spring although we didn't have much rain.

   **D**   The park looks beautiful this spring we didn't have much rain.

**For Numbers 18–20, read the paragraph, then choose the sentence that best fills the blank in the paragraph.**

Adapted from *A Pacific Coast Odyssey*, by David Green

**18**  Long ago, welcoming strangers was a way of life. _____.
His small hut stands open to the wilderness traveler. He doesn't even have to be there to play host. However, he was at his place when I arrived last night.

   **A**   Rex Williams is an example of that time.

   **B**   No one ever does it now.

   **C**   No other people in history ever welcomed strangers.

   **D**   This trip was too long and I'll never do it again.

**19**  We talked only briefly then. This morning, though, the good hiking hours of early sun are lost to Rex. His company and hotcakes-and-fried-egg breakfast make the delay worthwhile. _____ _____.

   **A**   I really didn't enjoy breakfast at all.

   **B**   Rex is a wonderful surprise in a long journey.

   **C**   I decided that I didn't like the cabin at all.

   **D**   Rex was too full to eat breakfast.

**20**  _____.
I took a short side trip into a ski town to resupply. I was welcomed, washed, and stuffed to the gills with food. My cook-stove, which gave out earlier on the trip, had its clogged part replaced in a local backpacking shop.

   **A**   I took a short side trip to Alaska.

   **B**   We tried very hard to fix the cook-stove, but it didn't work.

   **C**   I never did get to shower or wash my clothes.

   **D**   My food supply gave out before the John Muir Trail did.

**For Numbers 21 through 25, read the letter and look at the numbered, underlined parts. Choose the answer that is written correctly for each underlined part.**

(21) <u>September 12 2005</u>
Mr. James Blake, Proprietor
Best Shoes, Inc.
(22) <u>5757, Main Street</u>
(23) <u>Alston NY 21345</u>

(24) <u>Dear Mr. Blake;</u>

On August 30, 2005, I bought a pair of gym sneakers for my son. I paid for them with my credit card.

Your employee told us that the sneakers would wear well. He showed us the tag that said the same thing.

My son wore the sneakers to gym class only three times. Then, a large tear appeared across the front below the toes. I returned the sneakers immediately and the salesperson said, "Well, that's what happens." He refused to allow me to return the sneakers.

I would like to be sure that you are in the store the next time I come in. Please call me at 433-5500 to tell me when you will be there. I know that you will want to credit my account.

Thank you for your help.

(25) <u>Sincerely—</u>

Lin Chou

---

**21**
 A   September, 12 2005
 B   September 12, 2005
 C   September, 12, 2005
 D   Correct as it is

**22**
 A   5757 Main, Street
 B   5757 Main Street,
 C   5757 Main Street
 D   Correct as it is

**23**
 A   Alston, NY 21345
 B   Alston, ny 21345
 C   Alston NY, 21345
 D   Correct as it is

**24**
 A   Dear Mr. Blake
 B   Dear Mr. Blake:
 C   Dear Mr. Blake!
 D   Correct as it is

**25**
 A   Sincerely,
 B   Sincerely;
 C   Sincerely?
 D   Correct as is

## Section 4, Lesson 1 Answer Key

| | | | | |
|---|---|---|---|---|
| 1. B | 6. C | 11. D | 16. D | 21. B |
| 2. A | 7. C | 12. C | 17. C | 22. C |
| 3. A | 8. A | 13. C | 18. A | 23. A |
| 4. D | 9. C | 14. A | 19. B | 24. B |
| 5. B | 10. D | 15. B | 20. D | 25. A |

**To the Student: After you check your answers, record any incorrect answers in this chart. Then review the lessons that will help you to correct your errors.**

| Item | Answer | Lesson Number | Language Skill Category (for Review) |
|---|---|---|---|
| 1. | B | 8 | Punctuation/End mark |
| 2. | A | 8 | Punctuation/Quotation Mark |
| 3. | A | 8 | Punctuation |
| 4. | D | No error | |
| 5. | B | 8 | Punctuation |
| 6. | C | 3 | Verb tense |
| 7. | C | 5 | Comparison of adjectives |
| 8. | A | 3 | Verb tense |
| 9. | C | 4 | Pronoun/Subject |
| 10. | D | 4 | Pronoun |
| 11. | D | 4 | Negatives |
| 12. | C | 8 | Capitalization |
| 13. | C | 8 | Capitalization |
| 14. | A | 2, 6 | Run-on sentences |
| 15. | B | 7 | Sentences/Subordination |
| 16. | D | 6 | Sentences/Extra Words |

| | | | |
|---|---|---|---|
| 17. | C | 7 | Sentences/Subordination |
| 18. | A | 7 | Paragraph/Supporting Detail |
| 19 | B | 7 | Paragraph/Supporting Detail |
| 20. | D | 7 | Paragraph/Topic Sentence |
| 21. | B | 8 | Punctuation/Letter |
| 22. | C | 8 | Punctuation/Letter |
| 23. | A | 8 | Punctuation/Letter |
| 24. | B | 8 | Punctuation/Letter |
| 25. | A | 8 | Punctuation/Letter |

Note: These broad categories of language skills are broken down into subskill categories. Question numbers agree with the subskill titles.

## Language

### Usage

**Pronoun**

Nominative                  9

Objective

Possessive

Relative

Reflexive

**Antecedent Agreement**

TENSE

Present

Past                       6

Future

Perfect                 8

Progressive Tense

Subject/Verb Agreement

Easily Confused Verbs

Geographic Name

Title of Work

Punctuation

**End Marks**

Period

Question mark                        1

Exclamation point

**Commas**

Compound Sentence

Series

Direct Address                       5

Yes/No/Well

Appositive

Introductory Element                 3

Parenthetical Expression

**Semicolon**

QUOTATION MARKS

Quotation marks                      2, 13

First word in quotation

Comma with quotation

End Marks                            1

**Apostrophes**

Contraction                          10, 14

Possessive

**Letter Parts**

Date                                 21

Address                              22

City/State/Zip                       23

Salutation                           24

Closing                              25

## LESSON 2  Do you Know What a Sentence Is?

Anna, Tim, and all their classmates were surprised when they arrived in English class. The topic for the day was written on the board: *Do you know what a sentence is?* Many of the students had been speaking and writing English sentences for years. Of course they knew what a sentence was! Then Ms. Allen gave each student a piece of paper with some examples on it. She said, "Read these and decide if they are sentences."

But before *you* read those sentences, study the Words to Know.

**Words to Know**

| | |
|---|---|
| Subject | The noun or pronoun in a sentence. It performs the action or is linked by a being verb to the predicate. |
| Verb | A word that shows action or being. (More about "being verbs" in Lesson 3.) |
| Predicate | The part of the sentence that holds the verb and other words. |
| Fragment | An incomplete portion of a sentence. |
| Run-on Sentence | A sentence that should be interrupted with punctuation. |
| Substitute | Something that replaces something else. |

These are the sentences that Ms. Allen gave the class to read:

1. Once again, leaving late for work.
2. Run and sweaty and still late for work.
3. Being late for work even one more time.
4. And then the manager and the other workers and a messed up schedule.
5. The manager asked me to see him after work he had never done that before.

Ms. Allen asked, "Is there anything wrong with these sentences? Luis volunteered, "They sound wrong to me. The fourth sentence is too long." Ms. Allen continued, "Yes, there are a lot of words, but the writer actually has not given you *enough* information."

What's missing in sentences 1 through 4? As you think about the answer to the question, keep this in mind: (1) does each sentence tell you *who or what is the performer? Who is being talked about*? (2) Does each sentence tell you what was *done*? Also, how is sentence 5 incorrect in a *different way* from the others?

English sentences need two basic parts in order to be clear and complete. Each of the sentences below is complete—a person or thing (performer) is doing something. They're not very interesting sentences, but each one does have a person or thing, the subject, doing something.

Also, notice that every sentence starts with a capital letter and ends with a punctuation mark—a period. In other sentences, you will use question marks, exclamation points, or quotation marks. Remember these: ., ?, !, and " ".

A plane flies.

The dog barks.

The truck stopped.

Mac laughed.

Sheila rides a motorcycle.

Cars speed.

Sometimes you use a different word—a substitute—for the name of a person or thing. The substitute is called a *pronoun.* You use pronouns all the time. For example, the subjects are all pronouns in the five sentences below:

**Pronoun**

It flies.

It (or he/she) barks.

It stopped.

He laughed.

She rides a motorcycle.

They speed.

How are these sentences different? They are different only because each *subject* is a *pronoun.* You will have a chance to read more about pronouns later in this book.

Now look at a slightly more complicated sentence:

Our car makes a terrible noise.

What thing is this sentence about? It's about our *car.* You might already know that this part of the sentence is called the subject. The subject contains a person, place, or thing. What does the subject (performer) do? The subject, *car, makes* noise. *Makes* is in the part of the sentence called the predicate. The main word in the predicate is the verb or action word. The main word or verb in the predicate of this sentence is *makes.* Later we'll discuss verbs that do not do actions.

Look back to the five sentences before the Study Tip. Why aren't these sentences clear? What information is missing? Keep in mind what you read in the Study Tip. Each sentence should have a person or thing (subject) doing something (verb/predicate). Practice I asks you to add the missing information to each sentence.

## Practice 1

Directions: Rewrite the fragments and run-on sentences in the spaces below. The first one is done for you.

1. Once again, *I* was leaving too late for work. (In the example, the who/performer *I* was missing. Now the subject/performer has been inserted.)

2.

3.

4.

5.

Check your answers in the Answer Key before you go on.

You know that when we talk to family, friends, and even co-workers, our sentences are often incomplete, or fragments.

Example:

Meet for lunch?

Sure.

When?

About noon?

OK.

That is fine for informal, or casual conversation, but, for other occasions, you need to use *standard* (the most accepted) English usage when you speak or write.

## Back to Fragments and Run-on Sentences

Watch out for these errors: We sometimes confuse a group of words that includes an –ing ending word with a complete thought.

Examples:

Incorrect: *Treading the floors carefully so I wouldn't ruin the finish.*

Change to: *I treaded the floors carefully so I wouldn't ruin the finish.*

What has been added? Of course, the answer is the subject/performer.

Incorrect: *Striking the windshield with a terrible blow.*

Change to: *The large rock struck the windshield with a terrible blow.*

What has been added? Again, the sentence needed a subject/performer. What struck the windshield?

Run-on sentences do just as their name indicates. They go on and on with no end in sight.

> Incorrect: *The large rock struck the windshield we immediately called for a tow the truck took just a short time to reach us.*

> Change to: The large rock struck our windshield. We immediately called for a tow. It took just a short time to reach us.

What has been added? The simple answer is, punctuation! You needed to separate the three thoughts with periods. Later, in this lesson, you'll read more about how to combine short sentences, such as sentences two and three.

Combined:

> We immediately called for a tow and it took just a short time to reach us.

## Practice 2

Directions: Find the fragments and run-on sentences in this Practice. Correct the sentences on the lines provided.

1. Weaving in and out of crowded clothing racks.

   _____

2. Missing the plane and not boarding another one until morning.

   _____

3. Pouring rain, lightening strikes, and thunder.

   _____

4. I hate driving in the rain I pulled over under an overpass many others pulled over, too.

   _____

5. Having coffee, the taste was delicious. (Note special problem: According to this sentence, the coffee was enjoying the taste!)

   _____

6. When you speak. (Note: There is a subject and a verb, but this is still a fragment. How can you rewrite it?)

   _____

7. Pausing for a moment after walking a great distance.

   _____

8. Flour, sugar, baking powder, and eggs.

_____

9. School spending cuts causing much discussion this year.

_____

10. Jan broke her leg she couldn't walk the stairs at work.

_____

## Practice 3

Directions: In each paragraph below, find one sentence that is either a fragment or a run-on. Correct that sentence on the line provided.

1. (A) We already had two children, five and seven years old, when our twins were born, so we knew that we needed a larger apartment. (B) We never realized how complicated it was to move even a half-mile away. (C) In a different school district. (D) That was only one of the major changes.

_____

2. (A) In our new apartment, we have an extra bedroom. (B) Need it for the twins. (C) We're all enjoying the extra space, especially the second bathroom. (D) However, the building has no elevator to carry carriages and packages up and down two flights of stairs.

_____

3. (A) Our happiness didn't last long we took the older children to their new school. (B) As soon as we walked into the school, both children began to cry. (C) "Where are our friends?" they sobbed.

_____

Check your answers in the Answer Key before you go on.

## Practice 4

Directions: Add a subject/performer or verb/action word to each sentence below. More than one choice of words might be possible.

1. Because of the crowds, _____ leave for the airport very early.
2. Our _____ insists on efficiency at work.
3. The child _____ very hard and then tears came to her eyes.
4. We _____ to put off the discussion until the next meeting.
5. Marcello _____ to be on time, but he rarely succeeds.

As you learned, sentence fragments need a subject/performer or a verb to complete them. Sometimes, though, you can correct the sentence by coordinating the fragment with another thought.

> **Correct:** In our new apartment, we have an extra bedroom. We need it for the twins.

> **Also Correct and Coordinated:** In our new apartment we have an extra bedroom that we need for the twins.

The writer added a connecting word, *that*, to solve the problem. You will learn more about connecting words later in the book.

## More About Subjects and Verbs

What else do you have to know about subjects/performers and verbs/action words? You have to know that they have singular and plural forms. Subjects and verbs must match or agree in number. Compare these sentences:

1. Jorge drives to the adult learning center.
2. Malissa and Inga drive to the center, too.

How are these sentences different? In sentence one, how many performers are there? Yes, there is only one, Jorge. How is sentence two different? There are two performers, Malissa and Inge. You can say that the subject in sentence one is *singular*. The subject in sentence 2 is *plural* because more than one person is performing the action, *driving*.

The addition of an *s* on a singular verb/performer might seem strange to you. You are used to adding an *s* to a word to make it plural:

Car/cars

Book/books

House/houses

The words above are ***not*** verbs/performers. They are subject words. However, you do add an *s* to a verb/performer to show that it matches or is in agreement with the subject.

Examples:

> *An employee eats in the cafeteria.*

> *Employees eat in the cafeteria.*

How and why did the verb change? To match the singular employee, you use the singular verb/performer, *eats*. To match the plural employees, you drop the *s—eat*.

Practice 5

Look at these sentences. Decide which verb/performer is correct. Circle it.

1. Paper and pencils (sit/sits) on the desk.
2. Raoul (need/needs) a helper to finish.
3. Mark and Emilio always (skip/skips) that part of the task.
4. The customer on Terry's list (need/needs) a new truck.
5. This book (take/takes) a long time to read.
6. The flower (sit/sits) in water.
7. Savings accounts in each bank (pay/pays) different interest.
8. Ceil and Kerry (try/tries) to be on time.

Check your answers in the Answer Key before you go on.

## Answer Key: Section 4, Lesson 2

**Practice 1**

Your answers might be slightly different. Just be sure each sentence has a subject and a verb.

1. (See the sentence already rewritten for you.)
2. I ran and sweated, but I was still late for work.
3. My boss said I could not be late for work even one more time.
4. I angered the manager and the other workers and messed up the schedule.
5. The manager asked me to see him after work. He had never done that before.

**Practice 2**

Your answers may be different but still correct.

1. I found my little girl weaving in and out of crowded clothing racks.
2. Heraldo missed the plane and could not board another one until morning.
3. We experienced pouring rain, lightening strikes, and thunder.
4. I hate driving in the rain. I pulled over under an overpass. Many others pulled over, too.
5. I had coffee and the taste was delicious.
6. When you speak, use your loudest voice.
7. Jan paused for a moment after walking a great distance.
8. The recipe listed flour, sugar, baking powder, and eggs.
9. School spending cuts caused much discussion this year.
10. Jan broke her leg. She couldn't walk the stairs at work.

**Practice 3**

Your answers may be different. More than one choice of words is possible.

1. (C) The apartment was even in a different school district.
2. (B) In our new apartment, we have an extra bedroom which we need for the twins.
3. (A) Our happiness didn't last long when we took the older children to their new school.

**Practice 4**

Your answers may be different. More than one choice of words is possible.

6. Because of the crowds, we leave for the airport very early.
7. Our manager insists on efficiency at work.
8. The child thought very hard and then tears came to her eyes.
9. We agreed to put off the discussion until the next meeting.
10. Marcello promises to be on time, but he rarely succeeds.

**Practice 5**

1. Sit
2. needs
3. skip
4. needs
5. takes
6. sits
7. pay
8. try

## LESSON 3  More about Verbs

Anna was happy to think that the class on subjects, verbs, fragments and run-on sentences was not so hard for her. Tim, however, reminded her that there was much more to learn—and the rest wasn't very easy for him. He was thinking about the irregular verbs as he said, "I have *brung*—no, *brought*—this English book home every day. Some verbs are still hard for me!"

Anna, Luis, and Jorge met for coffee after class. They were surprised to see that their grades on the weekly English quiz were not very good. Jorge said, "I know my English is not so good, but I been speaking English for 12 years now and look at the grade I got!" Luis said, "Me, too! I done terrible!" Anna tried to reassure them that they would all do better in the future, but she could hear some errors in their conversation. Do you know how to correct the young men's English? Read on to find out.

**Words to Know**

| | |
|---|---|
| Tense | Time |
| Irregular Verbs | Verbs that do not follow the usual rules in how they are spelled |
| Progressive Tense | A verb tense that shows action that's happening now, before, or in the future |

**Verbs and Time**

Verbs also show *time*, or what we call *tense*. Look at these sentences:

**Example 1.** **Present:** Marie *plans* the family picnic each year.

**Past:** Marie *planned* the family picnic last year.

**Future:** Marie *will plan* the family picnic next year.

**Past with helping word, has, have, or had:** Marie *has planned* the family picnic each year. (Note: This is an action that started in the past but continues into the present.)

**Progressive:** Marie is planning the company picnic each year. (Note: This form shows action in progress.)

These tenses—present, past, future, and past with helping word—have *progressive forms*. Just add the correct time of *be* plus –ing to the verb to form the progressive tense:

Present Progressive: Marie *is planning* the family picnic each year.

Past Progressive: Marie *was planning* the family picnic each year.

Future Progressive: Marie *will be planning the family* picnic each year.

Past with helping word has, have, or had: Marie *had/has been planning* the family picnic each year.

**Example 2.** **Present:** Mike *walks* to the library.

**Past:** Mike *walked* to the library.

**Future:** Mike *will walk* to the library.

**Past with helping word, has, have, or had:** Mike *has walked* to the library.

**Progressive:** Mike is/was/will be walking to the library.

**Example 3.** **Present:** Jack *listens* to the radio.

**Past:** Jack *listened* to the radio.

**Future:** Jack will *listen* to the radio

**Past with helping word has, have, or had:** Jack *has listened* to the radio.

**Progressive:** Jack is/was/will/has been listening to the radio.

So far, this is probably very easy for you; you change verb forms—drive, drove, will drive—without even thinking about it. We say that these verbs change tense, or time, in an organized, *regular* way. Now, place a pronoun (a word that stands in for a person or thing) in front of the verb. For example, *I plan* or *they plan*. Then continue from there. See the chart below.

| Present | Past | Future | Past + helping word, has, have, had | Progressive |
|---------|------|--------|-------------------------------------|-------------|
| I plan | planned | will plan | has, have, had planned | have been planning |
| You walk | walked | will walk | has, have, had, walked | had been walking |
| They listen | listened | will listen | has, have, had walked | will be walking |
| We count | counted | will count | has, have, had counted have been counting | will have been counting |
| I use | used | will use | has, have, had used | had been using |

You have probably used all of these verb forms for some time. You never think about the changes because they come naturally to you. If you look at them very carefully, however, you will see a pattern.

| Present | Past | Future | Past + helping word, has, have, had | Progressive |
|---------|------|--------|-------------------------------------|-------------|
| They walk | They walk + ed | They walk + will | They walked (past form) + helping word (have walked) | They are walking (–ing form of walk, plus a form of *be*) |
| count | count + ed | count + will | counted (past form) + helping word (has counted) | am counting (–ing form of count, plus a form of *be*) |

What changes occur in these action words in the past tense and with helping words? Look again at the chart above.

- The answer, of course, is that you add an *ed* to form the past tense.
- You add a forward-looking word, such as will, to the present tense. That gives you the future tense.

- You add a helping word to the past tense to express the past time that continues into the present. (*They have walked to work for three years. They're still doing it.*) They are walking to work.

- You add an –ing ending to the verb, plus a form of *be*. That gives you the progressive tense or action in progress.

You do all of this without even thinking about it!

Why do we even bring this up if we use these words correctly? The answer is that people don't always use them correctly. English takes some strange turns. And that is why you need to be aware of the common verb use errors. We'll explore the topic further in the section entitled, **There's More?**

### Practice 1

Place these action words on the chart. The first word, *call*, is done for you.

| Present | Past | Future | Past + helping word has, have, had | Progressive |
|---------|------|--------|-----------------------------------|-------------|
| Call | called | will call | have called | was calling |
| Change | | | | |
| Check | | | | |
| Include | | | | |
| Use | | | | |
| Clean | | | | |

### Practice 2

Fill each space with one of these action words. The sentences will give you clues to the time of the verb. Change the verb endings when necessary.

load        guide        trip        enter        arrive        begin

1. Yesterday I _____ over that wire.

2. According to the chart, you will _____ the dishwasher every night this week.

3. As I _____ the room, I can see my favorite chair.

4. My newspaper has _____ on time every Sunday.

5. Your map _____ me to the campsite.

6. Sophia was _____ to understand the difference.

*There's More?*

It would be comforting to think that you now know everything you need to know about action words/verbs. Unfortunately, that is not the case. You recall that you worked with verbs that changed tense in a regular pattern—adding *–ed* to the past, and so forth. Now you need to learn about *irregular* action words/verbs. These are verbs whose spellings change a great deal in order to show tense. They are called, *irregular* verbs—for a reason.

Many errors in writing and speaking occur because of these irregular verb changes. Study the list that follows to see if you use the correct forms. As you study the list, what one characteristic do you see that remains the same with every verb? Hint: Look at the future tense.

| Present | Past | Future | Past + helping word, has, have, had |
|---------|------|--------|-------------------------------------|
| begin | began | will begin | have begun |
| bite | bit | will bite | have bitten |
| bring | brought | will bring | have brought |
| burst | burst | will burst | have burst |
| buy | bought | will buy | have bought |
| chose | chose | will chose | have chosen |
| dig | dug | will dig | have dug |
| do | did | will do | have done |
| drink | drank | will drink | have drunk |
| drive | drove | will drive | have driven |
| fly | flew | will fly | have flown |
| forget | forgot | will forget | have forgotten |
| freeze | froze | will freeze | have frozen |
| get | got | will get | have gotten |
| grind | ground | will grind | have ground |
| hang | hung | will hang | have hung |
| have | had | will have | have had |
| know | knew | will know | have known |
| lay (place) | laid | will lay | have laid |
| lend | lent | will lay | have lent |
| lie (recline) | lay | will lie | have lain |
| mistake | mistook | will mistake | have mistaken |
| ride | rode | will ride | have ridden |

| | | | |
|---|---|---|---|
| ring | rang | will ring | have rung |
| run | ran | will run | have run |
| see | saw | will see | have seen |
| send | sent | will send | have sent |
| shake | shook | will shake | have shaken |
| shine | shone | will shine | have shone |
| shrink | shrank | will shrink | have shrunk |
| sink | sank | will sink | have sunk |
| speak | spoke | will speak | have spoken |
| spring | sprang | will spin | have spun |
| steal | stole | will steal | have stolen |
| sing | sang | will sing | have sung |
| sting | stung | will sting | have stung |
| strike | struck | will strike | have struck |
| swear | swore | will swear | have sworn |
| swim | swam | will swim | have swum |
| swing | swung | will swing | have swung |
| take | took | will take | have taken |
| tear | tore | will tear | have torn |
| think | thought | will think | have thought |
| throw | threw | will throw | have thrown |
| wind | wound | will wind | have wound |
| wring | wrung | will wring | have wrung |

## Practice 3

Read the sentences for clues to the tense, or time of the verb. Choose the correct form of the verb in each sentence. Look back at the list whenever you are in doubt about the correct form to use.

1. I (did/done) my homework very carefully.
2. Mac has (sing/sung) in the choir for years.
3. Lydia and Tomas have (teared/torn) up their credit cards.
4. On my vacation, I (swimed/swam) a half mile every day.
5. I went home again because I had (forgot/forgotten) my license.
6. Our dog (shaked/shook) his wet fur furiously.
7. The recipe said that I should have (grinded/ground) the meat.

8. Betsy and David (drived/drove) over an hour a day to work.

9. The student (laid/lain) his paper on the teacher's desk.

10. Those birds have always (flew/flown) south.

11. My friend was furious at me because I (throwed/threw) his favorite hat away.

12. I can't (lay/lie) down after I eat.

13. Elio forgot what time he had (set/sat) the meeting for.

14. I forgot I hadn't (taken/took) any money with me.

15. Maurilio has (shined/shown) his shoes a dark brown.


## Section 4, Lesson 3 Answer Key

**Practice 1**

1. change *changed *will change *was changing
2. check *checked *will check *was checking
3. include *included *will include *was including
4. use *used *will use *was using
5. clean *cleaned *will clean *was cleaning


**Practice 2**

| | |
|---|---|
| **1.** tripped | **4.** arrived |
| **2.** load | **5.** guided |
| **3.** enter | **6.** beginning |


**Practice 3**

| | | |
|---|---|---|
| **1.** did | **6.** shook | **11.** threw |
| **2.** sung | **7.** ground | **12.** lie |
| **3.** torn | **8.** drove | **13.** set |
| **4.** swam | **9.** laid | **14.** taken |
| **5.** forgotten | **10.** flown | **15.** shined |


## LESSON 4  Something Else about Verbs

Jorge met Anna and Luis when he joined their English class. Jorge had come to the United States when he was seven-and-a-half years old. In Puerto Rico, where he was born, he had just learned to read well. Then his parents told him the family was moving to America. He was happy to go because his parents wanted to go there. Jorge had no idea how many challenges or problems he and his family would face. One of the challenges was learning to speak and write English correctly.

**Words to Know**

| | |
|---|---|
| Linking or Being Verbs | Verbs that do not act; they link the subject to a word in the predicate |
| Contraction | A word that is made up of two words, e.g., isn't = is not |
| Article | A word that points to a noun, e.g., the, a, an |
| Negative | A word that means *no* |

## Another Kind of Verb: *Being,* Not *Performing*

Up to now, Ms. Allen had discussed only one kind of verb: an action word such as *write, return, plan, arrive, make, look,* and so forth. The subjects or performers, as we have called them, did something, an action. Example:

The sheep provided valuable wool.

The action word/verb in this sentence is very clear: *provided*. Who did it? The *subject*, or *sheep,* did it.

Now you will learn about another type of verb. This kind of verb does not tell what the subject was doing. This verb tells what the subject was *being*. Some people call these *being verbs* while others refer to them as *nonaction* or *linking verbs*. You'll see why.

Example:

The other candidate *was* angry.

You can see that there is no action in the sentence, but there is a description of how the candidate *felt*—how he or she *was*. The verb, *was*, links *candidate* to the describing word, *angry*. Because of the linking verb, you can turn the sentence around and you can still make sense of the meaning. (Angry was the candidate.)

You will read more about words (such as *angry*) that describe in Lesson 5.

## Linking Verbs

| | | | |
|---|---|---|---|
| are | am | appear | become |
| is | feel | seem | smell |
| was | were | grow | taste |
| be | sound | remain | |

## Practice 1

Chose a linking verb in each sentence.

1. Angelo (is/are) the tallest person in our crowd.
2. We (was/were) not even close to his height.

3. Only one of us (were/was) tall enough to reach the low roof. (Hint: Don't be fooled by words between the subject and linking verb.)

4. Bill and Ann (is/are) always late.

5. This new word processing program (is/are) much easier to install than the last one was.


Practice 2

Fill each blank with a linking word from the Linking Verb Chart above. There may be more than one correct choice for some sentences.

1. My arms _____ tired from exercising.

2. Do you _____ as groggy as I do today?

3. I'll _____ office manager for a year at least.

4. The first apples of fall _____ tart and crispy.

5. Marge _____ sick.


Words Have Names and Jobs: More about Pronouns and Linking Verbs

All of the words in a sentence have both a *name* and a *job*. Look at the sentences below. Above each word is its *grammatical name* and its *job* in the sentence.

| Adjective/article and describing word (*job*) | Noun (*name*) and subject (*job*) | Verb (*name*) and action word (*job*) and (*job*) |
|---|---|---|
| / | / | / |
| The | airplane | landed |

| Noun (*name*) and subject (*job*) | Verb (*name*) and linking word (*job*) | Adj. (*name*) and describing word (*job*) |
|---|---|---|
| / | / | / |
| Marge | became | sick. |

Suppose you used another word for Marge. What would be a good substitute? Of course, the word that could stand in for Marge is the pronoun, *she*.

| Pronoun (*name*) and subject (*job*) | Verb (*name*) and linking word) (*job*) | Adj (*name*) and describing word (*job*) |
|---|---|---|
| / | / | / |
| She | became | sick. |

In fact, the job of a pronoun is to stand in for another word. You will need to know more about using pronouns correctly.

The chart below shows that linking verbs also show time, or tense.

The chart also combines *tense* with *number*. Again, using pronouns (I, you, he, we, etc.) as subjects you can see that the number of the subject (pronoun) changes the spelling of the linking verb.

**Linking Verbs**

| Present | Past | Future | Past with helping words have, has, had |
|---------|------|--------|-----------------------------------------|
| I (subject) *am* | *was* | *will be* | *have been* |
| You *are* | *were* | *will be* | *have been* |
| He, she, it, *is* | *was* | *will be* | *has been* |
| We *are* | *were* | *will be* | *have been* |
| They *are* | *were* | *will be* | *have been* |

You may have heard and spoken English for a long time. Most of what you have read above comes naturally to you. Imagine what it must be like to learn this as a second language—so many changes to memorize!

But don't become too comfortable. Common errors occur when people use linking verbs. How many times have you heard this double error?

*Me and Jim was* on our way to work.

The first error, of course, is a common pronoun error. You will learn more about this pronoun error later. For now, just remember to *state the other person's name first* and *choose I for yourself,* that is, *Jim and I.* Now, decide whether the subject—*Jim and I*—is a singular or plural subject. Yes, it is plural (there are two people in the subject) and it requires a plural linking verb. Look back at the chart. If you substituted a pronoun for *Jim and I*, which one would it be? Of course, *we* would be the correct pronoun. The subject we must agree in number (plural) with the plural linking verb.

*We were* on our way to work.

*We* is a plural subject and *were* is the plural linking verb.

## Practice 3

Read the sentences and decide if they are correct. Do the subjects and linking verbs agree in number? Change any words that are used incorrectly.

1. These hamburgers tastes so good.

2. We was here on time; where was you?

3. This surround-sound TV sounds much better than my old one sounded.

4. Ron, Fred, and Barney feels left out.

5. Both a painter and a plumber is needed.

6. Ellen and Lacy is cochairs of the event.

7. The dog is a terrier.

8. The scouts growed weary from raking the leaves.

9. The Santos' and their dog is home after a long walk.

10. The appliances appears to be broken.

### Special Forms of Pronouns + Linking Verbs

We often take shortcuts when we write or speak. We can take a shortcut using pronouns and linking words. A linking word can be combined with the pronoun to construct a new word, a *contraction*. In each case, one letter is left out of the combination. An *apostrophe* (') is used instead of the letter.

| Contraction | Example | Letter Left Out |
|---|---|---|
| I'm = I am | I'm here to help. | a |
| He's = He is | He's always right! | i |
| She's = She is | She's my best friend. | i |
| It's = It is | It's your turn. | i |
| You're = You are | You're wrong as usual. | a |
| We're = We are | We think we're a great team. | a |
| They're = They are | They're following us. | a |

 **NOTE**

Without the apostrophe, *its* is used to show possession. Example: The cat took the kitten to *its* new home.

The information above might not be a great challenge for you. However, the same problem—agreement in number—does remain a challenge. Sometimes we use a contraction when we should *not*. Examples:

*There's many problems* with your plan. = *There is many problems* with your plan.

What is wrong with this sentence? *Problems* is the subject and it is plural. A plural subject agrees with a plural linking verb. Change *is* to *are*. The words should be

*There are* many problems with your plan.

*Here's the magazines* you asked for. = *Here is the magazines* you asked for.

What is wrong with this sentence? *Magazines* is the subject and it is plural. Once again, you need to use a plural linking verb. Change *is* to *are*. The construction should be

Here are the magazines you asked for.

*Now Add Not*

What happens when the contraction is negative? Add *not* to the following:

is + not = isn't

are + not = aren't

will + not = won't

were + not = weren't

was + not = wasn't

*Avoid Double Negatives*

 **FYI**

You need only one negative in a sentence.

Incorrect: You *aren't never* going to finish that job. (*are not* plus *never*)

Correct: You aren't ever going to finish that job.

Incorrect: I *haven't* got *no* time. (*have not* plus *no*)

Correct: I haven't got any time.

Remember that *aren't* = are *not*. *Haven't* = have *not*. *Never* and *no* add a second, unneeded, negative to the incorrect sentences.

*Never, Never Acceptable*

Never use the contraction, *ain't*. Think about what it takes the place of and use the correct form instead.

| | |
|---|---|
| I ain't (am not) finished yet. | I'm not finished yet. |
| You ain't (are not) well yet. | You aren't well yet. |
| She ain't (is not) here every day. | She isn't here every day. |
| They ain't (are not) copied yet. | They aren't copied yet. |
| We ain't (are not) at the bus station yet. | We aren't at the bus station yet. |

Even though you will find *ain't* in some dictionaries, it is not correct usage, *ever*.

Practice 4

Find the errors in the following sentences. One sentence is correct as written.

1. My ideas isn't the worst I've ever heard!

2. Wasn't you and Miguel supposed to start at 8 a.m.?

3. I ain't ever going to make that mistake again!

4. I can't sign up at the community college until September.

5. There's plenty of grapes on the vine.

## Section 4, Lesson 4 Answer Key

### Practice 1

1. is
2. were
3. was

4. are
5. is

### Practice 2

There might be more than one correct choice for some sentences.

1. are, were, feel
2. feel
3. be, remain

4. taste, are
5. feels, grew

### Practice 3

1. taste
2. were, were
3. correct
4. feel
5. are

6. are
7. correct
8. grew
9. are
10. appear

### Practice 4

1. isn't (Use a plural linking verb, *aren't*, to agree with *ideas*.)
2. wasn't (Use a plural linking verb, *weren't*, to agree with the plural subject, *you and Miguel*.
3. ain't (*Ain't* is never acceptable. In this sentence, use *am not*.)
4. Correct as written
5. There's (*There's*, meaning *there is*, is singular. The subject, *plenty* is plural. Use *there are* plenty. . .)

## LESSON 5   Add Color and Interest to Your Sentences

Just as Anna, Luis, and Jorge have done, you have worked with simple sentences in earlier lessons. You have learned to recognize complete thoughts: subjects plus action or linking verbs.

The question is this: How can you make these sentences more interesting and colorful? The answer is that you can add descriptive words. When Luis first studied adjectives and adverbs, he said, "My first boss always corrected me when I said, "Jake did that job nice." I was describing what Jake did. What's wrong with that?"

Luis and you are about to find the answer to that question and many more about descriptive words.

**Words to Know**

| | |
|---|---|
| Adjective | A word that describes a noun or pronoun |
| Adverb | A word that describes a verb, an adjective, or another adverb |
| Comparison of descriptive words | The degree of difference (e.g., fast, faster, fastest) |

## Information, Please

We have said many times that a complete thought must have a subject and a verb. Then we should ask ourselves if that complete thought gives the reader enough information.

> My car chugs.

What information can we add to this sentence to give the reader more information and a better picture of the car?

> My old car chugs noisily.

Now we have a better picture of the car and what it does. The word *old* describes *car*, the subject/noun, and is called and *adjective*. The word *noisily* describes the verb, *chugs*, and is called an *adverb*. Both *old* and *noisily* add information to the picture the sentence forms. The question, of course, is this: If both adjectives and adverbs have the same job, that is describing other words, why do they have different names? This is the reason:

> The strong nest held three eggs easily.

Answer these questions.

1. What is the subject of the sentence? *Nest* is the subject.
2. What is the verb in the sentence? *Held* is the verb.
3. What word describes the subject? *Strong* describes nest. This is the adjective. Adjectives describe subjects/nouns.
4. Which word describes how the nest *held* the eggs? *Easily* describes *held*. This is the adverb. Adverbs describe verbs.

### A Small Complication

The above is easy to understand, but we need to add two items to the adverb's job.

> The strong nest held the three eggs *very* easily.

How *easily* did the nest hold the eggs? It held the eggs *very* easily. *Very* is also an adverb and it describes another adverb, *easily*. So, you need to know that adverbs can describe other adverbs.

And one more thing. . .

The extremely strong nest held the three eggs very easily.

How strong was the nest? It was *extremely* strong. *Extremely* is an adverb and it describes an adjective, *strong*.

To summarize, adverbs are very useful words. They describe verbs, adjectives, and other adverbs.

**FYI**

Many adverbs are easy to recognize because they end in –ly. Can you think of some examples of adverbs that end in –ly?

Examples:

Neatly
Brightly

Practice 1

Directions: Add three more –ly ending adverbs to the examples above. Then, write a sentence using each one. The first sentence is done for you.

1. Amelia packed her new suitcase *neatly*.

2.

3.

4.

5.

You know that an adjective is often linked to the subject. However, are there other adjectives used in sentences? Consider this:

My search is completed.

| Noun/Subject | Linking Verb | Adjective |
|---|---|---|
| / | / | / |
| My search | is | completed |

**STUDY TIP**

In the sentence above, *my* describes *search*, a noun. *My* is an adjective that tells whose *search* it is. However, you have learned that *my* is a pronoun. How can that be true? The answer is that some pronouns act as if they are adjectives. The kind of *job* they do in a particular sentence affects what they are called. Remember, words have names and they have jobs, too.

Another Example:

His car is a mess.

car (noun/subject) is (linking verb) mess (adjective describes car)

After reading the Study Tip above, what do you think *His* does in this sentence? In other words, what is its job? The answer is that its job is to describe car; it is a pronoun acting as an adjective.

*Use Adjectives and Adverbs Correctly*

Some adjectives and adverbs are often misused. You will want to study them in order to avoid these common errors.

## Well versus Good

*Well* can be used as an adjective when you talk about health.

I feel well now. (*Well* describes *I*.)

At all other times, *well* is an adverb and, as such, describes the action word.

My friend builds furniture well. (*Well* describes *builds*.)

Important: *Good* never describes an action. What kind of word does it describe in the next three sentences?

My boyfriend is a good driver. (Not, "My boyfriend drives good." *Good* cannot describe the action, *drives*.)

A good reader usually has a larger vocabulary.

A good place to live is not always that easy to find.

Use good paper to print that report.

You read these phrases: good driver, good reader, and good paper. The word *good* obviously describes people, places, and things. They are all nouns.

## Practice 2

Choose an adjective or an adverb to complete each sentence.

1. One of my friends eats (good/well).
2. Our new puppy has not felt (good/well) for weeks.
3. My sister is a (good/well) house painter.
4. That group sings (good/well).
5. I rewrote my resume and it worked (good/well) for me.

## Real versus Really

*Really* describes another descriptive word. Did you notice the –ly? Yes, this is an adverb. and it describes other descriptive words.

It is really cloudy today. (*Really* describes the adjective, *cloudy*.)

Manrillo's computer is really outdated. (*Really* describes the adjective, *outdated*.)

Aaron's excuse for being late was really lame. (*Really* describes the adjective, *lame*.)

*Real* describes a person, place, or thing—a noun.

This is a real antique. (*Real* describes the noun, *antique.*)

The house's siding is made of real wood. (*Real* describes the noun, *wood*)

The movie mystery had a very real script. (*Real* describes the noun, *script.*)

## Practice 3

Choose the correct word in each sentence.

1. Our dog is a (real/really) lovable part of our family.
2. The hat was (real/really) too small to protect me from the sun.
3. The morning meetings were (real/really) early.
4. One (real/really) problem is that our meetings are in the morning.
5. Why don't you take a (real/really) break—an extra 10 minutes?

### Nice versus Nicely

This is one of the most common errors in the use of descriptive words. Don't make this error!

The senator spoke *nice* at the town meeting.

Once again, you need to decide what job each word performs. *Nice* describes a person, place, or thing—a noun. *Nicely* describes an action. In the sentence above, what does *nice* try to describe? The answer, of course, is *spoke*. But *nice* cannot describe a verb; *nicely*, the adverb, does.

The council chairman spoke nicely at the yearly meeting.

If you wanted to describe the chairman as nice, what would you say?

The nicely chairman spoke at the yearly meeting.

OR

The nice chairman spoke at the yearly meeting.

*Nice* is an adjective and, as you know, adjectives do describe nouns or persons, place, or things. The second choice is correct.

## Practice 4

1. On a (nice/nicely) day, we walk to work.
2. "(Nice/Nicely) done!" yelled the fan.
3. The manager spoke (nice/nicely) at the district meeting.
4. The (nice/nicely) manager spoke at the district meeting.
5. He's really a (nice/nicely) person.

## Practice 5

Read the paragraph below. Choose a correct adjective or adverb in each sentence.

Today, young people need to know that they will have more than one job in their lifetimes. It is (real/really) likely that they will have many jobs over time. For some, this is a (nice/nicely) opportunity to avoid boredom in their work lives. It is also a (real/really) good opportunity to become a lifelong learner. These young people—as well as older workers—must expect to change jobs. In addition, they will have to feel (good/well) about changing the kind of work they do. They have to be (real/really) ready, and trained for change.

### An Important Change

There is another very important way that adjectives change in order to change the meaning in a sentence. The change is called *comparison of descriptive words*. You can see below just why that is a good term.

The commuter bus is *fast*.

My friend's new car is *faster*.

That racecar is the *fastest* one of all.

Obviously, each sentence talks about the degree of speed. The first sentence simply states a fact—a bus is fast. Sentence two states a comparison: the friend's car is faster than the bus. The important fact here is that two things are compared. In the English language, we add an –er to indicate that of the *two*, one is faster. Look at the third sentence and you read a higher level of comparison. Now it is clear that of the three kinds of transportation being compared, the racecar is the fastest. The word ending, -est, is used to show that comparison of three or more.

This simple comparison exercise is probably not much of a challenge for you. You use the words below, and many others, without a problem.

| Adjective | Comparison of Two | Comparison of More Than Two |
|-----------|-------------------|------------------------------|
| fast | faster | fastest |
| green | greener | greenest |
| blue | bluer | bluest |
| pretty | prettier | prettiest |

### Trouble Ahead

We tend to run into trouble in comparisons in two ways:

1. Sometimes adjectives change spelling in ways other than the addition of –er or –est to the base word. Some describing words are too long and become awkward when we place an extra syllable on the end. Consider this:

   That is the *advancedest* English course I've ever taken.

The writer or speaker compared all of the courses in a program. The person decided that one of many courses was the most advanced. *Advanced* becomes a very awkward word when you add –er or –est to it. What is a good choice here? The solution is to add *more* or *most* and keep the base word, *advanced*.

> That course is the most advanced I've ever taken. (The sentence indicates a comparison among three or more courses. The word *most* is used instead of adding –est.)

OR

> That course is more advanced than the one I took last semester. (The sentence indicates a comparison between two courses. The word *more* is used instead of adding –er.)

We sometimes, mistakenly, use *more* or *most* plus the –er or –est ending and that is too much of a good thing.

> That TV show is *more funnier* now than it was in the past.

Corrected:

> That TV show is funnier now than it was in the past.

Here are some other words that need to use *more* and *most* in comparisons.

| Adjective | Comparison of Two | Comparison of More than Two |
|-----------|-------------------|-----------------------------|
| enormous | more enormous | most enormous |
| difficult | more difficult | most difficult |
| beautiful | more beautiful | most beautiful |
| valuable | more valuable | most valuable |
| wonderful | more wonderful | most wonderful |

2. Some adjectives are spelled entirely differently when they are used to compare two or more things. Look at the chart below.

| Adjective | Comparison of Two | Comparison of More than Two |
|-----------|-------------------|-----------------------------|
| Good | better | best |
| Bad | worse | worst |

What's wrong with this sentence?

> That was the worse meal I've ever had.

Worse is used to a comparison of two things. I think we can assume that the writer has had more than two meals. How would you correct the sentence?

> That was the worst meal I've ever had.

Try this:

That book is the better of the group.

If the book is part of a group, you can assume there are more than two.

Corrected:

That book is the best of the group.

## Practice 6

Find an error in all but one of these sentences. Write a correction in the space provided.

1. She has children who are enormouser than mine. _____

2. This class is more difficulter than math. _____

3. Our baseball team looks good this year. _____

4. This is the worse meal I've ever made! _____

5. You'll never find a more wonderfuler friend. _____

6. My manager was more sympatheticer to my absence than she was to yours. _____

7. Tod's known as the most persistentest person in our group of runners. _____

8. I feel good today. _____

9. Jan lives nearest to work than Carl does. _____

10. Unfortunately, Jan is known as a most rudest person than Carl. _____

11. That episode was more funnier than any of the others. _____

12. Tommy is the better painter of the three men. _____

13. Tito plays the guitar good. _____

14. She's real unhappy. _____

15. The children ate nice at the family dinner. _____

16. Your book of jokes is more funnier than mine. _____

*Warning!*

A descriptive word or phrase should take its place next to the word it describes.

When descriptive words or phrases are misplaced, confusion results. Example:

The child yelled at her mother on the swing.

Who was on the swing, the child or her mother? You cannot say for sure after reading this sentence. Rewrite it:

The child on the swing yelled at her mother.

Try this:

Tom ran down the newly polished hallway in slippery boots.

Who was wearing slippery boots, Tom or the hallway? Be more precise by placing the descriptive phrase closer to the word it describes. You can do this in more than one way.

In slippery boots, Tom ran down the newly polished hallway.

OR

Tom, in slippery boots, ran down the newly polished hallway.


## Practice 7

Find the incorrectly placed descriptive phrases in these sentences. Rewrite the sentences and place the phrases closer to the words they describe.

1. The cow belongs to that farm with the black and white spots.

   _____

2. The photographer relaxed after taking 100 outdoor pictures in his studio.

   _____

3. I was finally able to hang on my wall my diploma.

   _____

4. Show Lois in the collar the frisky dog.

   _____

5. The drivers on the counter completed registration forms.

   _____


## Section 4, Lesson 5 Answer Key

### Practice 1

The adverb in each sentence is underlined.

1. Amelia packed her new suitcase <u>neatly</u>.
2. Little children love <u>brightly</u> colored pictures.
3. I am <u>actually</u> doing more reading now than I ever did before.
4. The book may be <u>too</u> long to finish in a few days.
5. We thought the man was <u>terribly</u> rude.

Practice 2

1. well
2. well
3. good
4. well
5. well

Practice 3

1. really
2. really
3. really
4. real
5. real

Practice 4

1. nice
2. nicely
3. nicely
4. nice
5. nice

Practice 5

1. really likely
2. nice opportunity
3. really good
4. good about change
5. really ready

Practice 6

1. more enormous
2. more difficult
3. correct
4. worst
5. more wonderful
6. more sympathetic
7. most persistent
8. well
9. nearer
10. a ruder person
11. was the funniest of them all
12. the best painter
13. well
14. really
15. nicely
16. is funnier

Practice 7

1. The cow with the black-and-white spots belongs to that farm.
2. The photographer relaxed in his studio after taking 100 outdoor pictures.
3. I was finally able to hang my diploma on my wall.
4. Show Lois the frisky dog in the collar.
5. The drivers completed registration forms on the counter.

## LESSON 6  Decisions, Decisions

Theresa called Anna to say hello but also to announce her exciting news. "I've decided what I'm going to study at the community college," she said. "You know how I've been trying so hard to change my eating habits. Well,

I've learned so much more about it, I want to help others with the same problem! I'm going to earn an associate degree in nutrition. What do you think?" Anna was very excited for Theresa. After all, Theresa had been trying to make a decision for a long time. Anna said, "I think you're doing the right thing. You'll probably find it so much easier studying something you're interested in. Good luck!"

Theresa asked, "And what about you? I can't wait until you get here! Have you decided what you'll study when you enter the community college?" Anna replied, "I'm almost positive that I'm going to work at a bank, so I'll start with the computer classes at the college. But first I have to pass the TABE Tests. Right now the English class is a challenge. I never knew there were so many different kinds of pronouns and so many ways to use them! As a matter of fact, I'd better get back to my studying."

**Words to Know**

| | |
|---|---|
| Reflexive Pronoun | Refers to another noun or pronoun in the sentence |
| Intensify | Increase in importance |
| Appropriate | Correct for the occasion |
| Antecedent | A word that is referred back to |
| Demonstrative | Identifying a person or thing |

## More about Pronoun Usage

### Show Emphasis with Reflexive Pronouns

Have you ever heard someone use a pronoun with the suffix *–self* or *–selves* on the end of it? When they are used correctly, *reflexive* pronouns, such as *myself, himself* and *ourselves* are very effective.

Examples:

I'll take care of that assignment myself.

We decided to paint the house ourselves.

He, himself, found it really difficult to do.

In each case, the reflexive pronoun *emphasizes* another word. In the sentences above, *myself* emphasizes *I. Ourselves* emphasizes *We. Himself* emphasizes *He.* The problem occurs when we use the reflexive pronoun *instead* of *I, me,* or *us.*

 **STUDY TIP**
Use *reflexive pronouns* to refer back to a personal pronoun or a noun. Reflexive pronouns intensify, or add importance to the personal pronouns. Look back to the three examples above. Are the pronouns singular or plural?

**Reflexive Pronouns**

| Singular | Reflexive | Plural | Reflexive |
|---|---|---|---|
| I | myself | We | ourselves |
| You | yourself | You | yourselves |
| He | himself | They | themselves |
| She | herself | They | themselves |
| It | itself | They | themselves |

**Very important tip:** The first column under **Singular** contains pronouns that can act as subjects. The first column under **Plural** contains pronouns that can act as subjects. None of the other pronouns can take that job; they can only refer back to subject words.

**Incorrect:** John and *myself* decided to paint the house. (*Myself* can't be used as the subject.)

**Correct:** John and *I* decided to paint the house.

**Incorrect:** The manager gave the assignment to *myself*. (*Myself* does not refer to the subject, *manager*, so it cannot be correct.)

**Correct:** The manager gave the assignment to *me*.

Practice 1

Directions: Read these sentences. Change any pronouns that are used incorrectly.

1. Juan said nobody could solve his problems but hisself.
2. Her mom and herself meet for lunch each Thursday.
3. I, myself, believe in you completely.
4. John and youselves can take next week off.
5. Dori and themselves came in without knocking.

## Avoiding Problems with Pronouns

Just by dividing pronouns into three groups, you will avoid, not all, but many pronoun problems.

As you know, words have names (noun, verb, and so forth) and they have jobs (subject, action or linking word, and so forth). You can explain pronouns in the same way. You know that pronouns (that is their name) take the place of names (that is their job). In addition, pronouns can be placed in three groups according to what they do.

| Pronouns that Act Subject | Pronouns that are Acted Upon (Receive Action) | Pronouns that Own or Follow the Linking Verb or Follow the Linking Verb |
| --- | --- | --- |
| I | me | my, mine |
| you | you | your, yours |
| he, she, it | him, her | his, her, hers, its |
| we | us | our, ours |
| they | them | their, theirs |
| who | whom | whose |

Look at these sentences. Some contain linking verbs and others have action verbs. The chart above tells you why each pronoun is correct.

*I* gave the appointment to *him*.    (*I* acts; *him* receives the action)

The lunch bag is *yours*.    (*yours* shows ownership)

Betty and *I* gave *you* an extra day off this week.    (Betty and *I* act; *you* receives the action)

Our new leader is *she*.    (*She* follows the linking verb *is* and equals the *leader*.)

Our greatest resource is he.    (*he* follows the linking verb *is* and equals *resource*)

**STUDY TIP**

As you work with the sentences below, remember this: The pronoun that follows a linking verb either (1) describes the subject or (2) equals the subject.

(1) Describes the subject: The new office is *ours*. *Ours* is an ownership pronoun. *Ours* describes office.

(2) Equals the subject: The fastest runner is *she*. *She* equals the subject.

**FYI**

The best test of the subject and the pronoun being equal is this: You can turn the sentence around and achieve the same meaning.

*She* is the fastest runner.

She is the new council president

He is our greatest resource.

The authors know that most people do not answer the phone by saying, "Yes, this is he/she." In many cases that would be too formal and not natural. You need to make a choice based on the situation. At those times, when being casual is not appropriate, you need to use the correct pronoun form.

## Review—Practice 2

Directions: Use all that you have learned to choose the correct pronoun in each sentence.

1. The man adopted a dog; the man loved (her, she) immediately.
2. Shirley and (me, I) start work at exactly 7 a.m.
3. A new schedule was set for Kira and (me, I).
4. Mike and (him, he) plan to share an apartment.
5. The detective wrote in his formal report, "It is (she, her) who committed the crime."

### Another Pronoun Problem

Another problem occurs when a pronoun comes later in the sentence but refers to something before it. The word to which the pronoun refers is called the *antecedent*. You learned that subjects and verbs must agree in number. The same rule applies to a pronoun and its *antecedent*. For example:

> A new employee will pick up their own uniform.

What is the subject of the sentence and is it singular or plural? *Employee* is the subject and it is singular. *Their* is a plural pronoun that refers to *employee,* the *antecedent*. But that can't be correct, can it? Either both words must be plural or both must be singular. There are two ways to correct this sentence.

### Corrections:

> A new *employee* will pick up *his* or *her* own uniform.

> OR

> All new *employees* will pick up *their* own uniforms.

More examples:

1. The employee told the repairman that his computer was down.

   Whose computer is down? Does it belong to the employee? Or does it belong to the repairman? Rewrite the sentence:

   The employee told the repairman that his, the employee's, computer was down.

2. Larry and Juan moved the equipment to the new office, but he could not stay past 6 p.m.

   Who could not stay? Larry? Juan? Rewrite the sentence:

   Larry and Juan moved the equipment to the new office, but Juan could not stay past 6 p.m.

Practice 3

Directions: Where necessary, rewrite these sentences for clarity. One sentence is correct.

1. Don't give new employees ID tags until *they* have been date stamped.

2. The manager told the receptionist *her* phone was not working. [Hint: Whose phone was not working?]

3. Each of our sons wants a car for *themselves.*

4. Before *they* are eighteen their friends get new cars!

5. Anybody in this group who thinks *they* are done are sadly mistaken.

A Problem to Solve: When to Use Demonstrative Pronouns

As it is used in the title, *demonstrative* means pronouns that *identify.* We use demonstrative pronouns to identify a person, place, or thing.

| Demonstrative Pronoun | What it Identifies |
|---|---|
| *This* book | A thing |
| *That* street | A place |
| *These* children | People |
| *Those* printers | Things |

*This book*, *that street*, *these children*, and *those printers* are all correct uses of the pronouns. The error most often heard is, "*Them* books are torn." If you think about the definition of the demonstrative pronoun, you'll see why this is incorrect. Only four pronouns identify people, places, or things. *This* and *that* (singular) and *these* and *those* (plural) are the correct forms. The word *them* is not on that list. In the example, is *books* singular or plural? The answer, of course, is plural. How can you correct the error?

These books are torn.

Or

Those books are torn.

The example below shows another error to be aware of when you use demonstrative pronouns. Remember that this kind of pronoun is supposed to identify another word. What's wrong with this sentence?

Incorrect: We bought a quilt at the outdoor market. *This* was a great find.

The question is, what was the great find, the quilt or the market? Rewrite the sentence correctly on the line provided. _____

_____

## Practice 4

Directions: Find the pronoun errors in this paragraph. Which phrase would you choose to correct phrase the error?

1. Them guys didn't come to the party. 2. We bought all of that food and it wasn't eaten. 3. Those soda was a total waste. 4. This guys won't be invited again.

1. **a.** This guys
   **b.** That guys
   **c.** Those guys
   **d.** Correct as written

2. **a.** those food
   **b.** these food
   **c.** this foods
   **d.** Correct as written

3. **a.** Them soda
   **b.** These soda
   **c.** This soda
   **d.** Correct as written

4. **a.** These guys
   **b.** Them guys
   **c.** This guys
   **d.** Correct as written

## Section 4, Lesson 6 Answer Key

### Practice 1

1. . . . but himself
2. . . . Her mom and she. . .
3. Correct as written
4. John and you. . .
5. Dori and they. . .

### Practice 2

1. her
2. I
3. me
4. he
5. she

### Practice 3

1. . . . Until the tags have . . .
2. . . . the receptionist that the manager's phone . . .

**3.** . . . for himself

**4.** Before their friends are 18,

**5.** . . . he or she is done is sadly. . .

or

All in this group who think. . .

Rewrite the sentence:

At the outdoor market, we bought a quilt, which was a great bargain.

Practice 4

**1.** C

**2.** D

**3.** C

**4.** A

## LESSON 7 Building Sentences and Paragraphs

Now it was finally time for Anna and the rest if her English class to go on to a new and important topic. They would apply all the lessons they had learned in Ms. Allen's class to writing sentences and paragraphs.

**Words to Know**

| | |
|---|---|
| Coordinate | Bring together |
| Subordinate | Treat as less important |
| Mentors | People who help, teach, and advise newer employees |
| Transaction | A business matter or operation |

## Building Sentences

Ms. Allen reminded the class about writing complete sentences. The first rule in building good sentences is to avoid fragments and run-on sentences. She asked the class to refresh their memories by looking at the following statements. "Is each one a sentence, she asked? Are any of them run-ons?" See if you can answer Ms. Allen's questions when you read the first Practice.

Practice 1

Directions: Rewrite any incorrect sentences.

1. A label on a new cereal.

2. Your car's gas tank filled and the mileage recorded and how much you spent.

   _____

3. The first month at my new job.

   _____

4. Our favorite program was on TV the last season's star had returned.

   _____

5. The emergency brake that is on the floor of the car.

   _____

6. Gloating and showing off my beautiful TV.

   _____

7. Many friends and they're all angry with me.

   _____

Check the Answer Key before you go on. Review Lesson 2 if you had more than one wrong answer.

*Parallel Thoughts*

After Ms. Allen asked the class to correct the above sentences, it was time to move on to another sentence writing skill. She used an example and asked the class to think about why the sentence was not as clear as it could be.

**STUDY TIP**

When you read the example, decide if the words and thoughts are parallel. That is, is each part of the sentence expressed in the same form? Read this example and think about what is wrong with it.

Incorrect: My truck route is long, tiring, and I'm bored.

The writer is describing his or her truck route. The linking verb, *is*, links the subject, *truck route* to descriptive words. *Long* and *tiring* are the descriptive words. What about the words *I'm bored*? Are they stated in the same way as *long* and *tiring*? How could you change *I'm bored* to match *long* and *tiring*? You can do that by changing the two words to one descriptive word.

Correction: My truck route is long, tiring, and *boring*.

Incorrect: If you're looking for a job, write an informative resume, write a good cover letter, and then, you'll be practicing interviewing.

Explanation: The sentence gives you three actions to take if you're looking for a job. Two actions take the same form: *write a resume* and *write a cover letter*. Now, how can you change the third item to match the first two? Cross out *and then, you'll be* and change *practicing* to a shorter form.

Correction: If you're looking for a job, write an informative resume, write a good cover letter, and practice interviewing.

Practice 2

Directions: How can you rewrite these sentences to make them parallel? The first sentence is corrected for you.

1. Once a week, Angelo asks his children to sweep the porch, put their clean clothes away, and then they have to wash the car.

   Corrected: Once a week, Angelo asks his children to sweep the porch, put their clean clothes away, and wash the car.

2. Before you buy a washing machine, think about the size of your family, the amount of room you have, and you should always think about how much money the machine costs.

3. My children love playing tag, riding bikes, and to swim.

4. Heraldo is a good student, a great runner, and he's good at playing the guitar, too.

5. The bird swooped down, picked up its catch, and flying back up toward the sky.

Practice 3

Directions: Read the paragraph. Find the sentence that includes the unparallel phrase.

1. At our restaurant, we have hired two cooks, three servers, and a greeter. 2. Each person has a new uniform, a clearly printed nametag, and is instructed for using the stove. 3. Next week we'll start training the wait staff.
   a. Sentence 1
   b. Sentence 2
   c. Sentence 3
   d. Correct as written

2. I like to bake bread. 2. My favorite steps are adding the flour and to knead the dough. 3. The baking bread makes the kitchen smell wonderful.
   a. Sentence 1
   b. Sentence 2
   c. Sentence 3
   d. Correct as written

3. We have so many projects to do at our house! 2. This weekend I'll go to the discount store for supplies and instructions. 3. The next weekend, I will empty the basement, scrape off the wallpaper, and fixing the hot water heater.
   a. Sentence 1
   b. Sentence 2
   c. Sentence 3
   d. Correct as written

When descriptive words and phrases are not in the right place in a sentence, readers are confused. One important rule is to place a describing word close to the word it describes.

Incorrect: Did you know about the service that was bad that I received?

Which word describes the kind of *service* this writer received? Of course, the word is *bad*. Place the word *bad* next to *service*, the word that *bad* describes.

Correct: Did you know about the bad service I received?

By placing the describing word (adjective) next to the word it describes, you solved a second problem as well. You eliminated unnecessary words, "that was bad that."

Incorrect: The magazine, *People*, sells all over the world and is widely read.

Correct: The widely read magazine, *People*, sells all over the world.

By placing the describing words, *widely read*, next to the word described, you have also eliminated two unnecessary words, *and is*.

## Practice 4

Directions: Place describing words next to the words they describe. Try to eliminate all unnecessary words in the sentences.

1. The rabbit under the wire fence was stuck. (Hint: What was stuck, the *rabbit* or the *fence*?)

   _____

2. The athlete at the stadium parks free.

   _____

3. The child ran down the steps in very high boots.

   _____

## Bringing Sentences Together

If you learn how to *combine related thoughts*, you will avoid choppy sentences. You will also eliminate unnecessary repetition.

## Practice 5

Directions: Read each set of two related sentences below. Combine each set into one sentence. The first one is combined for you.

1. A.  Each day, I brought lunch to work.
   B.  I always brought a ham and cheese sandwich for lunch.

Combined: Each day, I brought a ham and cheese sandwich to work for lunch.

2. A. We harvested corn this summer.

   B. We harvested corn from two acres.

   _____

3. A. Next summer we're taking a family vacation.

   B. Next summer we're taking a family vacation to Cape Cod.

   _____

4. A. If you want to succeed, make time for important tasks.

   B. Use your time wisely.

   _____

5. A. How can I do that?

   B. How can I learn to handle money well?

   _____

There are two other ways to write sentences so that related ideas are brought together. The first way uses simple words to *coordinate* ideas. The following are some of the coordinating words that are so often used:

| Coordinating Words | Coordinated Sentences |
|---|---|
| and | We can finish our work first, *and* then we can leave for the day. |
| but | You could take the car, *but* you could also take the bus. |
| yet | I put hours into creating a new filing system, *yet* no one uses it. |
| so | My computer doesn't have enough memory, *so* I'll buy another used one. |
| or | I will have the birthday party at home, or we'll take the children out for lunch. |

## Practice 6

Directions: To coordinate these sentences, choose a connecting word from the list above. Write the new sentence on the line provided.

1. I don't know where my time goes. I'll keep a chart of what I do.

   _____

2. It might be hard to start a new task. It's easier if you take one small step.

   _____

3. Get a notebook that you can carry with you. Keep your action notes in it.

   _____

4. I haven't finished my first task. Julio is finished with the third step.

   _____

5. Julio wants a promotion now. He will leave the company.

_____

You probably realized that the coordinating words connect thoughts of *equal* importance. Each thought could stand alone as a sentence. In a different situation, you might want to stress one idea over another. In that case, you would use a *subordinating* word. When you use a *subordinating* word, only one part of the sentence can stand alone as a complete thought. Here are some of the subordinating words you can use.

| Subordinating Words | Sentences |
|---|---|
| after | I thought I'd take a nap *after* I returned from work. |
| although | *Although* the weather person predicted snow, we still decided to go out. |
| since | I've had better job interviews *since* I improved my resume. |
| Because | You'll get that job *because* your computer skills are so strong. |
| When | *When* you get back, I'll have the back of the house painted. |

## Practice 7

Directions: Read the sentences above. In each case, decide which part of the sentence can stand alone. Which part is a fragment? The first sentence is done for you.

| Stand Alone | Fragment |
|---|---|
| 1. I thought I'd take a nap. | after I returned from work |
| 2. | |
| 3. | |
| 4. | |
| 5. | |

## Practice 8

Directions: Write three sentences. In each sentence, use one of the subordinating words listed above. Each sentence should have a part that can stand alone and a part that cannot stand alone (a fragment).

1.

2.

3.

A good paragraph follows at least two rules. First, the paragraph should contain a topic or main idea sentence. Second, the main idea sentence is followed by sentences that support the topic.

When you write a paragraph, be sure that it contains a main idea or topic sentence. That is the sentence that tells your reader what the paragraph is about. Keep this in mind as you read the paragraph below.

Example:

1. In most banks, head tellers are responsible for many daily tasks. 2. They set up both the work schedules and the teller line-up. 3. Head tellers also make sure that the many banking procedures and rules are followed. 4. In addition, they often act as mentors, or teachers for new staff.

**1.** Which sentence holds the main idea or introduces the topic?
   **a.** Sentence 2
   **b.** Sentence 1
   **c.** Sentences 3 and 4
   **d.** None of the sentences

Answer A is not correct. Sentence 2 gives the reader just one thing a head teller does. That is a supporting detail. Answer C cannot be correct because you are looking for just one topic sentence. Answer B is the right choice. Sentence 1 states the topic: head tellers have many responsibilities.

What do sentences 2, 3, and 4 do in this paragraph? Of course, they are the details that support the topic. These sentences name the tasks mentioned in sentence 1.

Practice 9

Directions: Read each paragraph. What would be a good topic sentence for each paragraph?

**1.** _____.

Only head tellers are allowed to enter the vault. They ensure that the correct amount of cash is in the vault. Head tellers also oversee large cash transactions.
   **a.** All tellers make sure that the correct amount of cash is in the vault.
   **b.** Head tellers teach employees to handle large cash transactions.
   **c.** Head tellers have special duties that other tellers are not allowed to perform.
   **d.** Only head tellers handle savings accounts.

**2.** _____

They may ask their tellers to process mail transactions. Some tellers are asked to replenish, or refill their cash drawers. Some tellers may be asked to do another important job and that is with the ATM machine.

The teller needs to sees that the ATM record agrees with deposits it has received and payments it has made.

   **a.** Some banks teach tellers to do additional tasks.

   **b.** Only inexperienced tellers do extra tasks.

   **c.** Every employee in the bank checks the ATM's records.

   **d.** Over the course of a day, tellers have only one thing to do.

## Practice 10

Directions: Choose the set of sentences that best supports the topic sentence.

Topic Sentence: When a person applies for the job of bank teller, he or she might not realize that the job may involve sales.

   **a.** Your job as a bank teller starts at 9 a.m. and ends at 5 p.m. You can expect to take about 45 minutes for lunch. In the afternoon everyone takes turns taking a 10-minute break. Lunches and breaks are taken in the employee break room.

   **b.** Tellers are being trained to see sales opportunities. They can refer the customer to someone else in the bank who has the special knowledge. Or, the teller might have already had training to handle the customer's request for a new service.

   **c.** Your employee handbook explains vacation schedules. In your first year with the bank, you may plan on a week's vacation. The bank vice president will set the schedule. You can request a certain week, but no promises can be made regarding your first week of vacation.

   **d.** Before you start a regular schedule, you will train at the bank. Usually, the training process for a new employee takes two weeks. Then you will be expected to "shadow" an experienced employee for another two weeks.

Be sure that all of the details in the paragraphs you write really do support the topic. You have already read the following paragraph. Read it again and look for the sentence that has been added. Does it support the topic?

When a person applies for the job of bank teller, he or she might not realize that the job may involve sales. Tellers are being trained to see sales opportunities. Sometimes lunch hours are changed from 1 p.m. to 2 p.m. They can refer the customer to someone else in the bank who has the special knowledge. Or, the teller might have already had training to handle the customer's request for a new service.

Which sentence does not support the topic? If you chose sentence 3, you were correct. That was easy to see. Lunch hours have nothing to do with the topic. Read the following paragraphs and follow the directions.

## Practice 11

Directions: Find the unrelated sentence in each paragraph. Write that sentence on the line provided.

1. A. Children love spending time in art museums that allow them to get involved with the art. B. In fact, some museums have stories that go along with the artwork. C. For example, children are asked to push buttons to see or listen to the artist's story. D. Children are guided through the park. E. In some museums, the visit may end with an actual art class. In this way, the children take home a piece of their own work.

---

2. A. A vote is coming up on increasing the number of hours we are allowed to work each week. B. Therefore, I am writing to ask you to cast a positive vote. C. We are all feeling the pinch of rising food and energy prices. D. In fact, some of us have even planned a children's clothing exchange in order to save some money. E. Last year the Christmas party lasted too many hours. F. Clearly, we deserve a chance to improve how we live.

---

Before you continue, check your answers in the Answer Key.

 **STUDY TIP**

Some words make strong connections between sentences and thoughts. They tie the thoughts together. Reread Paragraphs 1 and 2 above. Look for words at the beginnings of sentences that connect ideas within the paragraph.

Did you find these words?

Paragraph 1:

In fact, For example, In this way

*In fact* emphasizes or stresses an idea that came before. *For example* gives the reader another way to understand how children get involved. *In this way* gives the reader an example of how children experience the museum.

Paragraph 2.:

Therefore, In fact, Clearly

*Therefore* connects *why I am writing* to the first sentence. *In fact* emphasizes the pinch that people are feeling. *Clearly* emphasizes or stresses all the thoughts that came before this sentence.

Practice 12

Directions: The following paragraphs are each missing a sentence. Choose a sentence that best connects the ideas within the paragraph.

1. In 1963, President John F. Kennedy authorized the practice of awarding The Presidential Medal of Freedom. Before then, the medal was called The Medal of Freedom. Therefore, the people who have received this award have come from many different backgrounds. For example, Mother Theresa as well as the comedian and actor Bill Cosby received the award.

Others include General Colin Powell, the former U.S. Secretary of State, and The Native American leader Wilma Mankiller.

   **a.** The medal has always stood for outstanding contributions to peace, to the arts, or to other important deeds.
   **b.** The award, although important, is given only once in a great while.
   **c.** Awards have been given to three people only.
   **d.** The award never existed before President John F. Kennedy was in office.

2. **Annie Dodge Wauneka** (1910–1997) was one of the great Navajo leaders. She dedicated her life to help her people overcome the health problems that plagued the Navajo during her lifetime. Wauneka won many awards including the Presidential Medal of Freedom. The most common and deadly disease was Tuberculosis.
   **a.** Wauneka lived from 1917–2001.
   **b.** She educated her people about the prevention and treatment of diseases.
   **c.** She probably could have found the cure for the common cold.
   **d.** She was the one and only Native American leader who was a woman.

You can make your reader's job much easier by using words that move the paragraph along. For example, if a task should be done in a certain order, you might use the words *first*, *second*, *then*, *finally*. A recipe is the most common example of writing that gives information in a certain order. Here is a recipe for muffins. Usually you would see a list of ingredients, but for this lesson, we're interested only in the steps, or sequence. What words are used to tell you the sequence of steps?

*Bran Muffins*

Before you start the recipe, preheat the oven to 400°. First, in a mixing bowl, sift together flour, sugar baking powder, and salt. Set aside. Then, in a large mixing bowl combine the bran cereal and milk. Allow this to stand for about 5 minutes. The cereal should soften. Next, add the egg and oil and beat them well. Add the flour . . .

Although this is not the complete recipe, it is still clear that certain steps take place in a certain order. Which words tell you the sequence? Choose the words from the following list.
   **a.** recipe, next, beat, allow
   **b.** before you start, first, bowl, set
   **c.** before you start, first, then, next
   **d.** preheat, sift, combine, 5 minutes

Which answer did you think included all the sequence words? Clearly, the correct answer had to start with the words, *before you start*. No other steps could take place before that one. Only Answers B and C include that phrase.

The next choice was easy: *first* gives you the first step. The word, *then*, moves you to the next step. Which answer includes all of these sequence words? If you chose Answer C, you were correct.

As you read the next paragraph, look for sequence words.

> Can good friends and a loving family help a person to be healthier? Many doctors now think that the answer to that question is, "Yes!"
>
> To begin with, your family and friends might encourage you to live in a healthier way. The first thing they'll suggest is that you get a regular checkup with your doctor. Then, when your doctor suggests a better diet plus exercise, your friends and family might decide to remind you to keep up the good work. Finally, your friends might join you in your daily walk.

## Practice 13

Directions: Which words tell you the sequence of events in this paragraph?

a. then, can, to begin with, keep up
b. thing, finally, many doctors now, first
c. first, regular, to begin with, now
d. to begin with, the first thing, then, finally

Check the Answer Key for the correct answer.

## Section 4, Lesson 7 Answer Key

### Practice 1

Answers will vary.

1. I read a label on a new cereal.
2. You can keep a record of when you filled your car's gas tank, the mileage the car got, and the money you spent.
3. I loved the first month at my new job.
4. Our favorite program was on TV. Last season's star had returned.
5. The emergency brake is on the floor of the car.
6. I was gloating and showing off my new TV.
7. I have many friends, and they're all angry with me.

### Practice 2

Answers will vary. Notice that commas separate each item in a series.

1. Once a week, Angelo asks his children to sweep the porch, put their clean clothes away, and wash the car.
2. Before you buy a washing machine, think about the size of your family, the amount of room you have, and the amount of money you have to spend.

3. My children love playing tag, riding bikes, and swimming.
4. Heraldo is a good student, a great runner, and a good guitar player.
5. The bird swooped down, picked up its catch, and flew back up toward the sky.

## Practice 3

1. Each person has a new uniform, a clearly printed nametag, and instructions for using the stove.
2. My favorite steps are adding the flour and kneading the dough.
3. The next weekend, I will empty the basement, scrape off the wallpaper, and fix the hot water heater.

## Practice 4

1. The rabbit was stuck under the fence.
2. The athlete parks free at the stadium.
3. The child in the high boots ran down the steps.

## Practice 5

1. Each day I brought a ham and cheese sandwich for lunch.
2. We harvested two acres of corn this summer.
3. Next summer we're taking a family vacation to Cape Cod.
4. If you want to succeed, use your time wisely and make time for important tasks.
5. How can I learn to handle money well?

## Practice 6

Notice the comma before the coordinating word.

1. I don't know where my time goes, so I'll keep a chart of what I do.
2. It might be hard to start a new task, so it's easier if you take one small step.
3. Get a notebook that you can carry with you, and keep your action notes in it.
4. I haven't finished my first task, yet Julio is finished with the third step.
5. Julio wants a promotion now, or he will leave the company.

## Practice 7

| Stand Alone | Fragment |
| --- | --- |
| 1. I thought I'd take a nap. | after I returned from work |
| 2. We still decided to go out. | although the weather person predicted snow |
| 3. I've had better interviews. | Since I improved my resume |
| 4. You'll get that job. | because your computer skills are so strong |
| 5. I'll have the back of the house painted. | when you get back |

Practice 8

Answers will vary.

  **1.** Although I hate the crowds, I'm going Christmas shopping.
  **2.** Because you're first on my list, you'll probably get the best gift.
  **3.** After dinner is over, we should have a serious talk.

Practice 9

  **1.** c                              **2.** a

Practice 10

  **1.** b

Practice 11

  **1.** d                              **2.** e

Practice 12

  **1.** a                              **2.** b

Practice 13

  **1.** d


## LESSON 8 Capitalization and Punctuation

Ms. Allen's English TABE Test review class was coming to an end. The class had one more topic to discuss. She said, "Your work has improved in this class in every way—except one. Do you remember that we talked about always using end marks and capitals in your complete sentences? Well, we need to review those skills, because I'm still having trouble reading the papers that you write. Your ideas are excellent, but the lack of punctuation really makes it difficult for your reader—me."

Tim said, "Does this have anything to do with all those red marks on my papers?" The class laughed; Tim had a great sense of humor.

"Yes, that's exactly why you're seeing so much red on your papers!" Ms. Allen went on to explain more about punctuation.

**Words to Know**

| | |
|---|---|
| Reliable | Dependable |
| Mind-mapping | A way to organize information in picture form (See: http://www.mind-map.com/EN) |
| Represent | Stand for |

## Why Use Capital Letters and End Marks?

Sometimes writers forget how important punctuation and capitalization are for meaning. When we speak, we don't have to supply the punctuation and capitalization. Our voices fill in all the necessary information. We pause for commas (,). Our voices drop at the end of a sentence—indicating a period (.). Our voices rise for a question (?). We show emotion and that is the exclamation point (!). Obviously, on paper, we can't use our voices for end marks or capitals. We need punctuation marks and capital letters.

For the most part, the use of punctuation and capitalization simply makes sense.

As you have read, the period (.), question mark (?), and exclamation mark (!) are all end marks. They are the most common and the most easily used punctuation marks. Without end marks and capital letters, however, there would be nothing but confusion.

Example: would you like to be able to learn something the minute you need to would you like to get information from a reliable source any time anywhere then you should learn to get new information on the Internet

Place capital letters and end marks in the paragraph above. Check the Answer Key before you go on.

In this section, you will study end marks and capital letters at the same time. One does, in fact, signal the other. When you see a period or question mark or exclamation point, you know that a capital letter will follow. There are many uses for capital letters.

 **STUDY TIP**
Here is a list of capitalization rules. Look at this list whenever you are unsure about using a capital letter.
Capitalize:

- Names, such as place names, people's names, organization names, and languages. Examples: Arnold J. Green, American Association of Adult Educators, General Electric Company, Italian, The White House, The Declaration of Independence.

- The first word in a sentence.

- The first word of a direct quotation. Example: He asked, "Will you be ready on time?"

- The word *I*.

- A title, when it is part of someone's name: Lieutenant George Grant.

- The title of a book, play, magazine, or poem (just the first and important words in each, e.g., *The Competent Writer: A Plan of Attack*).

- Sections of the country, not compass directions. Examples: *I had lived in the East for many years. Go east on 10th Avenue.*
- Days of the week, months, and holidays. Example: *Christmas falls in the fourth week of December on Monday.*

## Practice 1

Directions: In the following paragraphs, place end marks and capital letters where they are needed. Do not worry about commas or any other punctuation marks.

1. if you ask me, our leader, bruce m wheeler, needs to learn more about leading a successful team work depends, to a great extent, on the skills of the leader our leader absolutely does not believe in setting rules would you rather have no rules or a few sensible rules of procedure and conduct anything less leads to total disorder

2. in june, our company will move to a new two-room office our moving list will include writing paper copy paper large rulers and markers yours should concentrate on furniture and lighting Ming will concentrate on the computers and other hardware the office can be moved quickly if we all cooperate do you think we can be ready by may 31

3. yesterday, i told my boss that i would be happy to work on the move he was very glad to get my message he's had trouble getting people to volunteer to help with the move what do you do when four of the five employees are uninterested

## Practice 2

Directions: What is the correct choice for the underlined word/s? Look for errors in punctuation (end marks) and capitalization.

1. Kim decided not to travel to <u>Chicago Brad</u> decided to go.
   a. Insert a comma after Chicago.
   b. Insert a question mark after go.
   c. Insert an exclamation point instead of a period.
   d. Insert a period after Chicago.

2. We'll meet at <u>market square</u> for Lela's birthday party.
   a. Insert a period after square.
   b. Insert capitals *M* and *S* on market square.
   c. Insert a comma between market and square.
   d. Insert an exclamation point at the end of the sentence.

3. Check with Dr. Peters before you stop taking your <u>medicine it</u> is dangerous to stop on your own.
   a. Insert a period after medicine and a capital *I* on *it*.
   b. Insert capital *M* on *medication.*

    **c.** Insert a question mark after medication.

    **d.** Insert a period after *medication* and capitalize *It.*

4. The advertisement said that you should take the item home to <u>try it</u> <u>bring</u> it back if it doesn't work.

    **a.** Insert a capital on *bring.*

    **b.** Insert a comma and capital *B.*

    **c.** Delete the word *it.*

    **d.** Insert a period after *try it* and capitalize *Bring.*

5. I love country <u>music do</u> you like it as much as I do?

    **a.** Insert a comma after *music* and capitalize *Do.*

    **b.** Insert a period after *music* and capitalize *Do.*

    **c.** Insert a question mark after *do.*

    **d.** Insert an exclamation mark and keep the letter *d.*

6. We graduate in <u>may I'm</u> so excited about starting classes at the Warwick Community College

    **a.** May.        College!

    **b.** May,        College!

    **c.** may.        College!

    **d.** May!        College,

7. Travel <u>South</u> to <u>new york city</u>.

    **a.** south        New York City

    **b.** South        New York City

    **c.** South        New York city

    **d.** South        new york City

## Practice 3

Directions: Read this paragraph. Then, add capital letters and end marks wherever they are needed.

    have you ever heard of mind-mapping it's a way to organize your thinking by using arrows, lines, pictures, and so forth you can write a schedule or plan the paper you have to write for school or the notes you take in school many people would rather make a mindmap (a picture of sorts) than make a list tony buzan came up with this idea when he was in college he found that it was much better for learning than his usual scribbled notes

## Another Reason for End Marks

You already know that every sentence must finish with an end mark. Did you know that you can avoid run on sentences by using a period? What is wrong with these sentences?

    My friend is always hungry she'll want to eat before we shop.

    My friend is always hungry, she'll want to eat before we shop.

These are both common examples of run-on sentences. A run-on sentence does exactly what its name says; it runs on from thought to thought with no punctuation or with the incorrect use of a comma. Did you notice that each part of this run-on sentence could stand alone? Each part is a complete sentence. How do you correct it?

My friend is always hungry. She'll want to eat before we shop.

OR

My friend is always hungry, so she'll want to eat before we shop.

Do you remember using *connecting words* (Lesson 7)? As you can see, in the sentence above, you can correct the run-on by using a connecting word (so) and a comma to combine the two sentences. Now it is a compound sentence, having two equal parts. Each part of the sentence before and after the comma could stand alone as a simple sentence.

You can also use another punctuation mark, a semicolon, to correct the two sentences above. Think of the semicolon as a weak period. The semicolon can be used to bring together two very closely related thoughts.

Examples:

My friend is always hungry; she'll want to eat before we shop.

The movie starts at 7:30 p.m.; don't be late.

I've bought the ice cream; you bring the cake.

 **FYI**
Keep this in mind. Thoughts connected by a semicolon might *otherwise* be connected using a comma plus the words *so, for, but, and, or, nor.*

## When Should I Use a Comma?

For many people, the comma is the most difficult form of punctuation. Just keep in mind that commas are meant to make the meaning of a sentence clear. You need commas for clarity, but you should not overuse them.

Comma Use Checklist

1. Use a comma after a salutation in a *friendly* letter.

Dear Abby,

 **FYI**
When you write a *business* letter, the correct punctuation mark is a colon. Dear Ms. Jacoby:

2. Use a comma when you address someone in writing.

> Felix, enjoy the Christmas holiday!

3. Use a comma after the closing in a business or friendly letter.

> Sincerely,
> Ruth

4. Use a comma after the introductory words, *yes*, *no*, or *well*.

> Yes, I understand the point you are making.
> Well, it was not my decision.

5. Separate items in a series with commas.

> Feed the cat, walk the dog, and clean the bird's cage.

6. Use a comma to separate an introductory phrase from the complete thought.

> Before we leave for the store, let's go over the list one
> more time.

**STUDY TIP**

Take a careful look at this last example. Writers sometimes make the mistake of thinking that the introductory words (Before we leave for the store) represent a sentence. They do not. When you finish reading those words, you want to ask, "What happens?" That is simply because it is an incomplete thought, a sentence fragment. Don't fall into the sentence fragment trap!

7. Insert commas to separate words that interrupt the flow of the sentence.

> A calculator, although I don't own one, is an essential
> tool today.

**FYI**

If you want to know if words interrupt the flow of a sentence, use this test. Can the words be left out? Leaving out the words will not affect the sentence's meaning.

> A calculator is an essential tool today

8. A comma separates two complete thoughts that are joined by a connecting word such as *but, for, or, and*.

> We will look at all the available rooms, and we will have to choose the largest one.

9. Insert a comma to separate the name of a city from the name of a state or country.

> Juan Moniz
> 196 Union Street
> San Francisco, CA 00000

10. Insert a comma to separate a direct quotation from the rest of the sentence. The comma, period, and the explanation mark are placed inside the quotation mark.

> Examples: "I'll never get to work on time in this <u>traffic,"</u> he complained.
> He shouted in his empty car, "I'll never get to work on time in this <u>traffic!"</u>
> "Margie, I know I won't make it on time," he said to his friend, "so please take a bus to <u>work."</u>

11. Insert a comma between the day and the year and between the year and the rest of the sentence.

> Mike will graduate on June 14, 2004, from Brightwater Community College.

## Practice 4

Directions: Read the paragraph below. To make the meaning clear, where would you insert commas? The checklist above will help you to understand the correct uses of commas.

> When you use the English language some rules are very clear. For example there is no argument about the word ain't. You should not use it—ever. Neither do you say "I don't never want to see that textbook again." However when it comes to commas we don't seem to be as confident sure or secure in making decisions. Now you will have the opportunity to study the important uses of commas and when you finish you will be very confident in your decisions.

Check your answers in the Answer Key. Correct your work by inserting any commas, you may have missed.

## Practice 5

Directions: For questions 1–5, decide if the underlined parts need correction. Write the correction or *correct as is* on the line provided.

1. How many times have you heard people complain about other people not communic<u>ating</u>.

   _____

2. Believe it or <u>not people</u> benefit from poor <u>communication</u>? _____

   _____

3. Poor communication allows people to hide their lack of <u>planning, others</u> can't see the whole picture. _____

4. <u>Or p</u>oor <u>communication, makes</u> it easier to deny what plan was made.

   _____

5. If you don't say things clearly, who can say you were wrong? _____

   _____

## Practice 6

Find and correct errors in capitalization, end marks, and comma usage. For practice, look for three sentence fragments among these sentences.

1. let's start at the beginning

2. I was ready to eat lunch

3. dear mom
   please send money.
   Love
   Sam

4. I'll mow the lawn fertilize it and pull the weeds

5. After seeing a really wonderful movie we stopped for coffee and dessert.

6. When I have finished and you are ready and the new equipment has arrived.

7. Because he was late six times this year John's pay was docked.

8. Dear Dr. Hernandez
   Please send my medical records to my new job.
   Sincerely,
   Mario Santamassina

9. If you think you will be available we'll meet on September 20 2005.

10. Are you ready for this commitment

**11.** "I cannot attend" she responded.

**12.** Before the event and after my promotion.

**13.** Almost everyone loves walking swimming and eating outdoors on summer days

**14.** That movie I must remind you is my favorite of all time.

**15.** After running after the children and entering the cool house.

### Review—Practice 7

Insert commas, end marks, and semicolons wherever they are needed. Look for run-on sentences and correct them.

**1.** Rod is taking a computer course an introduction to health care and a writing course

**2.** I'll be very busy at work all week please don't call me.

**3.** Shelley said that we should meet in the parking lot

**4.** Shelley said "Meet me in the parking lot."

**5.** I've already made plans so I won't be there.

**6.** Rain hail and snow followed us all the way home.

**7.** When you visit us you will travel on Route 95 for an hour.

**8.** The child needed to have a blood test he howled at the sight of the needle

**9.** His mother tried to comfort him but nothing she did seemed to work.

**10.** Jorge try the light switch does it work

## Quotation Marks

You have had some experience working with commas and quotation marks. You learned that quotation marks are used to set off the exact words said by a person.

Direct quotation: The President of the United States said, "We need to learn to work together to solve problems."

Indirect quotation: The President of the United States said that we need to learn to work together to solve problems.

What one word changes the direct quotation to an indirect one? The answer, of course, is the word *that*. The word *that* turns the statement into a *report* of what the president said.

In order to use quotation marks correctly, you need to know a number of rules.

## Quotation Mark Checklist

1. As you saw above, use quotation marks to indicate the exact words of a speaker. Important: Place the period inside the quotation marks at the end of the sentence. Also note the comma between the speaker and the words spoken.

   The policeman said, "Stay right and move along."

2. Some quotations are called "broken," because the name of the speaker interrupts the sentence.

   "Sure," shouted Audrey, "now that I'm finished, you want to help me!"

   "Now you're finished." said Benita, "You don't need my help,"

   In the first example, note the small letter on the first word of the second part of the quotation. In the second example, the second part of the quotation is actually a new sentence and requires a capital letter. Also look at the exclamation point. Just like the period, it is placed inside the quotation marks.

3. Place a semicolon after the closing quotation marks.

   I heard, "Pull over to the right"; so I did.

4. Never use two forms of punctuation at the end of a quotation. Use common sense to decide where questions marks and exclamation marks should be placed.

   Question Mark: Did Ms. Santos say, "Your final exam is next Thursday"?

   Exclamation Point: I was so furious when you said, "I never told you that the reconditioned equipment would work again"!

   If the entire sentence is a question, but the quotation is not, place the question mark after the closing quotation marks. If the entire sentence is an exclamation, but the quotation is not, place the exclamation point after the closing quotation mark.

5. Use quotation marks to enclose titles of poems, chapters, articles, or any part of a book or magazine. When the quoted title is followed by a comma, the comma should be placed inside the quotation marks.

   "To Brooklyn Bridge," by Hart Crane, was written in 1930.

## Review—Practice 8

Directions: Punctuate these sentences. Add capital letters where necessary.

1. The announcer said the manager must get the field in shape for the season

2. The announcer said that the manager must get the field in shape for the season

3. Two other people said that the manager must get the field in shape for the season

4. The announcer asked when will the manager get the field in shape for the season

5. Why didn't the announcer ask when will the manager get the field in shape for the season

6. Imagine if the announcer had said that the manager should get the field in shape for the season

7. The announcer shouted into the microphone the manager should get the field in shape for the season

Practice 9

Punctuate these sentences. Add capital letters where necessary. Some sentences need both capital letters and other punctuation.

1. "We asked them to come for dinner, she said

2. She said, We asked you to come for dinner, too"

3. The salesman said that we would receive our order within two weeks

4. I believe him do you

5. "If you are planning to drive the car back home" I said "Please be sure to check the tires first

6. After finishing the fourth chapter entitled "Getting Your Puppy Trained" I thought I could do a good job

7. After you drive the car out of the garage take out all the gardening tools she instructed

8. Did you say "Meet me in one hour"

9. "Did you hear that" Alice inquired

10. "Get off the stands. They're collapsing" the announcer shouted.

## The Apostrophe: A Review

You learned in Lesson 4 that an apostrophe takes the place of one or more letters in a contraction.

Examples:

Mac isn't (is not) meeting us until 9 p.m.

I'll (I will) call you when we're (we are) ready to leave.

It's (It is) too hot in here.

You also use an apostrophe to show possession. (a) Place the apostrophe before the *s* in singular words. (b) Place the apostrophe after the *s* in plural words. (c) Some words become plural by other spelling changes.

| Singular | Plural | Exceptions |
|---|---|---|
| the cat's meow | the cats' meows | |
| the book's pages | the books' pages | |
| the computer's keyboard | the computers' keyboards | |
| the lost shoe | the lost shoes | |
| the speaker's speech | | the speakers' speeches |
| the cow's pasture | the cows' pasture | |
| the woman's office | | the women's office |
| the baby's cries | | the babies' cries |
| the child's school | | the children's school |

Names follow the same rules.

| | |
|---|---|
| Ms. Paulsen's coat | The Paulsens' house |
| Mr. Downey's job | The Downeys' trip |

## Practice 10

Choose the correct word and punctuation in the parentheses.

1. (Its/It's) only 3 p.m.

2. Her 13-year-old (isnt/isn't) as old as she thinks she is.

3. That (restaurant's/restaurants) food is often stale.

4. In your backpack, carry the (childrens'/children's) water, some crackers, cheese, and trail mix.

5. When I (was'nt/wasn't) looking, the light turned red.

6. Call me when (it's/its) time to go.

7. The mother cat carried (it's/its) kittens to safety.

8. Even though Evan knows the manager of the company, he (should'nt/shouldn't) start the letter, Dear Mac.

9. The six town (councilors/councilors') decided to put off the decision.

10. We planned to drive the Blakes car to the beach.

## Section 4, Lesson 8 Answer Key

Example: Would you like to be able to learn something the minute you need to? Would you like to get information from a reliable source any time, anywhere? Then you should learn to get new information on the Internet.

Practice 1

1. If you ask me, our leader, Bruce M. Wheeler, needs to learn more about leading. A successful work team depends, to a great extent, on the skills of the leader. Our leader absolutely does not believe in setting rules. Would you rather have no rules or a few rules of procedure and conduct? Anything less leads to total disorder!

2. In June, our company will move to a new two-room office. Our moving list will include writing paper, copy paper, large rulers, and markers. Yours should concentrate on furniture and lighting. Ming will concentrate on the computers and other hardware. The office can be moved quickly if we all cooperate. Do you think we can be ready by May 31?

3. Yesterday, I told my boss that I would be happy to work on the move. He was very glad to get my message. He's had trouble getting people to volunteer to help with the move. What do you do when four of the five employees are uninterested?

Practice 2

| | | | |
|---|---|---|---|
| **1.** d | **3.** a | **5.** b | **7.** a |
| **2.** b | **4.** d | **6.** a | |

Practice 3

Have you ever heard of mind mapping? It's a way to organize your thinking by using arrows, lines, pictures, and so forth. You can write a schedule, or plan the paper you have to write for school or the notes you take in school. Many people would rather mind map (a picture of sorts) than make a list. Tony Buzan came up with this idea when he was in college. He found that it was much better for learning than his usual scribbling! If you can get on the Internet, look at this web site: http://www.mind-map.com/EN

Practice 4

When you use the English language, some rules are very clear. For example, there is no argument about the word ain't. You should not use it—ever. Neither do you say, "I don't never want to see that textbook again." However, when it comes to commas, we don't seem to be as confident, sure, or secure in making decisions. Now you will have the opportunity to study the important uses of commas, and when you finish you will be very confident in your decisions.

Practice 5

1. communicating?
2. not, people . . . communication.
3. planning. Others
4. Or, poor communication makes
5. Correct as is

Practice 6

1. Let's start at the beginning.
2. I was ready to eat lunch.
3. Dear Mom,
   Please send money.
   Love,
   Sam

4. I'll mow the lawn, fertilize it, and pull the weeds.
5. After seeing a really wonderful movie, we stopped for coffee and dessert.
6. Fragment
7. Because he was late six times this year, John's pay was docked.
8. Dear Dr. Hernandez:
   Please send my medical records to my new job.
   Sincerely,
   Mario Santamassina

9. If you think you will be available, we'll meet on September 20, 2005.
10. Are you ready for this commitment?
11. "I cannot attend," she responded.
12. Fragment.
13. Almost everyone loves walking, swimming, and eating outdoors on summer days.
14. That movie, I must remind you, is my favorite of all time.
15. Fragment

Review—Practice 7

1. Rod is taking a computer course, an introduction to health care, and a writing course.
2. I'll be very busy at work all week; please don't call me.
3. Shelley said that we should meet in the parking lot.
4. Shelley said, "Meet me in the parking lot."
5. I've already made plans, so I won't be there.
6. Rain, hail, and snow followed us all the way home.
7. When you visit us, you will travel on Route 95 for an hour.
8. The child needed to have a blood test. He howled at the sight of the needle. (A semicolon after *test*, followed by a small *h* on *he* would also be correct.)
9. His mother tried to comfort him, but nothing she did seemed to work.
10. Jorge, try the light switch. Does it work?

Review—Practice 8

1. The announcer said, "The manager must get the field in shape for the season."

2. The announcer said that the manager must get the field in shape for the season.
3. Two other people said that the manager must get the field in shape for the season.
4. The announcer asked, "When will the manager get the field in shape for the season?"
5. Why didn't the announcer ask, "When will the manager get the field in shape for the season?"
6. Imagine if the announcer had said that the manager should get the field in shape for the season!
7. The announcer shouted into the microphone, "The manager should get the field in shape for the season!"

## Practice 9

1. "We asked them to come for dinner," she said
2. She said, "We asked you to come for dinner, too."
3. The salesman said that we would receive our order within two weeks.
4. I believe him; do you?
5. "If you are planning to drive the car back home," I said "please be sure to check the tires first."
6. After finishing the fourth chapter entitled, "Getting Your Puppy Trained," I thought I could do a good job.
7. "After you drive the car out of the garage, take out all the gardening tools," she instructed.
8. Did you say, "Meet me in one hour"?
9. "Did you hear that?" Alice inquired.
10. "Get off the stands. They're collapsing!" the announcer shouted.

## Practice 10

1. It's only 3 p.m.
2. Her 13-year-old isn't as old as she thinks she is.
3. That restaurant's food is often stale.
4. In your backpack, carry the children's water, some crackers, cheese, and trail mix.
5. When I wasn't looking, the light turned red.
6. Call me when it's time to go.
7. The mother cat carried its kittens to safety.
8. Even though Evan knows the manager of the company, he shouldn't start the letter, Dear Mac.
9. The six town councilors decided to put off the decision.
10. We planned to drive the Blakes' car to the beach.

# SECTION 5 | Spelling

## Spelling Skills Assessment

**For Numbers 1 through 20, choose the word that is spelled correctly and best completes the sentence.**

**1** The child wore a really _____ costume to the party.

  **A** weard

  **B** weerd

  **C** wiered

  **D** weird

**2** We have _____ three weeks to finish designing and building the new office desk.

  **A** aproximately

  **B** approximately

  **C** approximmately

  **D** approximatelly

**3** The class had _____ the assignment, and they groaned.

  **A** herd

  **B** haerd

  **C** heard

  **D** hierd

**4** Our two apartments have the _____ amount of space, but the rooms are placed differently.

  **A** identicul

  **B** identicel

  **C** identicil

  **D** identical

**5** As we add new _____, our business grows.

  **A** technologies

  **B** technologys

  **C** technolagies

  **D** technoliges

**6** It's not unusual for a child to have an _____ friend.

  **A** imagenery

  **B** imaginary

  **C** imageniry

  **D** imagonary

**7** The community leader was _____ with an award.

  **A** acknowledgd

  **B** acknowledged

  **C** aknowludged

  **D** aknowledged

**8** Our service people are often called upon to show how _____ they are.

   **A** coureagous

   **B** couragaous

   **C** couragoeous

   **D** courageous

**9** Don't _____ to ask me for help.

   **A** hesatate

   **B** hesutate

   **C** hesitate

   **D** hisetate

**10** We never asked for _____ from him.

   **A** advise

   **B** advize

   **C** advice

   **D** advisse

**11** In order to live, an animal must _____ to its environment.

   **A** adopt

   **B** adapt

   **C** adept

   **D** effect

**12** The policewoman searched through all of the files for the _____ of the criminals.

   **A** identitys

   **B** identities

   **C** identaties

   **D** identuties

**13** Arriving in class unprepared is an _____.

   **A** embarrassment

   **B** embarrisment

   **C** emmbarrussment

   **D** embarassment

**14** Our _____ became good friends.

   **A** wifes

   **B** wivs

   **C** wives

   **D** wiffes

**15** Rita decided to prepare for a new _____.

   **A** ocupation

   **B** occupation

   **C** occuppation

   **D** ocuppation

**16** Mr. Sanchez _____ the book for me.

   **A** resserved

   **B** resurved

   **C** resirved

   **D** reserved

**17** I was so disgusted, I decided to _____ my resignation.

   **A** sibmit

   **B** submet

   **C** submit

   **D** sabmit

**18** The _____ of a cool breeze always feels so good.

   **A** circulasion

   **B** circulation

   **C** circulashun

   **D** curcalation

**19** All this rain will _____ the soil.

   **A** erode

   **B** arode

   **C** erude

   **D** urode

**20** Your bad mood _____ how I feel.

   **A** uffects

   **B** iffects

   **C** affects

   **D** effects

## Answer Key

| | | | |
|---|---|---|---|
| **1.** D | **6.** B | **11.** B | **16.** D |
| **2.** B | **7.** B | **12.** B | **17.** C |
| **3.** C | **8.** D | **13.** A | **18.** B |
| **4.** D | **9.** C | **14.** C | **19.** A |
| **5.** A | **10.** C | **15.** B | **20.** C |

**To the Student: After you check your answers, record any incorrect answers in this chart. Then review the rules that will help you to correct your errors.**

| Item | Answer | Section | Skill Category (for review) |
|---|---|---|---|
| 1. | | 5, Spelling | Long vowel |
| 2. | | 5 | Double letter |
| 3. | | 5 | R controlled |
| 4. | | 5 | Schwa |
| 5. | | 5 | Suffix |
| 6. | | 5 | Schwa |
| 7. | | 5 | Silent letter |
| 8. | | 5 | Root |
| 9. | | 5 | Schwa |

| | | | |
|---|---|---|---|
| 10. | | 5 | Similar word part |
| 11. | | 5 | Short vowel |
| 12. | | 5 | Suffix |
| 13. | | 5 | Double Letter |
| 14. | | 5 | Variant Spelling |
| 15. | | 5 | Double Letter |
| 16. | | 5 | R controlled |
| 17. | | 5 | Schwa |
| 18. | | 5 | Variant Spelling |
| 19. | | 5 | Schwa |
| 20. | | 5 | Homonym |

## Spelling Pretest Alignment

Vowel

| | |
|---|---|
| Short | 11 |
| Long | 1 |
| Schwa | 4, 6, 9, 17, 19 |
| R controlled | 3, 16 |

Consonant

| | |
|---|---|
| Variant Spelling | 14, 18 |
| Silent Letter | 7 |
| Double Letter | 2, 13,15 |

Structural Unit

| | |
|---|---|
| Homonym | 20 |
| Similar Word Part | 10 |
| Root | 8 |
| Suffix | 5, 12 |

# LESSON 1  How Do I Become a Better Speller?

**SKILL TIP**

*Some people seem to be "natural" spellers. For others, correct spelling is not an easy skill to gain. Spelling might be a problem for you. If so, try a different approach to learning.*

**STUDY TIP**

*Do you remember reading about different learning styles in "How to Use This Book"? That information also applies to becoming a better speller. You should think about how you prefer to learn before you start studying lists of spelling words.*

- *Do you prefer to move around as you study? Do it! Have your list handy and move around as you review the words. Spell the words out loud as you walk. Just be sure that you practice writing the words at some point.*

- *Do you learn more easily by listening? Use a tape recorder. Dictate a list of 10 words into the recorder. Then spell each word correctly as you look at the list. You might want to say each word in syllables. Listen to each word, and then write it. Check your work. Listen to the spelling until you can write it correctly.*

- *Do you learn new things more easily by seeing, reading, and writing? Then do that: Look at the word, read it in syllables, and then write it. Use different color pens for problem words, red for double letter words (accommodate), blue for silent letter words (knife), and so forth.*

- *Certain people learn best by using their hands and "feeling" the shape of the word. These learners actually create small sand boxes and trace the letters of the word in the sand with their fingers. It works! Just be sure to use paper and pen and write the word as the last step.*

Understand that you cannot learn to spell every word you need to know in a short time. Instead, take your time and do a small amount of studying at any one time. Try the following plan:

- Use your learning style as a tool.

- Keep a small notebook handy to record words that you have spelled incorrectly or that are new to you.

- When you enter a word into the notebook, divide it into syllables. Make sure that you are spelling and pronouncing it correctly. Check with a dictionary or use the spelling/dictionary tool on your computer.

- Look at the word. Say it in syllables.

- Think about whether a common spelling rule applies.

- Close your eyes and picture the word.

- Write the word. Check it. Write it again, if necessary.

- Review a word until you are sure you know how to spell it.

## What You Have to Know

To improve your spelling, you need to know about six things:

1. Vowels, a, e, i, o, u and sometimes y

    a. Vowel sounds can be *short,* as the *a* in *apple,* the *e* in *test,* the *i* in *pick,* the *o* in *top,* or the *u* in *up.*

    b. Vowel sounds can be *long,* as the *a* in *ape,* the *e* in *teen,* the *i* in *fine,* the *o* in *pole,* or the *u* in *use..*

    c. The vowel *y* provides different sounds depending on the word in which it is used: *scary* (long *e*), *rhythmic* (short *i*)

    d. Vowel sounds are sometimes dropped, or not clearly long or short. Listen to the *o* in *conclude* or the first *e* in *absence.* They are dropped vowel sounds. A dropped vowel sound is called a *schwa.* Listen to the word *a-po-lo-gy.* It has two schwas, one in the first syllable and one in the third syllable. Can you see where the schwa would be placed? In the dictionary, the schwa is printed this way: ə-po-lə-gy

2. Consonants, which are the rest of the alphabet

    a. Single consonants such as *d* and *g* in *dog*

    b. Combinations such as *sh* in *shut* and *ch* in *church*

    c. Sounds that have more than one spelling, such as the *j* sound in *jaw,* which becomes *dg* in *edge*

3. Combinations of consonants and vowels that sound the same but are spelled differently in different words: *partial, crucial.*

4. Silent letters as in *night*

5. Homonyms, or words that are spelled or pronounced the same but have different meanings, such as *stationary* (meaning *place*) and *stationery* (meaning *paper*)

6. Syllables, or how letters are put together in small units of sound. Any word that contains more than one syllable has an accent on one of those syllables.

Example: in´-stru-ment. This word is made up of three syllables. Say it out loud. Can you hear the *accented* or *stressed* syllable? Yes, the first syllable is stressed; therefore, it has an accent mark over it.

## Practice 1

Directions: Say each of these words. Put an accent mark over the syllable you hear stressed.

1. Span-ish
2. Com-put-er
3. Dis-tance
4. Yes-ter-day
5. Sig-na-ture
6. Re-luc-tant

## Rules

You read that sometimes learning a spelling rule helps. However, don't try to learn too many rules at one time. Occasionally, a series of rules go together naturally. One rule has to do with adding prefixes and suffixes to words. Prefixes and suffixes add meaning to words. Prefixes are added to the beginning of a word; suffixes are added to the end.

**Rule:** In most cases, you can add a prefix to a word without changing the spelling of that word. For example, add prefix *un-* to *necessary* and you have *unnecessary*.

| Prefix | Meaning | Root Word | New Word |
|--------|---------|-----------|----------|
| ir– | not | regular | irregular |
| un– | not | necessary | unnecessary |
| mal– | badly | nourished | malnourished |
| pre– | before | date | predate |
| post– | after | war | postwar |

## Practice 2

Directions: Use these negative prefixes to make new words. Choose prefixes from this list.

ir–    il–    im–    un–

1. possible
2. legal
3. regular
4. complicated
5. available

**Rule:** When you add a suffix that begins with a consonant, the spelling does not change (with few exceptions).

| Word | Suffix | New Word |
| --- | --- | --- |
| quick | –ly | quickly |
| careful | –ly | carefully |
| careless | –ness | carelessness |
| economic | –al | economical |

## Exceptions

| | | |
| --- | --- | --- |
| true | –ly | truly |
| due | –ly | duly |

**Rule:** When you add a suffix that begins with a vowel to a word that ends in *e*, drop the *e* before you add the suffix.

| Word | Suffix | New Word |
| --- | --- | --- |
| continue | –ous | continuous |
| fame | –ous | famous |
| decide | –ing | deciding |

**Exceptions:** Words that end in *ge* or *ce* must keep the final *e* in order to retain the soft sound of *g* or *c*.

| Word | Suffix | New Word |
| --- | --- | --- |
| notice | able | noticeable |

Another exception is the word *dye* (to color or stain).

Dye + –ing = dyeing

**Rule:** Suffixes change the spelling of words that end in y.

| Word | Suffix | New Word |
| --- | --- | --- |
| happy | –ness | happiness |
| necessary | –ily | necessarily |
| hearty | –ily | heartily |
| category | –ize | categorize |

## Practice 3

Directions: Use these prefixes to make new words. Choose each prefix from this list:

over–    under–    in–    ex–    pre–    post–

1. I needed to breathe deeply; first I _____haled and then I _____haled.
2. If you don't leave something out, it will be _____cluded.
3. There was one spectacular event that I _____looked.
4. We were told to appear for a _____trial hearing.
5. Danny thought that _____cover work might be very interesting.
6. Her father said, "Whatever you do, don't _____date a check!"

## Practice 4

Directions: Circle an incorrectly spelled word in each sentence.

1. The movie was not fameous for its good story.
2. Happyness means different things to different people.
3. She was noticably thinner after her illness.
4. I am truely sorry.
5. Carlessness is not an option.

**Rule:** When a one-syllable action word ends in a consonant preceded by a vowel (*run*), double the final consonant before you change the form of the word.

| | |
|---|---|
| run | runner |
| plan | planned |
| thin | thinner |
| swim | swimming |
| top | topping |

**Rule:** When a two-syllable word ends in a consonant preceded by a vowel and is accented on the second syllable (*occur*), change its form by doubling the final consonant (*occurred*).

| | |
|---|---|
| refer | referred |
| occur | occurrence |

**Rule:** In a two or three-syllable word, if the accent changes from the final syllable to a preceding one when a suffix is added (refer/reference), do not double the final consonant.

prefer          preference

confer          conference

## Practice 5

Directions: Circle the number of the incorrectly spelled word.

1. 1. unanimous 2. nominate 3. confer 4. suning
2. 1. abbreviated 2. painter 3. carelesness 4. satisfactory
3. 1. developped 2. prefer 3. funny 4. wonderful
4. 1. preferrence 2. reference 3. refined 4. necessary
5. 1. except 2. occurred 3. baddly 4. stun

## Practice 6

Directions: Read each sentence. Correct any incorrectly spelled word. If there is no error, leave the space blank.

1. It ocured to me to check the weather report before I left. _____
2. John was refered to me as a possible candidate for the job. _____
3. Your bad attitude has never deterred me. _____
4. I consider myself a runer, not just a fast walker. _____
5. Suning yourself day after day is not a healthful thing to do. _____

**Rule:** *i* before *e* except after *c*.

believe

receive

**Exceptions:** *e* before *i* in words that have a long *a* sound (neighbor).

neighbor

weigh

**More Exceptions:** weird, leisure, neither, seize

## Practice 7

Directions: Choose the correctly spelled word in each sentence.

1. I will feel great (relief/releif) once I have finished my report.
2. My boss has a (fierce/feirce) sense of loyalty to her employees.

3. "(Sieze/Seize) the day," is a famous saying.

4. Once he (deceived/decieved) Rubio, they couldn't be friends.

5. I hope we'll have more (liesure/leisure) time next month.

**Rule:** Rules for forming plurals of words.

1. Add an *s* to most words.

   | | |
   |---|---|
   | rug | rugs |
   | shoe | shoes |

2. Add *es* to words ending in *o* preceded by a consonant.

   | | |
   |---|---|
   | hero | heroes |
   | tomato | tomatoes |

3. Add only an s to words ending in o, preceded by a consonant, *but referring to music*.

   | | |
   |---|---|
   | alto | altos |
   | piano | pianos |

4. Add *es* to words ending in *s*, *sh*, *ch*, and *x*.

   | | |
   |---|---|
   | boss | bosses |
   | crush | crushes |
   | church | churches |
   | sex | sexes |

5. Change *y* to *i* and add *es* in words that end in *y* preceded by a consonant.

   | | |
   |---|---|
   | fly | flies |
   | story | stories |

6. Words ending in *-ful* form their plurals by adding *s* to the end of the word.

   mouthfuls

   spoonfuls

7. A compound word forms its plural by adding *s* to the main word.

   | | |
   |---|---|
   | mother-in-law | mothers-in-law |
   | babysitter | babysitters |

8. Numbers and letters form plurals by adding '*s*.

   | | |
   |---|---|
   | 7 | 7's |
   | m | m's |

9. Some words keep the same spelling for singular and plural forms.

   | | |
   |---|---|
   | sheep | chinese |
   | deer | trout |

10. Some words form their plurals by irregular changes.

| | |
|---|---|
| child | children |
| leaf | leaves |
| tooth | teeth |
| crisis | crises |
| thief | thieves |
| knife | knives |
| woman | women |
| louse | lice |
| alumnus | alumni |
| appendix | appendices |

## Practice 8

Directions: In each line, circle the word that is spelled incorrectly.

1. A. holiday B. bulletin C. knifes D. teeth
2. A. father-in-laws B. chairs C. bows D. towels
3. A. lice B. 6's C. childs D. bunches
4. A. gestures B. occurrences C. bulletin D. radioes
5. A. trays B. handsful C. clients D. women

**Rule:** *sede*, *ceed*, and *cede*. Only three words are spelled with a *ceed* ending:

exceed     proceed     succeed

Only one word is spelled with an *sede* ending:

supersede

All other words of this type are spelled with a *cede* ending.

## Practice 9

Directions: Choose the correct word in each sentence.

1. This manual (superceeds/supersedes) the first one we received.
2. (Procede/Proceed) to the corner and turn right.
3. At the meeting, Manuel (preseeded/preceded) me on the program.
4. Have you read about the states that wanted to (secede/seceed) from the union?
5. Your praise (exceeds/excedes) what I expected.

## Spelling Review

Practice 10

I. Directions: Find the word in each line that is spelled incorrectly. Write the word correctly. If all the words are correct, write, *no error.*

1. A. deferred B. hoping C. differences D. tomatos _____

2. A. preparing B. walking C. skiping D. running _____

3. A. ladies B. geese C. crises D. teeth _____

4. A. disappoint B. imature C. pianos D. candies _____

5. A. trucksful B. illiterate C. regularly D. overrate _____

6. A. content B. definitly C. unaccustomed D. truly _____

II. Directions: Find the incorrectly spelled word in each paragraph. Write the word correctly on the line provided.

1. In the absense of any bargains, we left the store. A friend had referred us to it. Now we know that we have to search for ourselves. When we find a real bargain, we'll buy the item. _____

2. Without hesitancy, we said to the salesperson, "That delivery time is not feasable. We don't even leave work until an hour later." She said, "We'll try our best." _____

3. Our changeing schedule is a problem. Many times, no matter how seemingly competent the salesperson, the item arrives before we get home. We've almost given up on completing the transaction. _____

4. We were complaining to a friend about our problem. He said, "I always ask for a guarantee of delivery at the promised time. I tell them that if I don't receive it, they lose my business. It has always worked." _____
_____

5. We've decided to start all over again. This time, we don't intend to loose the battle!

III. Directions: Find one incorrectly spelled word in each column.

| Column A | Column B | Column C | Column D |
|----------|----------|----------|----------|
| really | themselves | unfold | visible |
| magazine | omission | pronunciation | miniature |
| vision | studying | particular | whether |
| precede | weird | preferably | usually |
| nieghbor | efficiency | coming | defend |
| Wednesday | exhausted | stubborness | wherever |
| preference | thirtieth | unyielding | accomodate |
| reference | knowledge | height | challenge |
| salary | discipline | either | calendar |
| sufficient | noticable | women | ninety |

# Answer Key

## Practice 1

1. Spán-ish
2. com-pút-er
3. dís-tance
4. yés-ter-day
5. síg-na-ture
6. re-lúc-tant

## Practice 2

1. impossible
2. illegal
3. irregular
4. uncomplicated
5. unavailable

## Practice 3

1. inhaled, exhaled
2. included
3. overlooked
4. pretrial
5. undercover
6. postdate

## Practice 4

1. famous
2. happiness
3. noticeably
4. truly
5. carelessness

## Practice 5

1. D sunning
2. C carelessness
3. A developed
4. A preference
5. C badly

## Practice 6

1. occurred
2. referred
3. Correct as written.
4. runner
5. sunning

## Practice 7

1. relief
2. fierce
3. seize
4. deceived
5. leisure

## Practice 8

1. C knives
2. A fathers-in-law
3. C children
4. D radios
5. B handfuls

## Practice 9

1. supersedes
2. proceed
3. preceded
4. secede
5. exceeds

## Spelling Review

I

1. D. tomatoes
2. C. skipping
3. no error
4. B. immature
5. A. truckfuls
6. B. definitely

II

1. absence
2. feasible
3. changing
4. receive
5. lose

III

| Column A | Column B | Column C | Column D |
|----------|----------|----------|----------|
| neighbor | noticeable | stubbornness | accommodate |

## Commonly Misspelled Words

Review the words that you have misspelled in the past. Try to learn ten words at a time. Use the techniques outlined in the beginning of this section.

**STUDY TIP**
Many Web sites offer lists of frequently misspelled words. In addition, you can find spelling lists in a large number of books on the English language. See Appendix C.

A

| | | | |
|---|---|---|---|
| abscess | agitation | all right | assistance |
| accumulate | appreciation | argument | acquaintance |
| abnormal | absence | assent | amateur |
| abolition | accede | acknowledgment | attendance |
| affix | attendance | apparently | attorneys |
| adaptation | attendants | already | attribute |
| actually | aging | assessment | anxious |
| aggressive | apparatus | amplification | autumn |
| ageless | accommodation | appraisal | acquire |
| answer | adequate | anticipate | analysis |

| | | | |
|---|---|---|---|
| athletic | auxiliary | analyze | agreeable |
| audience | adjacent | aggravate | auditor |
| authentic | | | |

**B**

| | | | |
|---|---|---|---|
| biased | barely | bombard | bureau |
| believe | basically | bondage | burglaries |
| bachelor | belligerent | boundary | business |
| bacteria | benefited | boycott | biographer |
| bankruptcy | bimonthly | briefcase | bookkeeper |
| | bisect | bulletin | |

**C**

| | | | |
|---|---|---|---|
| cafeteria | challenger | colonization | controller |
| calendar | chameleon | colossal | consistent |
| campaign | colossal | commentator | classification |
| category | consensus | communal | corporal |
| changeable | column | computerized | correspondence |
| coincidence | candor | concession | courtesies |
| conscience | concede | conflagration | chronological |
| classified | courtesy | congenial | credentials |
| conscientious | census | congruent | cross-reference |
| canceled | certainty | connoisseur | criticism |
| collateral | conceive | connotation | crucial |
| conscious | chief | consultant | currency |
| cancellation | collaborate | continually | custody |

**D**

| | | | |
|---|---|---|---|
| debtor | development | dyeing | dossier |
| deceive | desert | disappear | deficit |
| decision | dessert (food) deroga- | discipline | develop |
| deferred | tory | defective | dispensable |
| dilemma | dissatisfied | definite | distasteful |
| deductible | disinterest | defendant | documentary |
| deliberate | de-emphasize | delicious | drastically |
| departure | descendant | desperately | durable |
| dependent | dissimilar | disrespect | |

# E

| | | | |
|---|---|---|---|
| economical | exonerate | explanation | exhibition |
| economy | embarrass | external | existence |
| effects | endurance | extravagant | extension |
| efficient | enormous | enzyme | exorbitant |
| elaborate | enthusiastic | entrepreneur | exceed |
| elasticity | enumerate | equipped | eyeing |
| emergency | envious | error | exhaustible |
| emigrant | evasive | evaluation | extraordinary |
| eminent | excitable | exaggerate | erroneous |
| endorse | exhibitor | exceed | exhilarate |
| emphasis | experiment | excel | extravagant |
| emphasize | | | |

# F

| | | | |
|---|---|---|---|
| facilitation | fastener | foresee | flexible |
| facsimile | fiendish | fourteen | foliage |
| faculties | filament | finally | forcible |
| falsify | finalist | financial | foreign |
| financier | finally | filmstrip | forfeit |
| forfeit | fluorescent | fissure | forty |
| fascinating | forty | flecks | function |
| familiarity | fiery | | |

# G

| | | | |
|---|---|---|---|
| gauge | ghetto | glamorous | guardian |
| gallery | glucose | grateful | guild |
| galvanized | gnash | guarantee | guidance |
| generalization | government | glamour | graft |
| geographic | grammar | grieve | gymnast |
| geological | gruesome | grievous | gravitational |

# H

| | | | |
|---|---|---|---|
| handicapped | height | hygienic | hosiery |
| handkerchief | helium | hypocrisy | height |
| hemorrhage | homage | harassment | hors d'oeuvre |
| harass | hemoglobin | hindrance | hostage |
| heterogeneous | hygiene | | |

## I

| | | | |
|---|---|---|---|
| idiomatic | inflammatory | insurance | irreparably |
| ignorant | influential | integrity | itemized |
| illegitimate | infraction | intelligent | integrity |
| impasse | inhuman | irrelevant | intermission |
| imminent | individual | incidentally | interpretive |
| illustrator | ingenuity | innuendo | intuition |
| immovable | innumerable | intercede | inverted |
| impenetrable | input | interruption | involuntary |
| imprisonment | interim | itinerary | irrigation |
| indispensable | inasmuch as | indict | irritable |
| inference | innocuous | inoculate | |

## J

| | | | |
|---|---|---|---|
| jealous | judgment | judgment | jurisdiction |
| jeopardy | jovial | judiciary | justice |
| journal | | | |

## K

| | | | |
|---|---|---|---|
| khaki | kidney | kindergarten | kinsman |

## L

| | | | |
|---|---|---|---|
| labeled | leisure | likewise | league |
| license | liable | lien | liaison |
| laboratory | libel | linguist | liquefy |
| ladies | legion | literally | logical |
| latter | liberal | loose | lovable |
| leased | liberate | lose | lucrative |
| legitimate | likeness | losing | |

## M

| | | | |
|---|---|---|---|
| maintain | mechanical | millennium | movable |
| maintenance | medieval | merely | muscle |
| manual | maneuver | mischievous | memento |
| marital | milieu | mislaid | miniature |
| mileage | miscellaneous | monkeys | misspell |
| minuscule | mediocre | mortgage | |

## O

| | | | |
|---|---|---|---|
| overweight | omitted | overview | outdated |
| offense | ordinary | optional | oceanography |
| omission | | | |

## P

| | | | |
|---|---|---|---|
| pamphlet | patience | playwright | principal |
| phony | parasite | pneumonia | psychiatric |
| privilege | patient | politician | persistent |
| panicky | peculiar | portable | prerogative |
| picnicking | people's | possession | publicly |
| procedure | physical | possibilities | persuade |
| paradigm | physical | preceding | presumptuous |
| plagiarism | physician | pitiful | privilege |
| proceed | practically | preferable | probably |
| parallel | permissible | preference | profit |
| potato | preceding | preparation | promissory |
| programmed | pseudonym | presume | phenomenal |
| pastime | perseverance | previous | pretense |
| potatoes | planned | preferably | pursue |
| pronunciation | | | |

## Q

| | | | |
|---|---|---|---|
| quantities | questionnaire | queue | quizzes |
| quartet | | | |

## R

| | | | |
|---|---|---|---|
| raisin | rescind | rhythmic | repetitious |
| rarefy | rhyme | reinforce | resemblance |
| realize | receive | recognizable | resilience |
| reasonable | resistance | reconcile | resources |
| rendezvous | rhythm | relevant | responsibility |
| rhetorical | recommend | rhapsody | rythm |
| receipt | restaurant | regrettable | |

## S

| | | | |
|---|---|---|---|
| sacrilegious | soldier | specialized | stationery (paper) |
| sieve | succeed | specifically | statistics |
| single | satellite | stationary | succeed |
| subtly | skeptic | seize | successor |
| salable | supersede | sponsor | summarize |
| salaries | schedule | surveillance | siege |
| salient | skillful | separate | strict |
| scenes | surprise | strength | subtlety |
| scissors | scissors | suggestion | suggestion |
| shield | similar | surreptitious | symmetrical |
| sincerely | souvenir | stationary (fixed) | |

## T

| | | | |
|---|---|---|---|
| taunt | threshold | tongue | thought |
| tariff | taxiing | tragedy | thoughtless |
| teammate | theater | temperament | thoroughly |
| telecast | totaled | tension | thunderstorm |
| telegram | technique | therefore | transportation |
| telegraph | technical | thesis | traveler |
| telescope | theory | thieves | trembling |
| temperamental | technology | tissue | troublemaking |
| tempt | | | |

## U

| | | | |
|---|---|---|---|
| unanimous | undernourished | uniform | unwieldy |
| unauthorized | undersea | unify | unnecessary |
| unbearable | underweight | unique | unmanageable |
| unconscious | undoubtedly | universe | unwieldy |
| uncovered | unfortunately | unusual | usage |

## V

| | | | |
|---|---|---|---|
| vaccination | valuable | valley | victory |
| vacuum | value | value | void |
| vague | vision | valueless | volcanoes |
| vain | valid | verify | vacancy |

vacillate      vinyl          vengeance      voluntary
vague          vacuum         verbal         voucher
valuing        volume         villain
vaccinate      vegetable      visible

## W

warrant        width          whether        woman's
waving         wiring         withhold       women's
weather        witnesses      wholly         worthwhile
wednesday      weird          wives          wrapped
welfare        wield          woeful         wretched
weird          woolly         wolves

## X

xerox          x-ray          xylophone

## Y

yardstick      yacht          yogurt         youngster
yarn           year           yoke           yourself
yield          yearly

## Z

zany           zero           zinc           zoo
zap            zest           zodiac         zone
zealous

# SECTION 6

# Vocabulary

## How to Develop Your Vocabulary

**Words to Know (a review)**

| | |
|---|---|
| Thesaurus | A book that lists related words: synonyms and antonyms |
| Synonym | A word that means the same or almost the same as another word |
| Antonym | A word that means the opposite of another word |
| Process | A number of actions directed toward a goal |

## Step One: Create a List of Your Own

If you want to improve your reading or English skills, you need to improve your vocabulary. Perhaps words don't come easily as you speak or write. You might not know the meanings of some words as you read. You know that you need to increase the size of your reading, writing, and speaking vocabularies.

If this is true for you, there is a way to meet your vocabulary needs. Like spelling, however, vocabulary improvement does not happen in a day. You will not improve by doing one lesson in this book. This is an ongoing process, but you can start building your vocabulary here and now.

### A Simple Idea

You might have heard this simple idea before because it does work. You probably can't carry a dictionary with you, but you can carry a small notebook. Each time you hear or read a word that you don't know, write it down. When you do have a dictionary available, look up the word and write the definition in the notebook. Using the word in a sentence is also a good idea. However, if you learn best by listening and speaking, you can do this. Say new words into a tape recorder as we suggested in Section 1. Say the word in a sentence. Remember to include both the synonyms and antonyms. Record sentences for both.

You can also look up the word in a Thesaurus, a book of synonyms and antonyms. (See Section 2, Lesson 4.) Looking at the Thesaurus can be very helpful to you. You know that you learn new things by making connections to what you already know. In the Thesaurus, you might find a synonym that you already know. You can connect the familiar word with the unknown word. The connection makes it easier to learn the unknown word. For example, suppose you didn't know the meaning of the word *familiar*. You look it up in a Thesaurus and find synonyms. They are, *well known, known, and common.* You already know the word *known.* You can now connect the synonym to the word *familiar.*

Take this a step further and look at the *antonyms* given for the word *familiar.* At least one of the antonyms will help you: The opposite of familiar is *unusual.* Put all of this information in your notebook or on your tape recording.

## Step Two: Think About How Much You Read

 **FYI**

*This step had its beginnings in Section 2, Lesson 1. Do you remember the section called, Reflections: Reading in my Daily Life? What were your answers to the questions on how much reading you do? This is a key to the size of your vocabulary.*

### The Secret: Read More

The more you read, the larger your vocabulary becomes. Why? That question was answered in Section 2 Reading, Lesson 4. Read about context clues again to refresh your memory, and we will review the skill below. As you read, you will always be trying to figure out the meanings of words. You will add to your vocabulary when you read the words in context.

In the meantime, take every chance you have to read. Read about subjects you enjoy. You are much more likely to read if there is something you want to know more about. Any kind of reading is acceptable. You might like fiction, or true stories, or biographies. Or you might be most interested in sports. Whatever it is, just READ!

Some people think that only books are acceptable. That's not true. If you have an interest in science, or current events, or auto mechanics or any other topic, there is a magazine for you. Don't forget newspapers. They are also full of topics of interest. Remember that you don't have to buy the magazine or newspaper. They are probably available at your local library.

## Step Three: Become an Expert at Finding Context Clues

We understand sentences and paragraphs because we *read words in a context.* You recall that context clues are the words and phrases around an unknown word that help to explain it. Review this important skill in Section 2, Lesson 4.

Example:

*In a city filled with many, many beautiful buildings, this one <u>edifice</u> was the tallest and most modern.*

Even if you do not know the meaning of the underlined word, you can still say what the sentence talks about. It talks about buildings. Two ways you can describe buildings are with the words height and style. What is an *edifice*? Of course, from the context of the whole sentence, you know it is another word for *building*.

*In a city filled with many, many beautiful buildings, this one <u>building</u> was the tallest and most modern.*

As you can see, having a larger vocabulary allows you to repeat an idea/thing (*building*) without repeating the same word (*building* becomes *edifice*).

Example:

*We have become more and more aware of the dangers <u>posed</u> by polluted water.*

What is the meaning of the word *posed*? Does it have anything to do with positioning yourself for a picture? No. It has to do with the dangers created or presented by polluted water.

 **STUDY SKILL**

A Thesaurus would be very useful to find synonyms for this word. You need to look up the base word, pose. (The Thesaurus does not list verbs with their endings.) You would find many synonyms. Some of them are create, cause, and produce. You would then add a d to match posed.

We have become more and more aware of the dangers created by polluted water.

Practice 1

Directions: Read the paragraphs. For each numbered blank, choose the word that best completes the meaning of the passage.

Paragraph 1: Our office couldn't decide to whether we should buy or __1__ a typewriter. We've already bought furniture. This year we don't really have __2__ money to buy all the equipment we need, so we may delay buying the typewriter. Next year, if our business is __3__, we'll buy a new computer instead.

1. **a.** get rid of
   **b.** put away
   **c.** repaint
   **d.** lease

2.  **a.** whole bunch of
    **b.** sufficient
    **c.** more than enough
    **d.** any

3.  **a.** still prospering
    **b.** going bankrupt
    **c.** not making enough for salaries
    **d.** still getting no orders

Paragraph 2: Both readers and listeners use __1__ techniques to figure out the meanings of new words. They listen to or read for the context, or __2__ in which the word is used. Writers, especially, will often use __3__ before or after a difficult word.

1.  **a.** incorrect
    **b.** effective
    **c.** hopeless
    **d.** weak

2.  **a.** no
    **b.** the setting
    **c.** the dictionary in the car
    **d.** only the computer

3.  **a.** antonyms
    **b.** synonyms
    **c.** opposites
    **d.** books

## More than One Definition: Multimeaning Words

A number of words in the English language have more than one meaning. These are words that are spelled the same but have different meanings. They are often called multimeaning words.

Example: homonym

His wife is a *major* in the Army National Guard.

Theresa decided on nutrition as her *major* in college.

The word *major* is used to show rank in the first sentence. In the second sentence, the word *major* tells what Theresa's main course of study will be.

Practice 2

Directions: Read the sentences. Then choose the word that best completes both sentences.

1. We usually _____ at the Town Hall once a year.
   My job is to _____ the ten pieces to make the auto part.
   **a.** check
   **b.** introduce
   **c.** assemble
   **d.** connect

2. On our trip, we stopped at an _____ to see the old ships.
   I don't want to _____ anything we might need for camping.
   **a.** overlook
   **b.** restaurant
   **c.** take
   **d.** camp ground

3. The engineer was afraid that the road might _____ under the high water.
   "Please, take your dishes to the _____!" his mother pleaded.
   **a.** drown
   **b.** sink
   **c.** bank
   **d.** garage

4. Don't forget that a pet is _____ on you for care.
   When I filled out a form, my employer asked if I had a _____.
   **a.** sitting
   **b.** car
   **c.** expensive
   **d.** dependent

## Synonyms

Practice 3

Directions: Choose the word that means the same, or about the same, as the underlined word.

1. adequate light
   **a.** bright
   **b.** sufficient
   **c.** too much
   **d.** additional

2. very <u>reluctant</u>
   **a.** happy
   **b.** related
   **c.** delicious
   **d.** unwilling

3. <u>preliminary</u> decision
   **a.** light-filled
   **b.** last
   **c.** first
   **d.** best

4. a great <u>challenge</u>
   **a.** test
   **b.** meaning
   **c.** lie
   **d.** uplifting

5. to <u>deceive</u> someone
   **a.** steal from
   **b.** leave
   **c.** lie to
   **d.** lead

6. feel <u>fatigued</u>
   **a.** tired
   **b.** dressed
   **c.** heavy
   **d.** famous

7. <u>accomplish</u> a task
   **a.** deny
   **b.** complete
   **c.** shirk
   **d.** unfinish

8. <u>cautious</u> attitude
   **a.** silly
   **b.** careless
   **c.** demanding
   **d.** careful

9. <u>preceding</u> page
   **a.** following
   **b.** enough
   **c.** later
   **d.** earlier

**10.** <u>majority</u> vote
   **a.** greater part
   **b.** lesser part
   **c.** even
   **d.** ranking part

## Section 6 Vocabulary Answer Key

### Practice 1

Paragraph 1

**1.** D lease
**2.** B sufficient
**3.** A prospering

Paragraph 2

**1.** B effective
**2.** B the setting
**3.** B synonyms

### Practice 2

**1.** C assemble
**2.** A overlook
**3.** B sink
**4.** D dependent

### Practice 3

**1.** b
**2.** d
**3.** c
**4.** a
**5.** c
**6.** a
**7.** b
**8.** d
**9.** d
**10.** a

**To the Student: After you check your answers, record any incorrect answers in this chart. Then review the skill category that will help you to correct your errors**

| Item Answer | Section 6 | Skill Category (for review) |
|---|---|---|
| Prac. 1 Par. 1<br>1. D | Vocabulary | Context Clue |
| 2. B | | Context Clue |
| 3. A | | Context Clue |
| Par. 2<br>1. B | | Context Clue |
| 2. B | | Context Clue |
| 3. B | | Context Clue |
| Prac. 2<br>1. C | | Multimeaning Words |
| 2. A | | Multimeaning |
| 3. B | | Multimeaning |
| 4. D | | Multimeaning |
| Prac. 3<br>1. B | | Synonym |
| 2. D | | Synonym |
| 3. C | | Synonym |
| 4. A | | Synonym |
| 5. C | | Synonym |
| 6. A | | Synonym |
| 7. B | | Synonym |
| 8. D | | Synonym |
| 9. D | | Synonym |
| 10. A | | Synonym |

## Vocabulary

### Word Meaning

**Synonym**                                Practice 3, Answers 1–10

### Multimeaning Words

**Multimeaning Words**                     Practice 2, Answers 1–4

### Words in Context

**Words in Context**                       Practice 1
                                           Paragraph 1, Answers 1–3
                                           Paragraph 2, Answers 1–3

# Posttests

## Reading

**Read these employment ads and answer Numbers 1 through 4.**

- Nurse Aides: Nurse Temps Inc. has jobs available statewide. Home care and hospital staffing. Will train. Call 1-000-000-0000.
- Customer Service: Earn while you learn. Full time. Must be able to work two nights until 10 p.m. Need good interaction skills. Basic computer knowledge a must. Apply in person to fill out an application. 400 Main Street, Yorktown, Monday to Friday, 9 a.m.–4 p.m.

**1** According to this ad for nurse aides, who should apply for jobs?

   **A** Only people who live in the northern part of the state

   **B** People who live in a different state

   **C** People who live anywhere in the state

   **D** People who live within a few blocks of the patient

**2** Nurse Temps supplies nurse aids to both

   **A** Home care patients and hospitals

   **B** Hospitals and schools

   **C** Schools and universities

   **D** Hospitals and day care

**3** If you were applying for your first job, which line in the Customer Service ad would make you very happy to read?

   **A** Apply in person to fill out an application.

   **B** 400 Main Street, Yorktown

   **C** Basic computer knowledge a must

   **D** Earn while you learn

**4** As it is used here, what is another word for "interaction?"

   **A** Play acting

   **B** Communication

   **C** Reaction

   **D** Computer skills

**Read this short biography of Eleanor Roosevelt. Then answer questions 5 through 8.**

Eleanor Roosevelt, wife of President Franklin D. Roosevelt, remains one of our most famous First Ladies. In fact, she has been called "First Lady of the World." She had a great impact on children, women, blacks, and on the United Nations. She spent most of her life in service to others.

Eleanor herself had a very difficult childhood. Her parents died when she was very young. Eleanor's grandmother raised her. Because her mother had told her that she was very homely, she suffered from doubts about herself for many years.

Eleanor raised six children while her husband built his political career. When Franklin became president in 1933, he was paralyzed from polio. Eleanor traveled for him in order to report what she had seen. She also wrote a daily newspaper column called, "My Day," and had her own radio program.

Eleanor used her position for many good causes. They included jobs for the poor and minorities. Eleanor was also the first to hold press conferences with women reporters. She gave talks all over the country.

After FDR died, Eleanor thought her "story was over." It wasn't. In 1945, the new president, Harry Truman, appointed her to the United Nations. She did important work at the UN, including helping to write the Declaration of Human Rights.

**5** Eleanor had a chance to help the world, especially as

   **A** A high school teacher in NY

   **B** A member of the United Nations

   **C** The wife of Harry Truman

   **D** The mother of three children

**6** Eleanor raised six children while her husband built his political career. Then what happened?

   **A** Eleanor's mother told her that Eleanor was very homely.

   **B** Franklin died and she wrote her column, "My Day".

   **C** Eleanor's grandmother raised her.

   **D** Franklin was paralyzed from polio. Eleanor traveled for FDR in order to report to him.

**7** After FDR died, Eleanor did some of her most important work. What did that include?

   **A** The Declaration of Human Rights

   **B** Entertaining foreign presidents

   **C** Working only from home

   **D** Becoming a nurse

**8** Eleanor's very difficult childhood

   **A** Made her most concerned about the problems of other people

   **B** Made it impossible to do anything with her life

   **C** Provided the reason for her poor relationship with her children

   **D** Made it impossible for her to help the world's poor

**Read this passage about choosing an occupation. Then answer Numbers 9 through 11.**

If you decide to change your occupation, or work, do some thinking and planning first. Ask yourself some key questions. What kind of job have you always wanted? What would make you happy and fulfill your ambition? Make lists to answer those questions.

Where can you get information about your choices? Think about the people you know. Does anyone you know have the job you would like to have? Talk to that person and get all the details you can. You may find out that the job is exactly what you want. Or, you may be surprised to find out that the job is not at all what you thought it would be. Obviously, this information is helpful and will save you much time in your search.

**9** Which statement best summarizes the advice in this passage?

    **A** Take the first job you see advertised.

    **B** Think and plan before you even look for the job.

    **C** Make lists and then lose them.

    **D** Talk to everyone who works.

**10** In the passage, another word for *job* is

    **A** List

    **B** Questions

    **C** Choices

    **D** Occupation

**11** If you talk to people about the job you want,

    **A** You'll always want the ones they have.

    **B** You may find that you don't want a certain job after all.

    **C** You'll never be surprised by what they say.

    **D** You'll never get a job.

**Read the passage and answer Numbers 12 through 14.**

We've all heard that too much sun without sunscreen is very dangerous. More people than ever have been diagnosed with skin cancer. Parents are advised to cover their children and put on the sunscreen.

Did you know, though, that there is another side to the sun story? Obviously, the sun makes us feel good and there's a reason for that. Sunlight helps our bodies produce a "feel good" substance. The sun also provides a very important vitamin, vitamin D. We need vitamin D for many reasons. One of the most important reasons is that vitamin D helps us to absorb the calcium that builds bones. Other reasons are now being studied:

1. Vitamin D helps to protect us against serious illnesses such as heart disease and some cancers.
2. Some scientists say lack of vitamin D leads to increased falls in people over 65.
3. Scientists also see an unexplained increase in bone and joint pain.

**12** Most people know that they should not stay in the sun for a long time without sunscreen. Which of the following sentences makes this statement true?

    **A** Sunlight always leads to skin cancer.

    **B** Sunlight gives us too much vitamin D.

    **C** Sunlight is dangerous in that it may cause skin cancer.

    **D** Sunlight is the only way to keep children healthy.

**13** The opposite of "absorb" is

    **A** Release

    **B** Build

    **C** Take in

    **D** Store

**14** The main idea of the second paragraph is that sunlight

    **A** Provides the vitamin D we need

    **B** Helps our bodies to absorb calcium

    **C** Is the most important vitamin for children

    **D** Both A and B above

**At most libraries, you can find the book you want on the library's computer catalog. Read this introduction to finding a library book. Answer Numbers 15 through 17.**

North Kingstown Free Library

Library Online Catalog

Use the catalog to find a library book, talking book, video, large print books, and more.

Type in your PIN number to open the catalog.

Your PIN number is the last four digits of your phone number.

If you are new to the library's catalog, click on the following link.

The link will print information that will help you get started.

Link: Help with Using the Library Catalog

*Adapted from North Kingstown Free Library introduction to the catalog.

**15** Which of the following phrases tell you that the library stocks more than books on its shelves? It offers

    **A** Free trips and auto rentals

    **B** Computers to buy

    **C** Needles and PINS

    **D** Library books, videos, and more

**16** Your PIN number

    **A** Helps you identify yourself

    **B** Is the way you pay for what you buy

    **C** Is your address

    **D** Is your license number

**17** Which words tell you how much it will cost to take books out of this library?

    **A** Will be much too difficult

    **B** Will be free

    **C** Will cost $10 per year

    **D** Will be available in the winter only

**18** Why won't you forget your PIN number?

    **A** Because it is your age

    **B** Because it is your address

    **C** Because it is part of your phone number

    **D** Because it is your social security number

**Read this story and answer Numbers 19 through 21.**

### Cliffhanger

Adapted, with permission, from Zen Stories

One day while walking through the wilderness, a man stumbled upon a fierce tiger. He ran but soon came to the edge of a high cliff. He was desperate to save himself. He climbed down a vine and dangled over the dangerous precipice. As he hung there, two mice appeared from a hole in the cliff. They began gnawing on the vine! Suddenly, the man noticed a plump wild strawberry on the vine. He picked it off and popped it into his mouth. It was incredibly delicious.

**19** In the sixth sentence, the word "gnawing" means

    **A** Wiring

    **B** Hanging

    **C** Desperate

    **D** Biting

**20** You can figure out the meaning of "precipice" by reading the words and sentences around it. The two clue words to the meaning are:

    **A** Gnawing and mice

    **B** Hole and tiger

    **C** Edge and cliff

    **D** Strawberry and vine

**21** The author had a purpose for writing this story. Which statement states the purpose?

    **A** Live each moment to the fullest, no matter how serious your problems are.

    **B** Never take a chance; never eat a strawberry that is not ripe.

    **C** Never go anywhere or do anything that is at all risky.

    **D** Wait for someone to come along who can solve your problems.

**Read this paragraph and answer Numbers 22 through 26.**

Do you think you are overweight? A study was done by the Shape Up America organization. The study showed some interesting facts about obesity. For example, Americans who are overweight know the health danger, but they don't think they are at risk. Does this remind you of another study? Yes, smokers know that cigarettes can kill. These same people think they will never get sick. In addition, the "Talk to Your Doctor" survey showed that doctors don't often bring up the topic of weight loss with patients. If they do, doctors don't always recommend life changes. Some changes might include exercise, diet, and medication, if necessary.

22  A study on being overweight was done by a group called

    **A**  Exercise for Life

    **B**  Shape Up America

    **C**  Weight Loss Problems

    **D**  Stop Smoking

23  According to this paragraph, the Shape Up America study showed some interesting facts about obesity. What is the *opposite* of obesity?

    **A**  Being smoke free

    **B**  Thinness

    **C**  Exercise

    **D**  Organization

24  The paragraph says that overweight people do not connect being overweight to their getting sick. This is compared to

    **A**  People who know that cigarettes can kill, but still smoke

    **B**  Doctors who don't know that being overweight can lead to getting sick

    **C**  People who do exercises that lead to back pain

    **D**  People who know that medicines will cure all their problems

25  In sentence four, "at risk" means

    **A**  Carefree

    **B**  In danger

    **C**  Helpful

    **D**  Not related

26  A survey and a health group that educate were mentioned in this passage. Who are they?

    **A**  "Talk to Your Doctor" and "He'll Talk Back"

    **B**  Shape Up America and "Overweight Americans"

    **C**  "Talk to Your Doctor" and Shape Up America

    **D**  "All-American Weight Loss" and Shape Up America

## Section 2 Reading Answer Key

| | | | |
|---|---|---|---|
| **1.** C | **8.** A | **15.** D | **22.** B |
| **2.** A | **9.** B | **16.** A | **23.** B |
| **3.** D | **10.** D | **17.** B | **24.** A |
| **4.** B | **11.** B | **18.** C | **25.** B |
| **5.** B | **12.** C | **19.** D | **26.** C |
| **6.** D | **13.** A | **20.** C | |
| **7.** A | **14.** D | **21.** A | |

**To the Student: After you check your answers, record any incorrect answers in this chart. Then review the lessons that will help you to correct your errors.**

| Item | Answer | Lesson Number | Reading Skill Category (for review) |
|---|---|---|---|
| 1. | | 2 | |
| 2. | | 2, 3 | |
| 3. | | 3 | |
| 4. | | 4 | |
| 5. | | 3 | |
| 6. | | 2 | |
| 7. | | 2 | |
| 8. | | 3 | |
| 9. | | 2 | |
| 10. | | 4 | |
| 11. | | 2 | |
| 12. | | 2 | |
| 13. | | 4 | |
| 14. | | 2 | |
| 15. | | 2, 3 | |
| 16. | | 3 | |
| 17. | | 2 | |

| | | | |
|---|---|---|---|
| 18. | | 3 | |
| 19. | | 4 | |
| 20. | | 4 | |
| 21. | | 5 | |
| 22. | | 2 | |
| 23. | | 2 | |
| 24. | | 5 | |
| 25. | | 4 | |
| 26. | | 2 | |

## Reading Skills Categories

*Interpret Graphic Information*

Signs

Maps

Dictionary

Index

**Reference Sources**

Graphs

Forms

Consumer Materials

WORDS IN CONTEXT

Same Meaning            4, 10, 19, 20, 25

Opposite Meaning        13, 23

Appropriate Word

RECALL INFORMATION

Details                 1, 2, 22, 26

Sequence               6

Stated Concepts        5, 7, 11

CONSTRUCT MEANING

Character Aspects

Main Idea              14

| Summary/Paraphrase | 9 |
| Cause/Effect | 3 |
| Compare/Contrast | 24 |
| Conclusion | 8, 16, 18 |
| Supporting Evidence | 15, 17 |

**Evaluate/Extend Meaning**

| Fact/Opinion | 12 |
| Predict Outcomes | |
| Apply Passage Elements | |
| Generalizations | |
| Effect/Intention | |
| Author Purpose | 21 |
| Style Techniques | |
| Genre | |

**Note: These broad categories of reading skills are broken down into subskill categories. Question numbers are aligned with the sub skill titles and the lesson to which you can return for a review.**

# Mathematics
## PART I: Mathematics Computation
## Note: No calculator permitted.

Date: _____    Start Time: _____

**1** $7\overline{)147}$

   **A** 210

   **B** 20

   **C** 21

   **D** 22

   **E** None of these

**2** $\$10.00 - \$4.50 =$

   **A** $4.50

   **B** $5.50

   **C** $6.50

   **D** $7.50

   **E** None of these

**3** $\begin{array}{r} 26 \\ \times 17 \\ \hline \end{array}$

   **A** 402

   **B** 442

   **C** 168

   **D** 444

   **E** None of these

**4** $\dfrac{3}{5} + \dfrac{1}{5}$

   **A** $\dfrac{4}{5}$

   **B** $\dfrac{4}{10}$

   **C** $\dfrac{3}{25}$

   **D** $\dfrac{2}{5}$

   **E** None of these

**5** 10% of 70 =

   **A** 10

   **B** 17

   **C** 7

   **D** 6

   **E** None of these

**6** $.1 + .01 =$

   **A** .11

   **B** .2

   **C** .12

   **D** .22

   **E** None of these

**7** $96 \div 6 =$

   **A** 33

   **B** 11

   **C** 13

   **D** 16

   **E** None of these

**8** $-8 - 15$

   **A** $-7$

   **B** $-23$

   **C** 120

   **D** 7

   **E** None of these

**9**   $5\dfrac{2}{3} - 4\dfrac{1}{3}$

    **A**   1

    **B**   $1\dfrac{1}{3}$

    **C**   $1\dfrac{2}{3}$

    **D**   2

    **E**   None of these

**10**   What is 15% of 20?

    **A**   10

    **B**   15

    **C**   5

    **D**   3

    **E**   None of these

**11**   $0.125 \times 0.04$

    **A**   5

    **B**   0.5

    **C**   0.05

    **D**   0.005

    **E**   None of these

**12**   $12 + (-9)$

    **A**   $-3$

    **B**   3

    **C**   21

    **D**   $-21$

    **E**   None of these

**13**   $17\overline{)204}$

    **A**   12

    **B**   13

    **C**   14

    **D**   15

    **E**   None of these

**14**   $\dfrac{2}{3} \times 15$

    **A**   $15\dfrac{2}{3}$

    **B**   8

    **C**   10

    **D**   20

    **E**   None of these

**15**   $85 \div -5 =$

    **A**   $-80$

    **B**   $-15$

    **C**   $-17$

    **D**   80

    **E**   None of these

**16**   $\dfrac{3}{4} \div \dfrac{3}{8} =$

    **A**   $\dfrac{9}{32}$

    **B**   $\dfrac{1}{2}$

    **C**   2

    **D**   $\dfrac{9}{12}$

    **E**   None of these

**17**   27 is 30% of what number?

    **A**   9

    **B**   81

    **C**   18

    **D**   90

    **E**   None of these

**18** $\dfrac{-45}{5}$

   **A**   −9

   **B**   9

   **C**   −5

   **D**   5

   **E**   None of these

**19** What percent of 40 is 8?

   **A**   20%

   **B**   8%

   **C**   5%

   **D**   3%

   **E**   None of these

**20** $30 - (-5) =$

   **A**   25

   **B**   30

   **C**   35

   **D**   −25

   **E**   None of these

**21** $4 \times \$13.75 =$

   **A**   $52.50

   **B**   $53.25

   **C**   $54.50

   **D**   $55.00

   **E**   None of these

**22** $1.957 + 1.091 =$

   **A**   2.948

   **B**   2.958

   **C**   2.048

   **D**   3.048

   **E**   None of these

**23** $28 \times 146 =$

   **A**   4088

   **B**   3658

   **C**   3988

   **D**   1450

   **E**   None of these

**24** $\dfrac{3}{4} \times \dfrac{2}{3} =$

   **A**   $\dfrac{5}{7}$

   **B**   $\dfrac{1}{2}$

   **C**   $\dfrac{6}{7}$

   **D**   2

   **E**   None of these

**25** $\dfrac{25}{4} =$

   **A**   $5\dfrac{1}{4}$

   **B**   $6\dfrac{1}{4}$

   **C**   $8\dfrac{1}{25}$

   **D**   $7\dfrac{1}{4}$

   **E**   None of these

# Part II: Applied Mathematics
## Note: Calculator permitted.

**Date:** _____     **Start Time:** _____

**1**  A model of a boat has a scale of 1 inch equals 12 feet. Suppose the mast of the boat is 3 inches tall. How tall is the actual mast of the boat?

    **A**   15 feet

    **B**   20 feet

    **C**   24 feet

    **D**   36 feet

**2**  A fiberglass fishing rod usually costs $85.00. It is on sale for 30% off. How much is the sale price?

    **A**   $59.50

    **B**   $63.75

    **C**   $68.00

    **D**   $73.50

**3**  Which of these is another way to write $5^4$?

    **A**   $5 \times 4$

    **B**   $5 + 5 + 5 + 5$

    **C**   $4 \times 4 \times 4 \times 4 \times 4$

    **D**   $5 \times 5 \times 5 \times 5$

**4**  Bob started cleaning the yard at 9:30 a.m. and worked for 3 hours and 15 minutes. What time did he stop?

    **A**   12:45 a.m.

    **B**   1:15 p.m.

    **C**   12:45 p.m.

    **D**   1: 45 p.m.

**5**  What type of angle is shown in the figure?

    **A**   obtuse

    **B**   right

    **C**   acute

    **D**   straight

**6**  The number of handshakes possible for a given number of people is shown in the table. How many handshakes are possible if there are 6 people.

| Number of People | Number of Handshakes |
|:---:|:---:|
| 2 | 1 |
| 3 | 3 |
| 4 | 6 |
| 5 | 10 |
| 6 | ? |

    **A**   14

    **B**   15

    **C**   16

    **D**   17

**The graph shows how people voted in a certain town. Study the graph. Then do Numbers 7 and 8.**

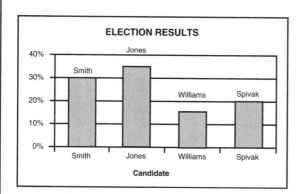

**7** Which candidate got 35% of the vote?

  **A** Smith

  **B** Jones

  **C** Williams

  **D** Spivak

**8** Which candidate got the smallest percentage of the vote?

  **A** Smith

  **B** Jones

  **C** Williams

  **D** Spivak

**9** Which number should go in the blank to make the equation true?

  $(2 \times 6) - (4 - 2) = 20 \div$ _____

  **A** 2

  **B** 4

  **C** 5

  **D** 10

**10** In which of these pairs of numbers are both numbers equivalent to 20%?

  **A** $0.2, \dfrac{1}{5}$

  **B** $0.20, \dfrac{1}{4}$

  **C** $0.02, \dfrac{1}{5}$

  **D** $0.02, \dfrac{1}{4}$

**11** In the diagram, $\triangle ABC$ and $\triangle DEF$ are similar. If $\angle BAC$ measures 40°, what is the measure of $\angle EDF$?

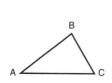
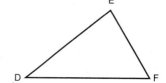

  **A** 40°

  **B** 50°

  **C** 60°

  **D** 80°

**12** A plumber charges $50 to come to your house, and $40 per hour on the job. The Johnsons spent $210 for the plumber to come to their house and fix a leak. How many hours did the plumber work there?

  **A** 3

  **B** 4

  **C** 5

  **D** 6

**13** Which of these cans is about $\frac{2}{3}$ full?

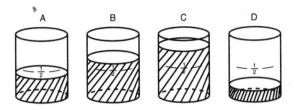

A  A

B  B

C  C

D  D

**A survey was done of how many pets people owned. The results are shown in the table.**

**Study the table and answer questions 14 and 15.**

| Number of Pets | Number of People |
|:---:|:---:|
| 0 | 12 |
| 1 | 20 |
| 2 | 10 |
| ≥3 | 8 |

**14** How many people owned more than two pets?

A  8

B  10

C  18

D  4

**15** What percentage of people owned one pet?

A  20%

B  30%

C  40%

D  70%

**The chart below shows the average high and low temperatures in a certain city for the months of March, June, September, and December.**

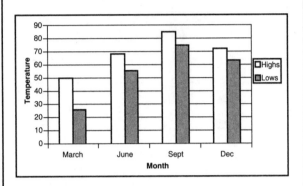

**16** Which of these is the best estimate for the mean (average) high temperature for the four months shown on the graph?

A  65°

B  70°

C  75°

D  80°

**17** During which month is the difference between the average high and low temperatures the greatest?

A  March

B  June

C  September

D  December

**18** How much fencing is needed to go around the perimeter of the yard?

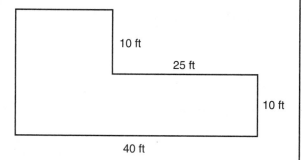

10 ft

25 ft

10 ft

40 ft

A   80 feet

B   85 feet

C   90 feet

D   120 feet

**19** Which of these figures is a pentagon?

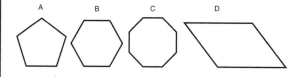

A        B        C        D

(A)  A

B   B

C   C

D   D

**20** Kathy rounded 6392 to the nearest 1000. Tom rounded the same number to the nearest 100. What was the difference between their rounded numbers?

A   200

B   300

C   400

D   500

**21** Phil took his pulse for 15 seconds. He counted 22 beats. What was his pulse rate per minute?

A   66

B   67

C   75

D   88

**22** Adam, Ben, Charlie, and David played the game of Parcheesi 75 times. Charlie won a third of the games. How many games did Charlie win?

A   3

B   25

C   30

D   35

**23** Which symbol goes in the blank space?

$3 \times 8$ _____ $30 - 5$

A   $<$

B   $>$

C   $=$

D   $\geq$

**24** What fraction is represented by point A on the number line?

0          1

**A**  $\dfrac{1}{8}$

**B**  $\dfrac{1}{4}$

**C**  $\dfrac{5}{16}$

**D**  $\dfrac{3}{8}$

**25** $(8 \times 10^4) + (3 \times 10^3) + (9 \times 10) + (6 \times 1)$

Which of these is the same as the number shown above?

**A**  8,396

**B**  80,396

**C**  83,096

**D**  800,396

**To the student. Check your answers and circle the question numbers you got wrong. Then go back to the lesson for that type of question and try to find out why you got the wrong answer. Double the number you got right to get your percent score. You should aim for 88–100 percent on the posttest.**

# POSTTEST ANSWER KEY, LESSON KEY, AND PROBLEM TYPE
## Part I: Mathematics Computation

| Question | Answer | Lesson | Type of Problem |
|---|---|---|---|
| 1 | c | 2 | Dividing Whole Numbers |
| 2 | b | 4 | Decimals |
| 3 | b | 1 | Multiplying Whole Numbers |
| 4 | a | 3 | Fractions |
| 5 | c | 5 | Percents |
| 6 | a | 4 | Decimals |
| 7 | d | 2 | Dividing Whole Numbers |
| 8 | b | 6 | Integers |
| 9 | b | 3 | Fractions |
| 10 | d | 5 | Percents |
| 11 | d | 4 | Decimals |
| 12 | b | 6 | Integers |
| 13 | a | 2 | Dividing Whole Numbers |
| 14 | c | 3 | Fractions |
| 15 | c | 6 | Integers |
| 16 | c | 3 | Fractions |
| 17 | d | 5 | Percents |
| 18 | a | 6 | Integers |
| 19 | a | 5 | Percents |
| 20 | c | 6 | Integers |
| 21 | d | 4 | Decimals |
| 22 | d | 4 | Decimals |
| 23 | a | 1 | Multiplying Whole Numbers |
| 24 | b | 3 | Fractions |
| 25 | b | 3 | Fractions |

# Part II: Applied Mathematics

| Problem | Answer | Lesson | Type of Problem |
|---------|--------|--------|-----------------|
| 1 | d | 11 | Measurement |
| 2 | a | 13 | Computation in Context |
| 3 | d | 7 | Numeration |
| 4 | c | 11 | Measurement |
| 5 | c | 12 | Geometry |
| 6 | b | 10 | Pre-Algebra and Algebra |
| 7 | b | 9 | Data Interpretation |
| 8 | c | 9 | Data Interpretation |
| 9 | a | 10 | Pre-Algebra and Algebra |
| 10 | a | 8 | Number Theory |
| 11 | a | 12 | Geometry |
| 12 | b | 13 | Computation in Context |
| 13 | b | 7 | Numeration |
| 14 | a | 9 | Data Interpretation |
| 15 | c | 13 | Computation in Context |
| 16 | a | 9 | Data Interpretation |
| 17 | a | 9 | Data Interpretation |
| 18 | d | 12 | Geometry |
| 19 | a | 12 | Geometry |
| 20 | c | 14 | Estimation |
| 21 | d | 8 | Number Theory |
| 22 | b | 8 | Number Theory |
| 23 | a | 10 | Pre-Algebra and Algebra |
| 24 | d | 7 | Numeration |
| 25 | c | 7 | Numeration |

# Language

For Numbers 1 through 3, decide which punctuation mark, if any, is needed in the sentence.

**1** "What is your work schedule next week" he asked.

    **A** !

    **B** ?

    **C** .

    **D** None

**2** I couldn't be any angrier with you

    **A** !

    **B** .

    **C** ?

    **D** None

**3** Vinnie can you meet me after work?

    **A** "

    **B** .

    **C** ,

    **D** None

For Numbers 4 through 7, choose the word or phrase that best completes the sentence.

**4** We _____ for an hour before the doctor saw us.

    **A** been waiting

    **B** are waiting

    **C** had been waiting

    **D** has waited

**5** It was cold, so I _____ a sweater with me.

    **A** bring

    **B** brought

    **C** bringed

    **D** had bringed

**6** _____ have been friends since elementary school.

    **A** She and me

    **B** He and I

    **C** Him and me

    **D** Him and her

**7** Manuel asked Teddy and _____ to his house for dinner.

    **A** she

    **B** I

    **C** we

    **D** me

For Numbers 8 through 13, choose the answer that is written correctly and shows the correct capitalization and punctuation. Be sure the answer you choose is a complete sentence.

**8**   **A** My wife and I had chose the same restaurant.

    **B** You and Mindy was holding up the line.

    **C** The food is ready when we arrived.

    **D** Our group was sitting in the main dining room.

**9**

   **A**   I didn't never want to do that again.

   **B**   He ain't ever going to, either.

   **C**   Jon has never been a good friend.

   **D**   You haven't never gotten a ticket.

**10**

   **A**   "As you leave, please lock the door, Matt said, "and I'll let you in when you get back."

   **B**   "Do you want us to get you anything while we're out" Andy asked.

   **C**   Matt answered, "I think we have everything we need"!

   **D**   "In that case, we shouldn't be away very long at all," said Andy.

**11**

   **A**   I have an English class on mondays and wednesdays.

   **B**   We also have a study group on Thursdays.

   **C**   There are Evening classes, but I don't take those.

   **D**   On sundays, my children and I swim at the Y.

**12**

   **A**   Last summer, we drove all the way to the grand canyon national park.

   **B**   Disney World is located in florida.

   **C**   In utah, you can drive from the City to the mountains in less than an hour.

   **D**   The bay is less than 30 minutes from us.

**13**

   **A**   Our town, one of the prettiest in the East, looks its best in the winter.

   **B**   Will you, a member of the community and a respected member.

   **C**   The biggest boy, and the biggest bully; he refused to move.

   **D**   If we're lucky, and we usually are it will snow by December.

**For Numbers 14 through 16, read the underlined sentences. Then choose the sentence that best combines those sentences into one.**

**14**   <u>We bought our grandson his first shoes.</u>
<u>We bought him a new stroller.</u>

   **A**   We bought our grandson his first shoes we bought him a new stroller.

   **B**   We bought our grandson his first shoes and a new stroller.

   **C**   Our grandson, we bought both a stroller and shoes.

   **D**   We bought our grandson his first shoes, we bought him a new stroller.

**15**   <u>I want to be the one to drive.</u>
<u>I leave early in the morning.</u>

   **A**   Or I leave early in the morning or I want to be the one to drive.

   **B**   I want to be the one to drive I leave early in the morning.

   **C**   I want to be the one to drive when I leave early in the morning.

   **D**   I want to be the one to drive. leave early in the morning.

**16**   He played baseball for our team.
         His brother played baseball for our
         team.

   **A**   He and his brother played. For
           our team.

   **B**   He played baseball for our team
           his brother played baseball for
           our team.

   **C**   He played baseball for our team,
           his brother played baseball for
           our team.

   **D**   He and his brother played
           baseball for our team.

**For Numbers 17 through 19, read the paragraph. Then choose the sentence that best fills the blank in the paragraph.**

**17**   We have a list of emergency numbers
         next to our phone for the babysitter.
         The first one is for our local fire
         department. _____.
         The doctor's number is listed also.
         Finally, we have the number for the
         Poison Center because you can never
         be sure what the children will get into.

   **A**   It's important to have emergency
           numbers.

   **B**   The second number is for the
           police.

   **C**   The second number is for the
           Poison Center.

   **D**   Our children never do anything
           that might be dangerous.

**18**   _____

         There are both good and bad things
         about going to school this way. Being
         able to keep your own schedule as you
         learn is important to some people.
         When you study is up to you. The
         computer doesn't care if you are
         learning at 5 p.m. or 5 a.m. Neither
         does your teacher.

   **A**   Are you interested in studying
           this course on-line?

   **B**   Your computer must be
           completely new.

   **C**   It's much easier to take a course
           on-line than in a school.

   **D**   Teachers of online courses don't
           give as much homework.

**19**   Are you independent enough for the
         responsibilities of online learning?
         There won't be a teacher to face in
         person. There are no second reminders
         about assignments. _____

   **A**   Although you will have an online
           teacher, there is no one at your
           side to help with homework and
           research.

   **B**   Although you will be doing all
           the work yourself, a teacher will
           come to your house to help.

   **C**   Although you will have an online
           teacher, you may never ask a
           question.

   **D**   Although you will have an online
           teacher, you will never have any
           homework.

**For Numbers 20 and 21, choose the answer that best develops the topic sentence.**

**20** Some companies have meetings to evaluate their employees.

   **A** Your company may cancel these meetings, so you probably don't have to do any planning. Never plan too far in advance. Things change all the time. Evaluations are not important anyway.

   **B** Bad service to your customers is definitely not a goal. Unfortunately, you probably won't talk about goals at the evaluation. So, don't bother writing anything down. You certainly shouldn't make any plans for the next evaluation. That would be a waste of time.

   **C** Don't worry about these meetings. You won't have to say anything to your next employer about your evaluation. No one really cares about how or what you did at your last job. Another company will never be interested in your goals.

   **D** After you go to one of these meetings, you can begin to prepare for the next one. Rewrite any notes that you took so that they're very clear to you. Look at any goals for the next six months that you and your manager decided upon. Plan how you will carry out the goals.

**21** How do you impress an employer who is advertising a job?

   **A** Always show up at the office. Don't try to make an appointment because you may not get one. Have your resume in your hand and just ask to see the boss.

   **B** Send your resume to the address given in the ad. Enclose your resume. Keep many copies of the same resume and one cover letter at home, ready to send out. Start your cover letter with your name, address, and age.

   **C** Don't expect to get the job if you send the same cover letter to everyone. Instead, read the ad to see what the company is looking for. Start your cover letter with something you have done that matches the skills the company is looking for. Of course, state your sincere interest in the job.

   **D** Even if the ad asks for a resume and cover letter, call instead. Someone will always give you an appointment. You can never say anything important in your resume or cover letter. It's important to do it in person.

**For Numbers 22 through 23, read the passage and look at the numbered, underlined parts. Choose the answer that is written correctly for each underlined part.**

Many people have learned to visualize in order to succeed at tasks. 22. Athletes <u>have knowed</u> this for a long time. Think of it this way: 23. <u>Its</u> mental exercise. Athletes use visualization to print success in their minds before an event.

22  **A**  had knowed
    **B**  has knowed
    **C**  have known
    **D**  correct as it is

23  **A**  Its'
    **B**  It's
    **C**  I'ts
    **D**  Correct as it is

**For Numbers 24 through 27, read the letter and look at the numbered, underlined parts. Choose the answer that is written correctly for each underlined part.**

September 16, 2005
Ms. Erina Davis, Manager
Kool-It Fans, Inc.
123 Main Street
Detroit MI

24. <u>Dear Ms. Davis,</u>
On June 1, 2005, I bought a fan at All-Appliance, Inc. in Detroit. The fan did not work from the first time I used it.

On June 2, I returned the fan to the store. The person who sold it to me refused to take it back. 25. <u>He says</u> I should just send it back to you because it's broken. I never even used the fan!

26. I am sending you the fan, but <u>I am to say the least</u> very disappointed in the terrible service from All-Appliance, Inc. Please return my money. I will buy the fan at another store.

27. Yours truly.

Michaela Bross

24  **A**  Davis:
    **B**  Davis;
    **C**  Davis!
    **D**  Correct as it is

25  **A**  He talked about
    **B**  He have said
    **C**  He said
    **D**  Correct as it is

| 26 | A | am going to say | | 27 | A | Yours Truly. |
|---|---|---|---|---|---|---|
| | B | am to say the least, | | | B | Yours truly, |
| | C | am, to say the least, | | | C | Your's truly, |
| | D | correct as it is | | | D | Correct as is |

## Language Posttest Answer Key

| | | | |
|---|---|---|---|
| 1. B | 8. D | 15. C | 22. C |
| 2. A | 9. C | 16. D | 23. B |
| 3. C | 10. D | 17. B | 24. A |
| 4. C | 11. B | 18. A | 25. C |
| 5. B | 12. D | 19. A | 26. C |
| 6. B | 13. A | 20. D | 27. B |
| 7. D | 14. B | 21. C | |

**To the Student: After you check your answers, record any incorrect answers in this chart. Then review the skills that will help you to correct your errors.**

| Item | Answer | Section | Skill Category (for Review) |
|---|---|---|---|
| 1. | | 4 | Quotation Marks/Comma |
| 2. | | | Exclamation Point |
| 3. | | | Commas/Parenthetical Expression |
| 4. | | | Tense/Progressive |
| 5. | | | Tense/Past |
| 6. | | | Pronouns/Subject |
| 7. | | | Pronouns/Object |
| 8. | | | Tense/Progressive |
| 9. | | | Negatives |
| 10. | | | Quotation Marks |
| 11. | | | Capitalization |
| 12. | | | Capitalization on Place Names |

| | | | |
|---|---|---|---|
| 13. | | | Appositive |
| 14. | | | Sentence/Coordinating |
| 15. | | | Sentence/Subordinating |
| 16. | | | Sentence/Compounding |
| 17. | | | Supporting Sentence |
| 18. | | | Topic Sentence |
| 19 | | | Connective/Transitional |
| 20. | | | Topic Sentence |
| 21. | | | Supporting Sentence |
| 22. | | | Tense/Perfect |
| 23. | | | Apostrophe/Contraction |
| 24. | | | Colon/Salutation |
| 25. | | | Tense/Past |
| 26. | | | Parenthetical Expression |
| 27. | | | Comma/Closing |

## Language

Usage

**Pronoun**

Nominative                6

Objective                 7

Possessive

Relative

Reflexive

**Antecedent Agreement**

TENSE

Present

Past                      5, 25

Future

Perfect                   22

# Spelling

**For Numbers 1 through 10, choose the word that is spelled correctly *and* best completes the sentence.**

**1** The words to the song soon became _____.

   **A** repetitive

   **B** repatitve

   **C** repitive

   **D** reputitive

**2** We can _____ here until the storm is over.

   **A** reman

   **B** remane

   **C** romaine

   **D** remain

**3** You should figure out the _____ from home to your job.

   **A** distence

   **B** distunce

   **C** distance

   **D** distince

**4** The children's _____ in the play was much better than we thought it would be.

   **A** purformance

   **B** paformance

   **C** performance

   **D** performanse

**5** Please remember to buy a box of _____ for the office.

   **A** tishues

   **B** tissues

   **C** tishoes

   **D** tishues

**6** People need _____ in their diets.

   **A** proteen

   **B** proten

   **C** protien

   **D** protein

**7** Some people have lived under an _____ government all of their lives.

   **A** opressive

   **B** oppressive

   **C** oporation

   **D** opressuve

**8** Tina wished they would answer _____ phone.

   **A** their

   **B** there

   **C** they're

   **D** the'yre

**9** It was definitely the _____ morning of the year.

   **A** chillyest

   **B** chilleyest

   **C** chilliest

   **D** chillyust

**10** In the winter, our family is _____ to colds.

   **A** susceptible

   **B** susceptibule

   **C** susceptibal

   **D** sisceptible

**For Numbers 11 through 20, read the phrases. Find the phrase that shows an underlined word that is _not_ spelled correctly.**

11  A  red <u>tomatoes</u>
    B  <u>ideel</u> weather
    C  <u>mailed</u> the letters
    D  <u>eventful</u> news day

12  A  <u>magnify</u> problems
    B  <u>mediocre</u> food
    C  <u>proudly</u> watched
    D  <u>priefer</u> chocolate

13  A  <u>couragus</u> soldier
    B  <u>dangerous</u> situation
    C  <u>distance</u> runner
    D  school <u>faculty</u>

14  A  <u>explore</u> the trail
    B  <u>wurth</u> the price
    C  <u>expert</u> witness
    D  <u>disturb</u> the peace

15  A  <u>unnecessery</u> doubt
    B  <u>solemn</u> gathering
    C  <u>subtle</u> color
    D  <u>reassured</u> patient

16  A  weekly <u>quizzes</u>
    B  hired <u>personnel</u>
    C  <u>aknowledge</u> a friend
    D  large credit card <u>debt</u>

17  A  a big <u>challenge</u>
    B  new <u>occupation</u>
    C  <u>acomplish</u> a task
    D  stamp <u>collector</u>

18  A  movie <u>reel</u>
    B  <u>treat</u> the patient
    C  <u>scent</u> the package
    D  <u>their</u> apartment

19  A  <u>combine</u> foods
    B  patient's <u>medacine</u>
    C  my <u>vitamins</u>
    D  it's <u>legal</u>

20  A  mirror <u>images</u>
    B  tries the <u>candys</u>
    C  sends <u>messages</u>
    D  immediate <u>tasks</u>

## Section 5 Spelling Answer Key

| | | | |
|---|---|---|---|
| **1.** A | **6.** D | **11.** B | **16.** C |
| **2.** D | **7.** B | **12.** D | **17.** C |
| **3.** C | **8.** A | **13.** A | **18.** C |
| **4.** C | **9.** C | **14.** B | **19.** B |
| **5.** B | **10.** A | **15.** A | **20.** B |

**To the Student:** After you check your answers, record any incorrect answers in this chart. Then review the skill category that will help you to correct your errors.

| Item | Answer | Section | Skill Category (for review) |
|------|--------|---------|------------------------------|
| 1. | | 5, Spelling | Short vowel |
| 2. | | 5 | Long vowel |
| 3. | | 5 | Schwa |
| 4. | | 5 | R-controlled |
| 5. | | 5 | Consonant/variant |
| 6. | | 5 | Silent letter |
| 7. | | 5 | Double letter |
| 8. | | 5 | Homonym |
| 9. | | 5 | Root |
| 10. | | 5 | Suffix |
| 11. | | 5 | Long vowel |
| 12. | | 5 | Short vowel |
| 13. | | 5 | Schwa |
| 14. | | 5 | R-controlled |
| 15. | | 5 | Similar word part |
| 16. | | 5 | Silent letter |
| 17. | | 5 | Double letter |
| 18. | | 5 | Homonym |
| 19. | | 5 | Schwa |
| 20. | | 5 | Plural |

## Spelling

### Vowel

| | | | |
|---|---|---|---|
| Long | 2 | 11 | |
| Short | 1 | 12 | |
| Schwa | 3 | 13 | 19 |
| R-controlled | 4 | 14 | |

### Consonant

| | | |
|---|---|---|
| Variant spelling | 5 | |
| Silent Letter | 6 | 16 |
| Double Letter | 7 | 17 |

### Structural Unit

| | | |
|---|---|---|
| Homonyms | 8 | 18 |
| Similar Word Part | 15 | |
| Root | 9 | |
| Suffix | 10 | |
| Inflectional Ending (Plural) | | 20 |

# Vocabulary

**For Numbers 1 through 7, choose the word that means the same, or about the same, as the underlined word.**

**1** <u>instant</u> answer

   **A** later

   **B** immediate

   **C** first

   **D** delayed

**2** <u>indebted</u> to someone

   **A** invited

   **B** allowed

   **C** grateful

   **D** afforded

**3** <u>descend</u> to

   **A** go up to

   **B** reach for

   **C** keep going straight to

   **D** go down to

**4** <u>anxious</u> feeling

   **A** nervous

   **B** happy

   **C** unconcerned

   **D** impatient

**5** <u>mischievous</u> child

   **A** well-behaved

   **B** mistaken

   **C** loud

   **D** naughty

**6** <u>irregular</u> outline

   **A** proper

   **B** uneven

   **C** irresponsible

   **D** infectious

**7** <u>remorseful</u> child

   **A** loud

   **B** regretful

   **C** unhappy

   **D** punished

**For Numbers 8 through 12, read the sentences. Then choose the word that best completes <u>both</u> sentences.**

**8** The child carried a new _____ to the game.
We had a _____ living in our attic for a long time.

   **A** glove

   **B** bat

   **C** uniform

   **D** cousin

**9** Our car slid down a very steep _____.
I hope you can drive me to the _____ so that I can deposit my paycheck.

   **A** hill

   **B** forest

   **C** bank

   **D** highway

**10** We like to _____ all of our opportunities before we decide on an action.

The men did a _____ in order to get the exact measurements.

  **A** survey

  **B** think

  **C** chart

  **D** map

**11** The teenager said, "I _____ drive the car anytime, now that I'm seventeen!"

Now that we have this huge crop of tomatoes, I'll have to _____ a lot of them.

  **A** can't

  **B** throw out

  **C** can

  **D** dig up

**12** You said you will _____ on my plants while I'm away.

How large a _____ should I write for this service?

  **A** board

  **B** watering can

  **C** light

  **D** check

**For Numbers 13 through 20, read the passage. For each numbered blank, choose the word that best completes the meaning of the passage.**

Listening __13__ a good memory. When you listen, you need to be able to keep words, ideas, and details in a __14__ order. In fact, when you were a small child, your being able to remember the sentences you heard was __15__ for learning to speak.

Many people don't listen very well when they are given directions __16__. The listener may miss several steps in the directions meant to take him or her from one place to another. The person giving the directions may __17__ an important step. Then, the listener must be __18__ enough to realize what has happened. The listener should stop the speaker and ask for __19__. Listening is definitely a __20__ process.

**13**   **A** requires

    **B** loses

    **C** looses

    **D** forces

**14**   **A** jumbled

    **B** sorted

    **C** sequential

    **D** approximate

**15**   **A** an unneeded skill

    **B** a requirement

    **C** only a fun way

    **E** talkative

**16**   **A** in writing

    **B** orally

    **C** at all

    **D** at night

| 17 | A | omit | | 19 | A | directions to a gas station |
|----|---|------|---|----|---|----------------------------|
| | B | remember | | | B | more of the same |
| | C | change | | | C | clarification |
| | D | drives away | | | D | a map |
| 18 | A | lazy | | 20 | A | two-way |
| | B | sleepy | | | B | one-way |
| | C | neglectful | | | C | no-win |
| | D | attentive | | | D | no-fun |

## Vocabulary Posttest Answer Key

| | | | |
|--|--|--|--|
| 1. B | 6. B | 11. C | 16. B |
| 2. C | 7. B | 12. D | 17. A |
| 3. D | 8. B | 13. A | 18. D |
| 4. A | 9. C | 14. C | 19. C |
| 5. D | 10. A | 15. B | 20. A |

**To the Student: After you check your answers, record any incorrect answers in this chart. Then review the skills that will help you to correct your errors.**

| Item | Answer | Section | Skill Category (for review) |
|------|--------|---------|------------------------------|
| 1. | | 6 | Synonym |
| 2. | | | Synonym |
| 3. | | | Synonym |
| 4. | | | Synonym |
| 5. | | | Synonym |
| 6. | | | Synonym |
| 7. | | | Synonym |
| 8. | | | Multimeaning |
| 9. | | | Multimeaning |

| | | | |
|---|---|---|---|
| 10. | | | Multimeaning |
| 11. | | | Multimeaning |
| 12. | | | Multimeaning |
| 13. | | | Context clues |
| 14. | | | Context clues |
| 15. | | | Context clues |
| 16. | | | Context clues |
| 17. | | | Context clues |
| 18. | | | Context clues |
| 19. | | | Context clues |
| 20. | | | Context clues |

## Vocabulary

Word Meaning

Synonym        1, 2, 3, 4, 5, 6, 7

Multi-Meaning Words

Multi meaning Words 8, 9, 10, 11, 12

Words in Context

Word in Context        13, 14, 15, 16, 17, 18, 19, 20

# APPENDIX A

# Testing Strategies and Tips

You read and answered questions about your test-taking "know-how" in Section 1 of this book.

You have seen test-taking strategies and tips in this book. The tips are important enough to read again. Using the tips below will help make you a better test-taker.

If you did not answer the questions in Section 1, you might want to go back there after you have read these suggestions. See how you feel about your skills and abilities now that you have completed this book.

1. **Visualize success for self-confidence and best results.**

   If you think you *can do* something, you have a better chance of being able to do it. If you think you can't do something, you have less of a chance of being able to do it. In short, tell yourself that you *can* do well. Talk to yourself using positive words, not negative ones.

2. **Prepare physically for the test day.**

   Preparing for the content of the test is not enough. You still might not do well if you are not well rested. So get to bed early the night before, or spend a quiet evening at home (it's probably not a good idea to go out to a party!).

3. **Identify key words in questions and directions.**

   During the test, look out for important words that will help you understand the directions and the questions. Don't rush through either the directions or the test questions. If you do, you might read them incorrectly. Then you will choose the wrong answers.

4. **Recognize pitfalls of multiple-choice tests.**

   Often the answers that you have to choose from in a multiple-choice test are similar. Read each one carefully and choose the best answer.

5. **Use a process of elimination to check multiple-choice questions.**

   If you are having trouble deciding on an answer to a multiple-choice question, first look at all the possible answers. See if any can be eliminated. Sometimes an answer just doesn't fit. You can eliminate it as a choice. Now you have fewer items from which to choose.

### 6. Relax by using breathing techniques.

When you sit down to take a test, you might feel nervous. Take a moment for a few deep breaths. Take them in through your nose and slowly exhale out through your mouth. This will help calm your nerves.

### 7. Take 1-minute vacations to relieve stress during test.

Another way to reduce stress during a test is to stop for a minute. Close your eyes and look at place that brings you peace or happiness. Put yourself there for a quiet moment. For example, if you love to be at the beach, try to see yourself sitting on the warm sand. Feel the sun beating down on your face. Think of the sound of the waves on the shore. Feel better already, don't you?

### 8. To finish the test on time, pace yourself during the test.

You might love to spend more than a minute on your minivacation, but don't. You need to think of the time limits of a test. Make sure you know how much time you can spend on each section. Stick to your plan. Don't linger too long on any question. If you have time, you can go back to it.

### 9. Know when to leave a question that is giving you trouble.

As we have said, you can't linger too long on any item. If you do, you will end up rushing through other questions. If you just can't seem to answer the question, move on. Come back to it later if you have the time.

### 10. Use any time that is left at the end to check your work.

If you do finish a test before the time is up, go back to items you have left blank. After that, check the rest of your work until time is up.

# APPENDIX

# B

# General TABE Information

The TABE is a multiple-choice test. The test is offered in either a Complete Battery or Survey version in Forms 7 and 8 and 9 and 10. The Survey version has one-half of the number of questions found in the Complete Battery version. The Complete Battery version consists of the following sections and number of questions:

- Reading—50 questions
- Mathematical Computation—25 questions
- Applied Mathematics—50 questions
- Language—55 questions
- Spelling—20 questions
- Vocabulary

TABE is one of several approved standardized tests that are used to determine if an adult qualifies academically for Federal Financial Aid.

Here are the current passing scores required for eligibility:

Test of Adult Basic Education (TABE):

Forms 5 and 6, Level D, Survey Version and Complete Battery Version.

Passing Scores:

Reading Total (768), Total Mathematics (783), Total Language (714).

Test of Adult Basic Education (TABE):

Forms 7 and 8, Level D, Survey Version and Complete Battery Version.

Passing Scores:

Reading (559), Total Mathematics (562), Language (545).

[FR Doc. 97-5686 Filed 3-6-97; 8:45 am] Dated February 28, 1997.

Website: http://www.ed.gov/legislation/FedRegister/announcements/1997-1/030797a.html

# APPENDIX C

# Resources

## English Language Reference Books

Bernstein, T. M. *The Careful Writer: A Modern Guide to English Usage.* New York: Atheneum, 1965.

Booher, D. D. *Communicate with Confidence: How to Say it Right the First Time Every Time.* New York: McGraw-Hill, 1994.

Brusaw, C. T., Alfred, G. J., and Oliu, W. E. *The Business Writer's Handbook.* (5th ed.) New York: St. Martin's Press, 1997.

Cazort, D. *Under the Grammar Hammer: The 25 Most Important Mistakes and How to Avoid Them.* (updated) Los Angeles: Lowell House, 1997.

Dutwin, P., and Diamond, H. *English The Easy Way.* (4th ed.) Hauppauge, NY: Barron's Educational Series, Inc., 2003.

Dutwin, P., and Diamond, H. *Grammar In Plain English.* (3rd ed.) Hauppauge, NY: Barron's, 1997.

Dutwin, P., and Diamond, H. *Writing The Easy Way.* (3rd ed.) Hauppauge, NY: Barron's, 2000.

Follet, W. *Modern American Usage: A Guide.* Edited and completed by Jacques Barzun and others. New York: Hill & Wang, 1998.

Kipfer, B. A. (editor) *Roget's International Thesaurus* (6th ed.) New York: Harper Collins, 2001.

*Merriam-Webster Collegiate Dictionary.* (10th ed.) New York: Merriam-Webster, 1998.

Mersand, J. and Griffith, F. S*pelling The Easy Way.* (2nd ed.) Hauppauge, NY: Barron's Educational Series, Inc., 1996.

Oliu, W. E., Brusaw, C. T., and Alfred, G. J. *Writing that Works.* New York: St. Martin's Press, 1980.

Sabin, W. A. *Gregg Reference Manual.* (9th ed.) New York: Glencoe McGraw-Hill, 2001.

*Merriam-Webster Dictionary.* (10th ed.)

Godden, Nell and Erik Palma, eds. (Princeton Review). *Grammar Smart: A Guide to Perfect Usage.* New York: Villard Books, 1993.

Strunk Jr, W. and White, E. B. *The Elements of Style.* (3rd ed.) Boston: Allyn and Bacon.

Turabian, K. L. *A Manual for Writers of Term Papers, Theses, and Dissertations,* (6th ed.) Chicago: University of Chicago Press, 1996.

Weiss, E. H. *The Writing System for Engineers and Scientists.* Englewood Cliffs: Prentice Hall, 1982.

## Information Technology

- Refer to Section 4, Lesson 4 for information on accessing the Internet.
- Refer to Section 4, Lesson 4 for information on using your library for researching on the Internet.
- Learn more about *distance education/learning.*
  Distance education provides instruction when students and teachers are in different places. They can be brought together by computers. Teachers and students communicate through e-mail.
- Inquire at your workplace about e-learning as a training solution. Companies offer training as needed through the use of computer courses. Computer Assisted Instruction (CAI) is used to help learners master specific skills.

## Community Services

Use your telephone book to find:

- Your local library
- Your community center (for education and recreation)
- Your Family Services organization
- Your Congressional representatives
- Your Local School Department
- Your local recreation department

## Educational Opportunities

You will find educational opportunities and solutions by calling the appropriate department of your local and state school system. Also, access your state's Web site for information. You might find any or all of the following.

State Adult Education Department (may sponsor distance education)

Adult High School

ABE/GED Programs

Career and Technical High School

Special Education

State Educational Opportunity Center

In addition, local libraries frequently offer literacy and ABE/GED classes as well as many other courses and programs.

# Index

Note: Boldface numbers indicate illustrations.

reference books, 53, 283
reflexive pronoun, 178–179
regular verbs, 160–162
reliable, 197
remainder, 74
represent, 197
resources, 283–284
rhombus, 121, **121**
right angle, 119, **119**
right triangle, 120, **120**
rounding numbers, 131–133
run-on sentence, 149, 151–154, 184, 200

scalene triangle, 120, **120**
scanning, in reading, 38
–*sede, cede, ceed*, 222
segments, line, 118
self-assessment of learning skills, 4–6
sentence structure, 149–156, 184–195
   capitalization in, 150, 197–210
   combining related thoughts in, 187–188
   commas in, 194–195
   complete, 184
   connecting words in paragraphs and, 192–193, 200, 202
   coordinate ideas in, 188
   descriptive word placement in, 175–176, 187
   emphasis and emphasizing words in, 192
   fragments in, 151–154, 184
   introductory words and phrases in, 201
   paragraph building from, 190–194
   parallel thoughts and, 185–186
   pronouns in, 150–151
   punctuation marks in, 150, 152, 197–210
   run-on, 151–154, 184, 200
   sequencing events with, in paragraphs, 193–194
   subject in, 149, 150, 154–155
   subordinate ideas in, 189–190
   verb in, 149, 150, 154–167
sequencing events in a paragraphs, 193–194
silent letters, 216

similar figures in geometry, 123, **123**
simile, 53, 54
skills assessment, 2–3
skimming, in reading, 38
solid shapes/figures, 122, **122**
spelling skills, 211–231
   assessment of, 211–214
   commonly misspelled words list for, 225–231
   exceptions to rules in, 218–222
   *i* before *e* except after *c* in, 220–221
   improving, 215
   plural words and, 221–222
   posttest and answers for, 270–273
   prefixes and suffixes in, 217–218
   rules for, 216, 217–218
   sede, cede, ceed in, 222
   syllables and, 219–220
   vowels and consonants in, 216
standardized, 85
subject, 149, 154–155
subordinate ideas in sentence, 189–190
subordinate, 184
substitute, 149
suffixes, 217–218
supporting details, reading for, 31–39
supports for learning, 10–12
syllables, 216, 219–220
synonym, 47, 233, 237–239

TABE, general information on, 281
tables, 103, **103**
   input-output, and algebra, 108–109
temperature, 112, 113
tense in verbs, 156–162
   number and, 165
test taking, 3–4, 18, 279–280
thesaurus, 47, 53, 233, 235
this, that, 182–183
time for learning, 13–16
time, units of, 112
tone in writing/reading, 56
transactions, 31, 184
trapezoid, 121, **121**
triangles, 120, **120**, 123–124, **123**, **124**

Venn diagrams, 101, **101**
verbs, 149, 154–167
   irregular vs. regular, 160–162